T0365093

THE

CHRISTENA DISASTER

FORTY-TWO YEARS LATER

—LOOKING BACKWARD, LOOKING FORWARD

THE
CHRISTENA DISASTER

FORTY-TWO YEARS LATER

—LOOKING BACKWARD, LOOKING FORWARD

A CARIBBEAN STORY ABOUT NATIONAL TRAGEDY,
THE BURDEN OF COLONIALISM, AND
THE CHALLENGE OF CHANGE

WHITMAN T. BROWNE, Ph.D.

iUniverse LLC
Bloomington

The Christena Disaster Forty-Two Years Later
—Looking Backward, Looking Forward
A Caribbean Story about National Tragedy, the Burden of Colonialism,
and the Challenge of Change

iUniverse books may be ordered through booksellers or by contacting:

iUniverse LLC
1663 Liberty Drive
Bloomington, IN 47403
www.iuniverse.com
1-800-Authors (1-800-288-4677)

ISBN: 978-1-4759-1868-7 (sc)
ISBN: 978-1-4759-1869-4 (hc)
ISBN: 978-1-4759-1870-0 (e)

Library of Congress Control Number: 2012907996

Printed in the United States of America

iUniverse rev. date: 11/19/2013

CONTENTS

Preface 1
A Word of Testimony for the Book
About the Boat Once Called *Christena* xiii

Preface 2
Recalling A Tragedy xvi

Preface 3
The Sound of, Christena Sink! Christena Sink! Still
Reverberates In My Head xx

Preface 4
Documentation of Our History is Crucial xxiv

Author's Preface
We Have Changed but the
Pain and the Emptiness Persist xxx

Chapter One
Nightmare on the Christena 1

Chapter Two
Of Dreams, Visions and Superstitions 21

Chapter Three
First-Hand Accounts 1 36

Chapter Four
First-Hand Accounts II 57

Chapter Five
   Newspaper Reports 123

Chapter Six
   Photographic Reflections..160

Chapter Seven
   Innocence, Ignorance, and Reality................................176

Chapter Eight
   Politics and the Disaster 190

Chapter Nine
   Commission of Inquiry Report 211

Chapter Ten
   Questions That Were Not Answered 235

Chapter Eleven
   Riding Out the Storm 258

Appendix I
   The Launching of the *Christena* 280

Appendix II
   The Labor Spokesman..282

Appendix III
   The Labour Spokesman..285

Appendix IV
   The Labour Spokesman..287

Appendix V
   List of Persons Identified
   (One of Original Lists From 1970)................................290

Appendix VI
    List of Missing Persons:
    (One of the Original Lists from, 1970)..........................293

Appendix VII
    List of Survivors (One Early List From, 1970)................300

Appendix VIII
    List of Persons Reported Missing (unconfirmed)............304

Appendix IX
    Witnesses Who Gave Evidence Before the Commission......305

Appendix X
    The St. Kitts-Nevis Observer...309

Appendix XI
    The Kitts-Nevis Observer..314

Appendix XII
    St. Kitts-Nevis Observer...319

Appendix XIII..322

Index...335

The Christena Incident Geography I

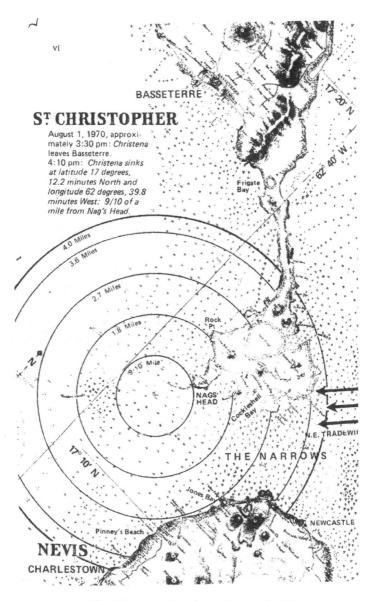

BASSETERRE

ST CHRISTOPHER

August 1, 1970, approximately 3:30 pm: *Christena* leaves Basseterre.
4:10 pm: *Christena sinks at latitude 17 degrees, 12.2 minutes North and longitude 62 degrees, 39.8 minutes West: 9/10 of a mile from Nag's Head.*

17° 20' N

62° 40' W

Frigate Bay

4.0 Miles

3.6 Miles

2.7 Miles

1.8 Miles

Rock Pt

9/10 Mile

NAGS HEAD

Cockleshell Bay

N.E. TRADEWII

17° 10' N

THE NARROWS

Jones Bay

NEWCASTLE

Pinney's Beach

NEVIS

CHARLESTOWN

The Christena Incident Geography II

ACKNOWLEDGEMENTS

This is a third version of the book, and hopefully, the best of them all. Each time it has appeared, there have been people who talked with me, suggesting new ideas to improve the book. Also, this time around, Mr. Phipps, Drs. Farrell, Maynard, and York, were invited to add their memories of, and reactions to, the incident, along with its aftermath. I thank these persons sincerely, and everyone else who has shared his or her reflections on the Christena incident with me. Thanks also to all the people who have kept the story alive and vibrant by asking to read it again, or who have sought to share it with others, especially from another generation.

Meanwhile, my family members who continue to believe in, and support my writing effort, are always deeply appreciated. And, I cannot end my expression of thanks and appreciation without extending a special, "Thank You," to Sue and John Morris of Editide, in Maine; to *The Barbados Advocate, The Labor Spokesman, The Democrat, and The St. Kitts-Nevis Observer.* Thanks too, to my publisher, iUniverse.

While I thank all these people and businesses, for having made special contributions to my work, if anyone sees short-comings in the final document, the blame is mine. Please forgive me. I too, am infected with human frailties.

Whitman T. Browne, Ph. D.

PREFACE 1

A Word of Testimony for the Book About the Boat Once Called *Christena*

by Dr. Gosnell York

Like so many of my compatriots (encompassing both islands of our beloved Federation of St. Kitts-Nevis), the mysterious sinking of the *Christena* some four decades ago was a national tragedy that led to psychological trauma beyond words—the wounds of which, perhaps, will never heal. Years later, it still creates a sinking feeling in our spirits and, in my case at least, it brought back the most unpleasant of memories and even drew tears from my eyes as I reread, in somber silence, the gripping account that Whitman Browne has so compellingly and competently shared with us in his book, *The Christena Disaster Revisited (2001)*.

When the tragedy struck, snuffing out hundreds of innocent lives, including some of my own classmates, I was a student at Basseterre High School (formerly the St. Kitts-Nevis Grammar School) at the time; and when I reread the book most recently

(April 2011), hardly being able to decipher the print on some of its pages through my tear-filled eyes at times, I was on an American Airlines flight, at a window seat, travelling back from a conference at the University of the Virgin Islands to Jamaica where I was located at the time.

In some ways, it seems as if I have no way of entirely avoiding boats. For one thing, our story of slavery in the Caribbean in general, and that of St. Kitts-Nevis in particular, makes little or no sense other than in relation to Columbus and his boats—and then to the many boats which were subsequently used to haul millions of our kicking and screaming ancestors from Africa to provide unpaid and unwilling labor on the various sugar and other plantations throughout the Americas. In addition, I myself, like so many of my compatriots, successfully made my way, on at least one occasion, from St. Kitts to Nevis and back on what later turned out to be that ill-fated boat which we called, *Christena*.

And now writing this testimony while based in a post-apartheid South Africa, I cannot help but think of that boat which was used to ferry Mr. Mandela and many others to Robben Island off the coast of Cape Town to the south of where I am currently located—to that infamous island, now made even more popular, perhaps, by hordes of visitors from both home and abroad, where Mr. Mandela and others were held captive against their collective wills for years on end, because of their stubborn commitment to the conviction that the right to full human flourishing of all South Africans, regardless of color, creed or culture, and in open defiance of the pathology of apartheid (as it then was) is a fundamental human right.

As a boat-conscious person, and like many others of my compatriots, then, I continue to laud Dr. Browne for helping to keep alive, through the power of both pen and print, the cherished memories of our parents, our brothers, our sisters, our cousins, our neighbors, our classmates, and our friends, who perished in the sea, because of a boat that sank.

May they continue to rest in peace.

Dr. Gosnell York
Faculty of Humanities, Development and Social Sciences
University of KwaZulu-Natal, South Africa
Professor *Extraordinarius* (Adjunct Professor)
College of Human Sciences, University of South Africa
Adjunct Professor, Northern Caribbean University, Jamaica
External Examiner, UWI (Mona)

PREFACE 2

Recalling A Tragedy

by Dr. Josiah Maynard

Some tragedies are so far-reaching in their impact on our consciousness that we can recall where we were and what we were doing at the time of their occurrence. A few that come to mind include President John F. Kennedy's assassination, the bombing of the Twin Towers in the U.S., the Asian tsunami, the Haitian Earthquake, and for Nevisians, especially those over forty, the sinking of the *Christena*.

Yes, it's been forty-two years! I was forty-two years younger and living in St. Lucia. It was a Saturday evening, August 1, 1970, around 6:00 p.m. I had just finished investigating a strange sound that I had heard a few moments before, of something like a heavy object falling in deep water making a gurgling sound as it sank. My curiosity led me to search for its source. I ran down the stairway, saw nothing and was left puzzled as to what it was. Moments afterwards my neighbor shouted to me to turn on my radio. He didn't say where to and what to listen for. He was right. The additional information was not necessary. Every radio station on the island was carrying the same report. It was about a tragic incident that had just occurred in the twin island State of St. Kitts-Nevis—my home State. A horrific tragedy had just taken place there and the entire Caribbean area was reeling from the sad news. The *Christena,* our once thought unsinkable ferry, had gone down, and over two hundred persons, young and old, had drowned. For 11 years *Christena* ferried the people of St. Kitts and Nevis the eleven plus miles across the pond. On that fateful Saturday afternoon, anyone of us could have been on the boat and been part of that tragedy.

For me, the questions came thick and fast. But the answers were difficult to come by. Was weather a factor? How many persons were on the boat? Did it have engine trouble? There were fatalities; did I know any of them? Even if I tried to call Nevis in search of answers, telecommunication between the islands at that time was difficult and costly. In time, however, the radio began to provide some of the answers. Weather was not a factor and there was no engine trouble. One reason was rumored as the lone cause of the disaster—overcrowding. Only later, as a result of further research on the incident, was it discovered that although overcrowding could have been a factor, it was not the only or major reason for the sinking.

The disaster pointed to many gaping holes in the ferry's safety system. It also exposed a number of deficiencies in what should have been better defined quality-assurance protocols in the government's operation of the ferry. Were there emergency protocols? Were passengers informed of what to do in case of an emergency? If overcrowding was indeed the cause, there should have been hell to pay by the individual(s) who allowed it to happen. Why were the life vests bolted down and virtually inaccessible to passengers? I don't think we ever got an accurate final tally of the number of souls lost in that tragedy. Meanwhile, for those who died that afternoon, these questions and their answers are late—very late. But are we better prepared today for a similar disaster? Did we learn anything from the incident to prepare us for a next time—God forbid?

I lost friends and political-sparring partners including Tony Nisbett, Sonny (Rabbit) Walwyn, Sam Sweeney, Orville Morton; a former student named Lorraine (Gertie) Griffin, and students who were currently in school, such as, Olga (Donny) Browne, Linda Mc Wilkin, and Marilyn Morris, my wife's cousin.

With the sea being visible from any point in St. Kitts-Nevis, children of school age shouldn't have to die from drowning in a boating accident. Learning to swim should become part of the school's curriculum. It's a vital life skill every boy and girl of the State should possess as long as we'll be using boats to ferry us across the pond. We are insular. For any move off the island we are compelled to use the water unless we build a bridge. Let the curriculum reflect the environment in which the students live. That's Education 101. Are we embarrassed to be identified as a nation of swimmers? Forty plus years have passed and we have done few things differently to prepare for a similar emergency. Of course we cannot avoid disasters a hundred percent of the time, but their impact can be mitigated by proper planning. As an independent nation we ought to plan so much more.

Meanwhile, a whole generation of Kittitians and Nevisians has grown up with cursory knowledge about this national tragedy. Except for monuments in Charlestown (Who reads monuments anyway?) and a poorly attended annual memorial service commemorating the event, hardly anything is known about it by the younger generation.

My friend and former colleague, Dr. Whitman Browne, is the only person I know who has written extensively on this tragedy. Shortly after its occurrence he went around St. Kitts-Nevis collecting data from survivors, victims' families, government officials and others concerned. He produced an initial definitive, vivid and dramatic book entitled *The Christena Disaster In Retrospect (1985)*. Sixteen years later, he published an updated version of the said book, *The Christena Disaster Revisited (2001)*. Now in an attempt to keep the story alive and to commemorate the forty-second anniversary of the tragedy, Dr. Browne has moved to make another printing of the book available. It will be especially useful for those who are not familiar with this portion of their national history. However, even those who were there can read the story again. It can become a keepsake for the now generation, while its content can serve as useful information for the next. Own it, read it and become informed. Treasure your national heritage. You know what they say about those who don't know their history. Don't let it happen to you.

Josiah Maynard, Ph.D.
Formerly, Superintendent of Schools
North Caribbean Conference of Seventh-day Adventists

PREFACE 3

The Sound of, Christena Sink!
Christena Sink! Still Reverberates
In My Head

by Dr. B. Osmond Farrell

"Christena sink! Christena sink! Christena sink!" These words still reverberate in my head after forty-two years. Despite the passage of time they continue to linger there. I still remember that afternoon quite vividly. Throngs of old and young persons went racing along the rough, partially paved main road of Jessup Village to the beach nearby. There, we gazed anxiously across the glistening, turquoise sea toward Nags Head, hoping to see the boat rising in the horizon.

In that now hushed and solemn atmosphere, people began murmuring that perhaps the boat had not sunk; or if it did, perhaps the casualties were few. However, that was not to be. The *MV Christena* not only sank, but took with it approximately two hundred and forty citizens—a significant percentage of the population in the twin island State of St. Kitts and Nevis.

The impact of the tragedy was instantaneous. It has also become long-lasting. Children were made orphans. Some parents buried their children. Every household on Nevis lost some relative, friend, or neighbor. In some instances it was not clear who were victims until it was suddenly evident that certain houses in villages and the town remained shuttered because their owners were resting in a watery grave. In the sad aftermath, others looked at unattended crops and straying animals and these informed them that certain people were not returning. They too were victims of the disaster.

The toll exacted by the Christena Disaster was of more than a physical nature. Nevisians, more than Kittitians, suffered from the incident. By nature, Nevisians are not an overly suspicious people, but some can be quite superstitious. A significant number of persons believed there were warning signs and ill omens everywhere before and during the disaster. Mrs. Martin of Jessups, for example, would normally spend Friday night on St. Kitts, finish her selling on Saturday, then return to Nevis on Saturday afternoon. On that Friday afternoon she simply gave away her goods to friends and customers so that she could catch the ferry and return to Nevis before the next day—Saturday, August 1, 1970. For some unknown reason, Mrs. Martin did not want to be caught traveling to Nevis the Saturday afternoon. On that afternoon, William Hutton was travelling with his children from St. Thomas to Nevis. It would have been much cheaper to get into Basseterre and catch the ferry to Nevis. However, Hutton remembers that he did not even give the idea a second thought. He simply paid the money and caught the plane over. When he heard that the ferry sank, Hutton reflected on the fact that he was saved by his travel choice to Nevis that afternoon. There were numerous other strange stories and incidents related to *Christena*. Accordingly, many people have come to believe the ferry's sinking was a matter of destiny—some were destined to die while others were to be spared the horror of death. Since I accompanied the author when he interviewed some of the survivors from Jessups, my village (one of the hardest hit areas), I heard many tales of foreboding dreams and warnings of danger.

Although a natural skeptic, I believe many of their stories. I had to. I have a story too. You see, on August 1, 1970, I too, was dressed to make that trip to St. Kitts. I was being sent to buy ice for my mother who was then an ice-cream vendor. The ice produced by the ice plant on Nevis was very limited. Accordingly, a number of the ice cream vendors on Nevis purchased ice from the ice plant in St. Kitts, which produced much more than its counterpart on Nevis. After I had dressed for the trip, it was very disappointing to be told by my mother that I should undress because I would not be going to St. Kitts. Her reason was, "I have a strange feeling. I just don't feel good about you going." Later, when news broke that the boat had sunk, my mother shared the strange dream she had. Based on my swimming skills, had I gone to St. Kitts that Saturday, I would not have been around today. It was only after my close friend and neighbor, James Joseph Claxton, barely in his teens, who made the trip to St. Kitts to buy ice for the same purpose was declared drowned, did I come to appreciate that my mother's order probably gave me a second chance at life.

It was a difficult, painful, haunting experience. Notwithstanding, the people of St. Kitts-Nevis, the smallest nation in the western hemisphere did find the social, psychological, and physical stamina, to weather what is still arguably one of the Caribbean area's most tragic sea disasters in recent times. In his book, *The Christena Disaster Forty-two Years Later*, Dr. Browne brilliantly captures the journey, the actual sinking, and the haunting consequences of that disaster. The lessons taught from a historical, social, political, economic, and cultural perspective are highly instructive and enlightening. Further, as we celebrate the forty-second anniversary of the *Christena* Disaster, there are lessons to be learned by old and young, as we revisit the story. Today, passengers get on one of the many boats nonchalantly, as they travel between Nevis and St. Kitts, without giving it any thought. Or, in the case of the "sea-bridge," one simply drives on to the barge with his car and rides between the islands, as easily as going to the next village.

This high level of comfort may once again lead to one's guard being let down, which could, in turn, have devastating effects. We had become so comfortable about travelling safely on the *Christena*, that after 11 years there was a growing belief that the ferry was unsinkable. An allusion to this point was made recently by the Deputy Prime Minister of St. Kitts-Nevis, Sam Condor. He was travelling to Nevis on August 1, 2010, to observe the 40th anniversary of the *Christena* Disaster at the Christena Memorial in Charlestown. Minister Condor noted that the boat on which he travelled to Nevis, took the names of the passengers, but did not leave the list of names on land. It was taken aboard the ferry. He reminded the audience that the world still does not know the exact number of people who died on the Christena. Strange as it might seem, Condor reminded the audience that had the modern vessel sunk, August 1, 2010, once again the exact number of victims might not have been known.

The nineteenth century American poet and philosopher, George Santayana, is credited with the saying: "Those who cannot remember their past are condemned to repeat it." The nation of St. Kitts-Nevis cannot endure another *Christena* type disaster, now, or in the near future. A good way to help ensure that one does not happen again in our lifetime is to study the story and circumstances surrounding the *Christena* Disaster. It is a story of struggles, fears, courage, and resilience. There are also messages of hope for all times. These are brought together in a vivid, captivating manner by Whitman Browne, in this work, *The Christena Disaster, Forty-two Years Later.*

B. Osmond Farrell, Ph.D.
Professor, Communication Studies
Montgomery College, Maryland

PREFACE 4

Documentation of Our
History is Crucial

by Jeffrey Phipps

Eighteen thirty-four is one of the dates associated with the ending of slavery in the former British Caribbean colonies. Also linked with the abolition of slavery, when the event actually occurred, is 1838. For St. Kitts-Nevis and most other British Caribbean islands, that became the August Monday holiday. Many persons aboard the *Christena* on Saturday, August 1, 1970, were going across to enjoy the holiday weekend on Nevis, and be at the horse races that Monday, August 3. With the new freedoms that came for Afro-Caribbean people, there was also the arduous task of rebuilding lives and finding meaning for living. A then largely broken people, though stripped of their identity and spiritual beliefs, became committed to a retooling of themselves using subliminal injections and other strategies, as they reached back to their subjugated African culture, traditions, and belief systems. In time, they brought multiple ideas together, in an emerging complex cultural paradigm.

Since the plantation economy failed on Nevis, by the 1970s a viable peasantry had emerged on the island. Many women on the island continued the market traditions that African descendents can still trace back to Africa, after hundreds of years. For Nevisians that became a well-organized economic system designed to feed themselves and also the citizens of the sugar producing sister island of St. Kitts. With plantation workers on St. Kitts, and a growing peasantry on Nevis, the system allowed for a vibrant symbiotic trading relationship between the two islands for many years. Nevisian traders called "Turn-hands" (Tun-han) provided food, including meat, ground provisions, fruits of all kinds, and livestock, such as sheep and cattle, for St. Kitts. The Kittitian traders provided much needed haberdasheries for their Nevisian neighbors. Nevisians were able to purchase sugar cheaply from St. Kitts. Many Nevisians also travelled to St. Kitts regularly because the exploiting British colonial system had conveniently riveted the islands together, making St. Kitts the dominant partner and metropole—the place to which Nevisians travelled for most government and other official services they needed. Consequently, travel between St. Kitts and Nevis has had a long history.

Before the *Christena,* there were various schooners and motor vessels including the *M/V Anslyn* and the *M/V Rehoboth.* Reflecting on that long history of inter-island travel, we dare not forget that glorious era of the sail-boats, when Nevisians knew and depended on such names as *Oceana, Lady Nisbett, Crown, Princess Royal, Sakara, and Gotham.* Those ships all ferried committed and independent entrepreneurs daily to conduct their varied business on St. Kitts. Hundreds of other Nevisians also made that regular journey because the political, social, and economic systems demanded it. To further facilitate and heighten travel between the islands, the St. Kitts, Nevis and Anguilla Government launched the 160 ft vessel *Christena* in 1959. Chief Minister Bradshaw purchased the ferry from Sprostons Ltd, of British Guiana. Once the new boat was in place, it gradually displaced the sailboats, particularly since by that time shipping sugar cane to St. Kitts was a dying business. The *Christena* started well. It also improved the comfort, efficiency, and the reliability of travel between St. Kitts and Nevis. Nevisians, and to a lesser extent Kittitians began to think they finally had a trusted and reliable vessel that would help them increase and ensure their safety as they travelled and traded between the islands.

While trade between St. Kitts and Nevis flourished, migration from each island also intensified its flow. Neither the peasant economy on Nevis nor the sugar plantation system on St. Kitts was attractive and vibrant enough to avert that movement. Further, the well-greased and growing economic engine between the islands came to a sudden halt on August 1, 1970. On that afternoon, a fully loaded *Christena* met a horrible fate. It capsized and sank suddenly off Nags Head, the Southeastern tip of St. Kitts. The incident resulted in the death of more than 200 persons—fathers, mothers, sons, daughters, teachers, traders, nuns, and mere babies resting in the arms of their parents. It was a tragedy that overwhelmed nationals and visitors alike.

While I was growing up on St. Kitts, I would always hear bits and pieces of the story about the *Christena*. However, like much of our history, that story was predominantly oral and it was never presented in the schools as part of our history curriculum. A serious study of the *Christena* incident and its impact on the islands was not available in our educational system. Later in my life, I was fortunate enough to work with Frank Tyson (also known as Frank Matthew). He was the first mate on the Motor Vessel *Christena* at the time of its demise. When I came to know Frank, now deceased, I found him a unique person and a very competent individual, at his profession, as harbor pilot for the St. Christopher and Nevis Port Authority. Unfortunately, Frank's early maritime experience came on board the *M/V Christena*, where he worked his way up to first mate. Interestingly, Frank was the first person to admit that he was untrained as a first mate then, and ill prepared to handle a sea disaster of such magnitude, when the *Christena* sank.

Some years after I met Frank, I overheard a family friend discussing a book about the *Christena* incident, and also the author of the book, Whitman T. Browne. The discussion tweaked my interest, and since I am a filmmaker, I began to think it would be a meaningful experience to grasp the opportunity, produce and direct a feature-length documentary on the *Christena* story. Somehow, I have come to feel connected and to sense an overpowering kinship with the incident. This posture did not come about merely by virtue of my being a Kittitian and citizen of the Federation of St. Kitts-Nevis. The desire came because when Frank Tyson was alive; he reported his first-hand account of the incident to me—over and over. He was very unhappy with how the story ended. From time to time Frank wished aloud that he was better trained and more thoroughly prepared for his job as first mate. He was also haunted by the specter of the ship, *Hawthorne Enterprise,* which left St. Kitts just after *Christena* and passed them struggling in the water. How could they have seen people floundering in the water and simply left them there?

It wasn't until I started interviewing for the film that I began to understand fully the depth and magnitude of the *Christena* disaster. Candid conversations with survivors and offspring of the victims impacted me in ways I could never have anticipated. I faced admonitions, threats, and accusations such as, "Why would you want to document a part of our history that is so painful and to some persons is considered ancient, sacred, and forbidden history?" At times I have wondered why Caribbean people neglect their own history but exalt that of other people, particularly those who colonized them? Further, why do we so often seem reluctant to pass on critical information from one generation to the next? Ironically, this can be a strategy by which to instruct our progeny, so they learn to link their future with the past.

Dr. Whitman T. Browne authored two books about the Christena incident. One, *The Christena Disaster In Retrospect*

(1985), and the other, *The Christena Disaster Revisited (2001)*. He should be commended for his effort because the two books have kept this story alive at a time when only few people, including Captain Sonny Skeete, Livinstone Sargeant, Dulcita David, Camella Caines, and Captain Arthur Anslyn continue to remember. Even the government has at times appeared to have forgotten the story. The work by Dr. Browne was a bold step in jump-starting the thrust toward documenting and preserving St. Kitts-Nevis contemporary history. It has, from time to time, reinvigorated the national discourse about a horrific tragedy that changed our islands forever.

Dr. Browne's books have also served as a useful testimony to the power of historical preservation and the need to continue such an effort in former colonies. As descendants of Africans, we are more than an oral people. It was our ancestors who wrote the first books on religion, spirituality, medicine, botany, and architecture. There is a variety of archeological and other evidence that supports this view. Snippets of these historical records are still available to be seen in imperial museums worldwide. The people of St. Kitts-Nevis should appreciate their indebtedness to Dr. Browne for documenting an important part of the islands' story, reflecting so uniquely on some of the traditions of our ancestors. It has also been inspirational to me, as a filmmaker; and I am aware that other individuals in the literary and artistic communities have paid attention. Through the years, every nation can create a list of horrors and triumphs. St. Kitts-Nevis is not different. What sets a people apart is how they use these events as markers, and to define themselves in the world. Do we present ourselves as a nation of weak dependent people, or as a nation of confident inspired people? Each generation in a nation must give careful thought to the foundation it lays; and to the meaning embedded in the stories it passes on.

The *Christena* story of August 1, 1970, tells me about the mettle of our people, even when they were tested painfully and severely again, just as they were tested many times before, in

1639, 1810, 1935, 1943, 1967, and then in 1970. Each time Kittitians and Nevisians rose to the challenge displaying both an unusual resolve and resilience. Despite the severity of the challenges, they managed to survive into the future. Meanwhile, there is little doubt that the *Christena* Disaster sowed the seeds for political autonomy in Nevis, demographic shifts in both islands, safer travel, between them. also political independence. Despite some successful outcomes and achievements since the *Christena* incident, a tragedy of such magnitude should never be allowed to happen again, because of incompetence and little readiness on the part of the government and people.

Jeffrey Phipps
Filmmaker.

AUTHOR'S PREFACE

We Have Changed but the Pain and the Emptiness Persist

Forty-two years have dragged by for many Nevisians and Kittitians since the sinking of the ferry *Christena* in 1970. Along the way, and during those years, there have been physical, social, political and demographic changes all around the islands. Notwithstanding such shifts through time, the emptiness and the pain from the disaster persist. The anger and vehemence Mr. Phipps met and reported in 2010, brought back memories of the time when I started to investigate the *Christena* incident as a research and writing project, back in 1982. Some of the people I encountered then were not welcoming. They simply wanted to forget the whole affair and move on with their lives, the parts of their lives that were sound and functioning well enough to keep on. For some of those people, talking about the *Christena* matter was not envisioned as worthwhile.

There were many people too pained to discuss their stories about how they were impacted by the ferry's sinking. Then, there were those who wondered aloud why anyone would want to investigate and write about such a horrible event—so many young Nevisians died, so many families were disrupted, and so many people were left barely holding on to life, at the edge of insanity. Some persons were accusative while others simply refused to speak with me. Because I was on Nevis that fateful afternoon, I witnessed the horror caused by the sudden disaster, and have tried to understand why some people reacted the way they did. During the late 1980s and early 1990s, when a fellow Nevisian visited and sought to dramatize the *Christena* event in a staged play, the entirety of Nevisian society seemed to shout a resounding, "No!" There was little interest in reliving the ferry's sinking. Time had not moved far enough to heal the pain. It was all still too vivid, too painful, and too unbearable. Now, forty plus years after, I am surprised that Jeffrey Phipps, who is interested in making a film about the incident, is still being pushed away. Seemingly, reflections on the incident continue to bring pain to the lives of some people. Just as it was, 1, 5, 10, 15, or 20 years after the incident, even today, merely pausing long enough to focus and talk about the *Christena* tragedy, even for a brief moment, becomes unbearable and disruptive to their emotional stability.

Such reactions forty-two years after, by people who survived the tragedy and persons who lost close friends and relatives as a result of the tragedy, represent the depth of the psychological wound the *Christena* incident inflicted on those lives. I think of Thelma Parris and Camella Caines, two young women on Nevis who know they had mothers, but for the past forty years have not seen them, because both mothers went down to a watery grave when the *Christena* sank in 1970. Both of these women were very young, when their mothers were snatched away suddenly. Other people filled in to raise them, and the fill-in mothers appeared to have done a good job in raising two sober and responsible women, each having a complex story to tell about loss and love, but about pain too, because at times when they are alone, on days such as Mothers' Day and Christmas, there must have been some deep yearnings for the mothers who left them so suddenly.

Then, there is my fellow Nevisian and friend, Livinstone Sargeant, who barely survived the tragedy. The event occurred at the height of his cricketing career. Had Sargeant died then, Nevis would have lost another native son, and one of its greatest cricketers, ever. However, fate came through for him. Others in the water saw Sargeant and recognized he was in danger, so they moved in and helped him. It was through the patience and cooperation of others that he made it to land and walked away alive. Notwithstanding, that incident impacted Sargeant's life profoundly. He remains forever grateful, and has never forgotten how close his life came to being snuffed out that afternoon. Today, he does not say very much about that afternoon. He was able to continue to demonstrate and display his cricketing prowess; however, Livinstone Sargeant has remained a cautious, somewhat reserved person, and he avoids as much as possible, talking about the day and circumstances in 1970, when he came so very close to dying. The terror of that situation continues to haunt his life. Although he survived, there is no reason to boast, so Sargeant continues to remain quiet on a matter he does not take pleasure in talking about. Death reached out to grab him. It was very much a miracle that he survived and forty-two years after can reflect on, and contemplate the experience, even though he refrains from talking about the matter.

Captain Sonny Skeete was in Nevis the afternoon *Christena* sank. However, his alertness, seamanship, and commitment to the people of St. Kitts and Nevis brought him to the center of the *Christena* disaster and its aftermath. On the afternoon of August 1, 1970, Skeete was directly involved with the rescue of many people thrown into the sea when the ferry *Christena* floundered. He was with the fishing boat, *Sea Hunter 1*, when it was brought to his attention that *Christena* had run into trouble on its way to Nevis, and floundered. Skeete and the captain of the *Sea Hunter* did everything possible to save passengers from the water. It was a desperate situation on both sides—for the scores of persons struggling or dying in the water, and for the rescuers on the *Sea*

Hunter 1, trying to help them. Even as the sun set and darkness fell, the *Sea Hunter* was still there trying to see in the dark, so that even one more person could be rescued and given life, amidst the death and gloom around.

Later, Skeete did all he could as a witness in the *Christena Enquiry*. He gave evidence about what he saw and heard that afternoon. After it was all over, Skeete was convinced that a number of things took place the afternoon when *Christena* sank, which were not fair to the people of St. Kitts-Nevis. Even today Skeete reflects soberly on the *Christena* matter. He is also very willing to talk with Mr. Phipps or anyone else, to share his reflections on what happened, the role he played, and the things he felt went wrong about the rescue effort forty-two years ago. Meanwhile, no one in St. Kitts-Nevis has done as much as Captain Skeete, to keep the memory of *Christena* alive. He was the person who, single handedly, many years ago, started the sea memorial ceremony off Nags Head to commemorate the *Christena,* and the more than 200 Nevisians and Kittitians who died when the ferry sank back in 1970. Because of Skeete's effort and commitment, Nevis now holds an annual August 1, *Christena* Memorial Ceremony. As a spin-off from the annual sea memorial ceremony, suggestions were made to the Nevis Island Government, under Vance Amory, that some form of broader *Christena* memorial be devised to involve more Nevisians. In 1998, a special *Christena* Memorial was constructed by the Concerned Citizens Movement (CCM) Government, at the waterfront in Charlestown, Nevis. That was a move in the correct direction, having a structure to mark the *Christena* event. Nevis government now has more than one permanent Christena monuments, accessible to citizens and visitors alike. However, the role and foresight of Sonny Skeete in the preservation of Christena's memory should always be applauded.

When the *Christena* sank in 1970, thousands of people on both St. Kitts and Nevis cried and mourned their loss. The number of Nevisians dead was greater, but it was a time on both islands when everyone cried. There were friends, relatives, teachers, and students, who died from St. Kitts and from Nevis. However, the length to which Nevisians have gone to keep the *Christena* matter alive has not been seen in St. Kitts. Over the years, there has been less and less attention to the memorial, from the Government and people in St. Kitts. For example, the markers for the *Christena* graves on St. Kitts, at the Springfield Cemetery have been removed, and the graves are being reused. Probably the politics of the *Christena* matter, as it emerged during the 1970s, helped to shape government's reactions to the event, on both islands. Right after the *Christena* event, the political leadership on Nevis used it to thrash, criticize, and blame the government on St. Kitts. During the 1980s, for example, Ivor Stevens made the comment that those *Christena* years, when he was attacking the government on St. Kitts, were some of his greatest, though not very productive years. Maybe the political conflicts and related criticisms have caused the government on St. Kitts to avoid dealing with the *Christena* matter. However, it is now forty-two years after the initial incident. The leadership of the islands has changed, and the tone of the acrimony between the two islands has diminished. Probably, this is a good time for the government and people of St. Kitts to appreciate the *Christena* event for is place in the islands' history. It was a Nevis and St. Kitts matter. The two peoples travelled and died together that afternoon. No longer should the *Christena* tragedy be memorialized only on Nevis or by Nevisians alone. It was a shared experience then; whatever is done to recall the event should also be a shared experience now. As a people with a long history of shared destiny, after forty-two years of haunting memories and times of dreaded, painful reflections, the people of St. Kitts-Nevis can now move to find new meaning in an old hurt.

For St. Kitts-Nevis the *Christena* tragedy became more than a regrettable, painful event. It was a complex historical experience that jolted and pushed the two island societies toward an age of change and new realities. As the 1970s dawned, Nevisians were frustrated and angry because they saw themselves being treated more and more like colonial subjects by St. Kitts. Nevisians hated Robert Bradshaw, leader of the government in St. Kitts, with passion, but that hatred seemed tainted with fear and a certain measure of respect for the man. On many occasions, one saw Bradshaw travelling to and from Nevis on the *Christena*. He had no special protection, and quite often he would engage Nevisians travelling on the ferry in conversations about a variety of topics. One discovery about Nevis' evolving politics was very revealing. During September-October, 1970, when the pioneers of the Nevis Reformation Party (NRP) debated over the name for their political party, names including the word "Revolutionary" were selected. The late 1960s, through the 1980s, was a time of both revolutionary thought and action in the Caribbean. Who can forget Anguilla, Dominica, Trinidad, and of course Grenada? However, no one wanted to offend Bradshaw with names that seemed outlandish and too far left. Accordingly, the political pioneers for Nevis, working to grasp some of the change suggested by a new level of cohesion on the island, opted for the more neutral political party name, Nevis Reformation Party. In a way, the NRP, a new political party for Nevis, established October, 1970, was a radical formation on the island. It captured the attention of Nevisians, young and old, from town and from country, as no party did before. Meanwhile, NRPs leadership teased, dared, and frustrated Bradshaw, the Labor Party, and the government in St. Kitts. The NRP on Nevis used some of the very tactics against Bradshaw, that he used earlier to galvanize the people of St. Kitts against planter-class politics and domination on St. Kitts, during the 1940s and 1950s.

In that struggle for political change and healing on Nevis, the politicians spent ten long and hard years, reminding Nevisians about their pain from the tragedy. At one time in 1974, for example, Ivor Stevens wanted to frustrate Bradshaw's thrust toward independence for St. Kitts-Nevis, so he spoke to the

House of Assembly for some 25 hours, in favor of secession. Ironically, Fitzroy Bryant argued later that when he spoke for as long as he did, Stevens prevented a vote on the secession issue. All of Stevens' speech was not about the *Christena* disaster and it tragic impact on Nevisians, but some of it was.

For the whole of the 1970s, and even as Bradshaw lay dying in 1978, the NRP attacked his independence plan, achieved the initial stages of autonomy for Nevis, then joined with the St. Kitts-based opposition party, the People's Action Movement (PAM) in 1980, to push aside the Labor Party Government. By collaborating with the PAM in 1980, the NRP played a critical role in rewriting the history of St. Kitts-Nevis. By 1983, NRP and PAM, two political parties dead set against independence for St. Kitts-Nevis, up until 1980, had the unique honor of leading the islands into independence, on September 19. Ironically, that date is 3 days beyond Mr. Bradshaw's birth date, September 16—but, a day the government under Labor Party leadership, acted to institutionalize as National Heroes' Day. This was certainly with the intent of honoring the memory of Mr. Bradshaw, their hero-politician, while St. Kitts-Nevis prepare to celebrate independence, on September 19.

It has been forty-two years since the *Christena* tragedy, and there have been many changes on the islands—a number of them propelled by the independent politics spurred by the island's response to the tragic event of 1970. Nevis now has its independent assembly. It took many tries, but the roads on the island are better than ever before, in the island's history. As of 2006, sugar is no longer produced in St. Kitts or Nevis, on a commercial basis. Related to this, has been the demise of the traditionally strong belief in, and a weakening of labor unionism on St. Kitts. Meanwhile, the St. Kitts sugar factory, which shaped society, politics, and the economy in the islands since 1912, ground to a halt in 2006. Travel between the islands has improved ten-fold, and at this point in the islands' history it goes both ways. It is no longer just Nevisians going to St. Kitts. Kittitians are now coming to Nevis, too. And, also related to this, are signs that the animosity and malice between the two islands are thawing. The airport in St. Kitts is no longer the white elephant it once was. Real planes are now flying from there. Nevisian students no longer have to attend the sixth form in St. Kitts. They now have their own sixth form college and are taking their place in academia.

Unfortunately, the changes on the islands during the last forty-two years have not all been positive. Some have been evil and very destructive to the islands. Before the *Christena* incident, drugs and guns were hardly heard of on St. Kitts-Nevis. Seemingly, the progressive changes that came to the islands brought with them painful costs that are still being realized. Also, like the other nations of the world, St. Kitts and Nevis have had their encounters with the dreadful AIDS disease. Nevisians have two elections while Kittitians have one. Meanwhile, the cost of elections in both islands has become prohibitive, to the point that politicians are increasingly being set up for sale, and finding wealthy buyers too! The result is that slowly but surely, the poorer citizens are being pushed aside, as wealthy bidders call the tunes. They pay the political pipers, too. And, the changes in the islands' politics get even more complex when we examine the matter of voting. Hundreds of St. Kitts-Nevis citizens now make it home, from other countries, to participate in the elections. However, their dual citizenship allows them to vote in St. Kitts-Nevis, and that other country, but none is allowed to stand as a candidate for elections at home. The migrant citizens are welcome to vote, but not to be voted for—that is unacceptable and should be illegal.

In spite of the fact that many aspects of life on St. Kitts-Nevis have changed dramatically, during the past forty-two years, to the point that the islands can be described as having been transformed, when one speaks in reference to the before, and the after, *Christena* tragedy. However, not every dimension of life, not every aspect of human nature that was touched and moved by the sinking of the ferry changed rapidly and dramatically, during the past forty-two years. There were aspects of human life and mind that became so drained and horrified by the pain, death, sudden, and long separation, that meaning for such victims lingered and stayed glued to the *Christena* tragedy. In her letter to the mother she barely knew, Camella Caines reflected on her experience of pain and emptiness while coming of age and taking on the challenges of this world, having barely known one's birth mother. Any life after such an experience as the *Christena's* sinking in 1970, where thoughts of death and such sudden loneliness come to one's life while still a young girl, the change and its meaning will come slowly. So, Camella Caines wrote and still speaks about the pain and emptiness that overshadowed her life and will not go away. The dramatic change; the optimism about tomorrow; and all those dreams, with their capacity for progress, always remained ripe for development, but never in reach of the planning done. There could never be a going home to a birth mother. Those special girl stories about growing up, falling in love, that first kiss, and all those thousands of other things to tell; talk to a mother about, and to feel the assurance of her warm knowing touch, did not happen. Her mother Christene Dore died too soon on *Christena*. She was merely 32 years old.

Thelma and Romeo Parris are two of eight children another mother on the Christena, left behind, when she too was suddenly snatched away from them. As fate would have it, there have been good family and friends who came into the lives of these children to fill that emptiness left by a mother who died suddenly and young, leaving all her children behind, lonely and forlorn. On that fateful day, she left them in the morning for her usual trip to sell in St. Kitts. But she died suddenly that afternoon.

The reality of the situation is that those children, alone, can really explain their experiences since their mother left and went away. Their challenges must have been varied and probably very complex. But, who can face life, and simply go on quietly into time, after the impact the *Christena* tragedy must have had, and continues to have, on their lives? For forty-two years, they have been forced to bear the pain; to hear stories over and over about who their mother was, and to build impossible dreams about what life with their own mother could have been. Both Romeo, who was shipped off to St. Kitts, and Thelma, who was allowed to stay in Nevis with the other siblings, talked about an overpowering displacement in their lives, that, despite their rescue and nurturing by others who loved them, they carry the pain of motherless children, too burdened by time to forget it all. Maybe, over time, the pain from that loss has been lessened. However, the meaning of *Christena's* sinking, to their lives, may still be too broad and too deep for those beyond the experience to appreciate and comprehend, except by being one of the many children, whose mothers died suddenly, leaving them alone, early in their lives. None of the children was on the ferry that afternoon but they are all still stressed and pained, forty-two long years after. Who can forget a mother who went to work so that she could feed her eight children, but on that August afternoon, was overwhelmed by water and fate. She never came back. Despite that early, crippling experience, many of the children found the desire and the fortitude to move on with their lives. Today, they are still very grateful for the individuals and communities which came together and rescued them, so that they could move beyond the horror of *Christena*, forty-two unsettling, dreary years ago.

I was living on Nevis the afternoon the *Christena* sank. That scene of Nevisians crying on the street, from New Castle to Charlestown, for some six miles, is still very vivid in my mind, forty-two years after. The operation of removing the first dead bodies from Charlestown pier was tentative, somewhat disorganized, and was virtually led by nurses, not the men. At that time very few people living on Nevis had ever seen 38 dead bodies in one place, all of them women. Meanwhile, there was another rescue and recovery operation connected with the *Sea Hunter 1*, at Jones' Bay. Assisting on land were people such as the government secretary on Nevis, George Bradley, along with Arthur Evelyn, Ivor Stevens, and some others. Of course,

Sonny Skeete was aboard the *Sea Hunter 1*. Throughout that night there were concerns about whether family and friends survived the tragedy. The unpreparedness of Nevis to manage and deal with such an event effectively, was very glaring. The emergency system was inept and broken. Communication was virtually nonexistent. Despite the boast by the PAM that one of its leaders, Dr. Simmonds, was the only medical doctor on the island initially, what was never said was that Nevisians had a doctor at the hospital that night because the *Christena* sank and it was impossible for Dr. Simmonds to travel back to St. Kitts on the boat's return trip. Meanwhile, it was quite a task to get other medical personnel over from St. Kitts. Cars lined up along the sides of the unlit airstrip, and shone their lights to aid landing at the airport, but the attempt failed.

During the following day, Sunday August 2, 1970, one saw sad, mournful, and angry scenes at the yard of the Alexandra Hospital. Melon-Gene Griffin was writhing in horror and grief. She had been inside the make-shift morgue at the hospital and saw the corpse of her daughter, Gertie Lorraine, who worked as a nurse in St. Kitts. There was Charles Freeman, walking in the hospital yard with a coffin on his head, intending to recover the body of his wife, Augusta, or his sister, Tamar. I did not see Robert Bradshaw, but there were stories about how angrily Nevisians reacted to him, blaming Bradshaw for the great loss of Nevisian lives on the ferry. There were also stories of him crying publicly, when he grasped the enormity of the loss on the island. Also, for the first time, while on Nevis, Bradshaw was accompanied by body-guards.

Among the dead were many of my friends and acquaintances. Gertie Lorraine, was from my village, Butler's. Tony Nisbett, Sonny "Parks" Walwyn, and Carmen Joseph, were among my many friends, who died suddenly that afternoon. Ms. Joseph had gone to St. Kitts because she was making final arrangements for a trip to the Virgin Islands for her summer vacation. She was a young teacher at Combermere School. On the afternoon she drowned Ms. Joseph was wearing a pair of sea shell earrings I had recently made and presented her. I attended more than one of the many funerals held throughout the island. Ms. Joseph's funeral was one of them.

To all who were in St. Kitts and Nevis in August, 1970, the *Christena* event was very riveting and compelling. It disrupted the normal flow of life, throughout the islands. The politics and the relationship between the islands shifted decidedly over time. From the afternoon of August 1, and for a long time after, the government's radio station ZIZ played only somber, solemn, sacred music. However, that hardly mattered to anyone since both islands were bewildered and in mourning. No one wanted to hear calypsos, love songs, or rock-n-roll. They were not in the mood for music of revelry. Travel between the islands was interrupted temporarily. The agricultural and fishing trade between the islands took another 10 years before it could recapture its former vigor. Unfortunately, it would never be as vibrant or as successful again. Meanwhile, thousands of pounds and dollars were channeled to St. Kitts-Nevis as aid from Kittitians and Nevisians living elsewhere. A number of young and older Nevisians who lost family members in the tragic sinking of the ferry were invited to leave Nevis and live abroad. In time, the large number of young Nevisians who died on *Christena,* along with the associated emigration, were critical factors that helped in causing a downturn in Nevis' population up to about the 1990s. As World War 1, did in France, when the *Christena* sank in 1970, it created the conditions for a lost generation of Nevisians.

At the dawn of August 1, 2012, forty-two years after the *Christena* tragedy, both St. Kitts and Nevis have been profoundly transformed, not only by the *Christena* incident, but also by time and other complex circumstances. The islands are now an independent nation, and more closely aligned in relations between the two people. Most people will now agree that the islands have progressed in almost every sense of the word: education and access to education, home ownership, employment, and a shifting demography. The population became more vibrant, there was wider media access and greater exposure to the world, while enjoying access to improved technology and more money. There was also a modernization of all aspects of the islands' infrastructure.

But, modernization and the growing grasp at materialism in Caribbean islands, including St. Kitts-Nevis, have come at disruptive, stressful, and great social costs. Back in 1970, forty-two years ago, Alvin Toffler, noted that culture shifts can disrupt and push human lives beyond normal patterning, forcing them out of the usual control. Today, we can look back and appreciate that the *Christena* incident still evokes painful memories for many Nevisians and Kittitians. However, the loss that came from the *Christena*, may not be as threatening to the future stability of these islands, as they plunge into modernity, with its vulgar forms of capitalism, culture shock, greed, and all their discontents. The islands now depict more displays of wealth, but less realization of happiness. Today, there is much more fear and uncertainty in the islands, than were experienced forty-two years ago. For many among the younger generations, the *Christena* story is unknown, despite its profound meaning in St. Kitts and Nevis history. It has become of more interest to many Nevisians and Kittitians to survive as alienated individuals, in a Caribbean world that has become increasingly threatening and hostile to human longevity. My hope for Nevisians and Kittitians is that they find the social, psychological, moral, physical, and legal know-how to move beyond their present morass, and what former President Jimmy Carter once referred to as, "a malaise of the soul," the ultimate social failure in a nation. Such a condition sets the stage for a more crippling disaster than the *Christena* experience—and one the present population may find more difficult to endure and survive. However, lessons can be learned from the *Christena* incident, despite its faded memory to some. It can still be instructive in the matter of future survival, for Nevisians, Kittitians, and for other Caribbean people. On the issue of learning for resilience and survival, forty-two years ago is still quite recent.

Chapter 1

The Christena Nightmare: Gives a vivid and compelling account of the circumstances that surrounded the sinking of the St. Kitts-Nevis ferry, *Christena,* on August 1, 1970. It takes the reader back to the boat's departure, the sinking, and the rescue effort.

Chapter 2

Of Dreams, Visions, and Superstition: Here is a review of the attempts by citizens of St. Kitts-Nevis to grapple with, explain, and make sense of the sudden tragedy that had come to overwhelm their lives. There were persons who claimed to have experienced foreboding of the painful event in their dreams. Twelve different stories are related.

Chapter 3

First Hand Accounts I: To date, three attempts have been made to tell, and keep the *Christena story alive: The Christena Disaster in Retrospect (1985), The Christena Disaster Revisited (2001), and now, The Christena Disaster Forty-Two Years Later.* Included in the chapter are many of the first-hand reports from people who were impacted by the ferry's sinking. Some of them were interviewed during 1980-1983, and again in 1998-2000.

Chapter 4

First Hand Accounts II: The stories here were created from interviews of people who survived the sinking, or had some link to it. Most of these stories are based on the 1998-2000, interview updates. One aim of the chapter is to tell where some of the *Christena* victims are, and how they have done in life since 1970.

Chapter 5

Newspaper Reports: A review of newspaper articles published shortly after the ferry's sinking. They were chosen from, *The Labor Spokesman* and *The Democrat*, then the leading papers in the islands. *The Democrat* is sympathetic to the views and ideas of the People's Action Movement (PAM) political party. In contrast, *The Labor Spokesman*, is sympathetic to the ideas and positions of the Labor Party.

Chapter 6

Photographic Reflections: This section of the book consists of a collection of photographs. It is a deliberate attempt by the author to put faces to names, plus, present aspects of the times, events, and places in pictures.

Chapter 7

Innocence, Ignorance, and Reality: The chapter reflects on how colonialism desensitized the people of St. Kitts-Nevis, to their objective interests, particularly up to 1970. That situation left the people too inept to deal with their own reality. Consequently, both the government and people of St. Kitts-Nevis were ill-prepared to deal with such a tragedy. The ferry's crew was untrained and none of the security systems was in order. We are now forty-two years beyond the disaster, but there is still uncertainty about how many passengers were really aboard the ferry.

Chapter 8

Politics And The Disaster: What at first seemed an unfortunate sinking of the inter-island ferry, soon became woven into the increasingly tense, inter-island politics. For the next ten years and beyond, the *Christena* tragedy remained an important factor in St. Kitts vs. Nevis politics. Eventually, it contributed to fundamental shifts in political relations between the two islands.

Chapter 9

The Commission of Inquiry Report: This is a reprint of the one-man *Commission Report* about the *Christena* incident, based on the inquiry conducted by J. D. B. Renwick, appointed by Premier Robert Bradshaw. Mr. Renwick once worked in the court system of St. Kitts-Nevis as a magistrate.

Chapter 10

Questions Still Unanswered: The chapter provides a critical analysis of the government's conclusions as to how and why the ferry sank.

Chapter 11

Riding Out the Storm: The final chapter delves into how the islands and their people strategized to survive the tragedy and move beyond its compelling grasp, into a changed future.

Appendices 1-13

Thirteen related documents: Each of these documents contains some information about the ferry *Christena or the Aftermath of the Sinking,* beginning with the boat's arrival in St. Kitts-Nevis during 1959. The documents include names of people who died and who survived the sinking. The name of the people who testified at the official inquiry are also included. Some of the more recent reflections on, and reactions to the incident and its aftermath are also included here.

Whitman T. Browne, Ph. D.
St. Thomas, VI
February 8, 2012.

CHAPTER ONE

Nightmare on the Christena

It was about 3:30 the afternoon of August 1, 1970. The sea was calm, blue, and inviting. A warm Caribbean sun still shone brightly, as the crowded ferry *Christena,* loaded with an expectant weekend crowd, swayed, rolled, and danced across the ocean on its usual afternoon run from St. Kitts to Nevis. However, the die of doom had been cast. The *Christena* was on its final run between the islands, with an illegal passenger load, more than twice its registered capacity of 155. She would never make the crossing to Nevis that afternoon. Rather, the ferry suffered a tragic and catastrophic fate when it sank suddenly, tossing everyone aboard to the mercy of a forever waiting sea. That afternoon, in a sudden, unguarded moment, almost 250 persons died a horrific, untimely death.

When the story of the ferry's sinking became known, a blanket of gloom swept over the people of both St. Kitts and Nevis. The terrible news, combined with the falling shadows of evening, quickly drove the sun and mirth from the lives of Nevisians and Kittitians at home, and everywhere else in the world. Everyone had a relative, friend, or neighbor, who had been snatched away with *Christena,* not to be seen at home, in the villages, on the streets, at the churches, or on the job again—forever!

1

Long after the sun returned, the smiles and joyful spirit of the people did not. Rather, the shadows and the gloom stayed in the lives and being of the people. They would not go away! The emotional shroud brought on by such sudden deaths just would not be lifted. Two entire societies, one on Nevis, the other on St. Kitts lay dazed, trapped by a common tragedy. So, too, were relatives and friends throughout the Caribbean and elsewhere in the world. Like battered, bruised, and disoriented travelers, they all lay worn, burdened, and groping in shock. Many persons struggled with fear while others were writhing in anger. There were also those among an aching people who dangled dangerously on a precipice of insanity. What a time it was for Nevisians and Kittitians to find themselves numbed by overpowering gloom and helplessness!

It was Saturday before August Monday, usually a joyful holiday, since it memorialized the abolition of slavery in the islands, back in 1838. Many persons were beginning to savor the long summer holiday from school. Weddings were planned. Travel abroad to visit family, friends, and lovers was on the minds of many. There were also preparations ongoing for horse races on Nevis. Other plans for bacchanal were afoot to commemorate the joyful memory of the freedoms that have come since the abolition of slavery, and growing dreams of more political empowerment. Many Nevisians had also travelled to St. Kitts to shop, trade, or for other reasons. August Monday was still two days away.

However, for all those people heading for the ferry that afternoon, Nevis was now! Some did not want to miss the horse races scheduled on the island for Monday. Many Kittitians and "people from away," migrants returning home for vacation, also wanted to be on Nevis. They intended to check out the races, see the island, and reunite with family and friends—just have a good time back home. Despite the ferry's limited passenger capacity (155 passengers), more than 300 persons were waiting to board. They all were bound for Nevis and intended to get there by ferry that afternoon. Nothing gave a hint of imminent danger. Even the calm, blue, waiting sea belied the impending horror about to visit the islands. Further, harmless-looking ripples caressed the surface, as the ferry *Christena* rocked gently at the pier, waiting to receive the long line of Nevis-bound passengers. Some were dressed in bright holiday outfits. Others, such as butchers and hucksters, in work clothes. And, there were those in ordinary dress too. But the three nuns in religious regalia stood out, as the waiting group began a slow, funeral like march, to the *Christena*, before it left at 3:30 p.m., that afternoon; the scheduled time for its departure from St. Kitts. There was usually no cut off time and hardly any need to hurry. If you made the boat you could get on. No matter the size of the group, few passengers were ever turned back from the ferry. There were many occasions, including that afternoon, when it went back to the pier for one more passenger.

A sign on the ferry said 155 passengers. But, on such afternoons, no one counted passengers or tickets in advance on the *Christena*. As many people as were waiting, could board the boat. A commuter just had to be there before the ferry left. That was the practice. Despite the many premonitions, there was no reason seen that Saturday afternoon, why things should be different. Talk about the large crowd at the pier was drifting across Basseterre. Since Nevis was where the action was, none of the fun lovers wanted to miss it. They were determined to take the hour ride across. Captain James Ponteen was around with friends. He was firing a rum with the boys, when he heard about the crowded situation at the pier. Back then, there was one ferry. It made one trip to each island in the morning and one trip to each island in the afternoon. There were very few occasions then, when the ferry made an extra trip—even when everyone was certain it was overcrowded. That afternoon, it appeared that Ponteen decided to leave the pier a few minutes early to avoid some of the crowd. Consequently, the *Christena* left the Treasury Pier in Basseterre just before 3:30. However, when the captain learned that one of his huckster friends was late and she could be seen rushing across the pier with her baskets, he backed up to allow her on board. The friend, Pappy Liburd, and two other persons who were destined to participate in that *Christena* event made it aboard. Pappy's leap onto the ferry was very athletic. The crowd aboard, including Captain Ponteen, applauded her. After the stragglers were on board, *Christena* headed toward Nevis. None of those aboard, joking, drinking, or simply looking across to Nevis expectantly, was aware that afternoon's trip would be the ferry's final crossing. Probably no one even thought about it then. Pappy Liburd seemed in good spirits because as soon as she settled down, Pappie opened a bottle of liquor and started to drink. When another passenger chided her, Pappy simply replied in her Nevisian tongue, "A wha eh be" (So what?).

On that fateful afternoon, *Christena's* passenger load consisted of a wide range of age groups, lifestyles, and backgrounds. Sonny (Parks) Walwyn and Orville Morton were government officers from Nevis who worked in St. Kitts. Also on board, were Nurse Arthurton, of Charlestown, who was stealing a day off, and Nurse Lorraine Griffin from Butler's, on a weekend off from the hospital in St. Kitts. There was Carmen Joseph, too, a teacher from Newcastle. She was planning her trip to the US Virgin Islands for summer vacation. From Brickkiln were Linda McQuilkin, a recent graduate from St. James School, and Donnie Browne, a student at Charlestown Secondary School. However, those were just a few of the passengers who were present at that great gathering on the *Christena*. The ferry began to dance dangerously from one side to the other, right from the start of its journey. Some of the passengers who survived the incident, suggested it appeared the captain got little response from the controls.

Seemingly, the *Christena* behaved as if it were an unwilling participant in destiny. Later, as part of the investigation, four divers went down to the *Christena*. They found that the throttle was still in the full-forward position. The rudder and other steering apparatus were also intact. Despite the uneven dance of the ferry, its three hundred plus passengers soon began to pass the time casually, expecting to arrive in Nevis safely and on-time. Some chatted and joked with friends. Others were having a small holiday party in the Captain's cabin. Meanwhile, there were some who cautiously changed position, moving upstairs as water came inside the lower section of the ferry, each time it rolled from one side to the other.

Orville Morton, a well-known Nevisian cricketer was celebrating his birthday, thus the small party aboard. That party along with Pappie on the deck, appeared to have been the extent of the drinking of liquor aboard that afternoon. Morton had sent someone to buy more liquor, but that person missed the ferry. Still, a feast sans booze was in progress. Some of the passengers had also brought goat-water aboard. It was then, and still is, a popular holiday dish in St. Kitts and Nevis. Most of the feasting was taking place inside the captain's cabin. But, a few passengers, including, Anthony Nisbett of Brick Kiln Village, were seen eating outside the cabin's door. Meanwhile, it was becoming more noticeable that water continued to enter the lower portion of the ferry. It was increasingly uncomfortable for passengers traveling in the second-class section of the boat. Still, no sudden disturbance of the water had become evident. However, as *Christena* neared Nags' Head, the last section of St. Kitts, before it entered the open channel between the islands, the rolling movement grew more pronounced and vigorous. Suddenly, the ferry lost all sense of balance. For the first time that afternoon, some passengers began to question their wisdom in deciding to make the trip under such crowded condition. At that point, however, all aboard were in, and totally committed to the ensuing fate.

It was just after 4:00 p.m. The captain had turned the controls over to his first mate, Frank (Matthew) Tyson. It was time to collect the fares and that was done by Captain Ponteen. As the captain moved about the ferry collecting fares, he could hear comments about the frightening movement of the ferry. It was because of concern for the comfort and security of passengers why Captain Ponteen suggested crew members adjust the position of some the cargo. The captain also asked some passengers to change places, in an attempt to bring equilibrium to the ferry. Despite the precarious situation, some of the passengers moved reluctantly. Others did not move at all. After all, they had seen the ferry dance on the water before.

Notwithstanding, concern increased when none of the adjustments the captain made steadied the *Christena*. Accordingly, Doldria Nolan, a passenger from Mt. Lily, Nevis, suggested to the captain that he try sailing the ferry closer to land. Captain Ponteen's response was, "It's calm enough to make it the way we are going." Unfortunately, Doldria and two of her sisters died in the accident. They knew how to swim but had no experience swimming out in the ocean, almost one mile from land. Rupert Wade and Earle Parris were traveling in a fishing boat behind *Christena*. They had gone to St. Kitts to sell fish and were on their way back to Nevis. As they sailed in the wake of the ferry, they could not avoid noticing how it rocked and rolled in the water. The two men soon observed the rhythm in the dance of the ferry had increased to a danger point. They became convinced that the *Christena* could not travel much further in that manner. It would not make it to Nevis in safety without some mishap.

When Rupert left St. Kitts that afternoon his intention was to beat the ferry across to Nevis. He and Earle had a head-start. They were certain *Christena* would meet them in Nevis. As fate had it, however, their engine developed some trouble and slowed them down. Thus, the *Christena* passed them and at that point was in the lead. Once the engine was running again, Rupert decided to retake the lead. But as he closed in on *Christena*, his seaman's instinct would not allow him to pass and leave the seemingly doomed ferry behind. Rupert's girlfriend, baby, a cousin, and many friends were aboard. He just could not sail on to Nevis when it seemed that something very ominous was about to happen.

Unfortunately for Rupert, he never saw the family he had on board the ferry again. Although he was there when it all happened, his child, his girlfriend, and his cousin, died that afternoon. He could not save them. However, his quick thinking and committed perseverance contributed to saving many of the people who did survive the disaster. Once Rupert realized that tragedy was imminent, he acted. He and Earle signaled the ferry to cut speed. They also suggested that it sail closer to land. Earle and Rupert were certain their signals were seen by the crew of the *Christena,* but there was no change in its trajectory, speed, or unusual movements. It did not matter how the men from the fishing boat tried, there was no response to any of their signals. Rupert remained at the helm of the fishing boat. His companion Earle had strict orders to keep his eyes glued to the ferry. Based on what they saw, the two men in the boat expected passengers to start plunging into the water at any moment. Their wait was not long.

Earle sounded the alarm as the *Christena* rolled violently. At first it was one man. Then other passengers started falling into the sea. Even when the sea is rough, the extended guitar-head portion of St. Kitts provides added shelter for the sea before crossing the channel between the islands. As boats move into the open sea, away from Nags Head, the very area where *Christena* was sailing, they move into the Narrows' Channel. Since there is no more shelter from the extended area of St. Kitts, rougher movement of the water becomes evident. That was part of the problem the ferry encountered, as it made its burdened journey to Nevis, August 1, 1970. It barely survived the sheltered portion of the journey. Now, the ferry was unable to negotiate and survive the increased swells encountered in the open channel. The danger mounted and the death knell rang right after the ferry entered the channel. Suddenly, the *Christena* was sinking. Everyone aboard was having an encounter with death—staring death straight in the face. At that point the ferry had taken on its limit of water. The captain's skill, luck, or prayers could not prevent disaster. The accident occurred just about one mile, or 1.5 km off Nags Head.

The Nightmare

The ferry made its final roll. Then the nightmare began. Passengers jumped or fell into the sea as the boat started to sink. First the right side, then her stern plunged into the sea. Passengers could be heard crying, praying, or cursing in response to their sudden dilemma. Former passengers were swimming, thrashing in horror, or just lying there in the water. Others were clinging to the ferry as it lingered briefly on the surface, sinking slowly. Many of the passengers were already dead, the pressure of the water having trapped them inside. When the force of water slammed the cabin door shut, all the passengers feasting inside called out in desperation for help. However, there was confusion everywhere and no one could help them. Meanwhile, buoyant benches inside the ferry, designed as vehicles to life and safety, became weapons of death, as they floated about inside the boat striking anyone in their path. Swimmers who fell clear of the sinking ferry tried to swim away as fast as they could. Overcome by great fear, other passengers clung to the *Christena's* bow. At the same time, passengers such as Livinstone Sargeant, Joseph Budgeon, the first-mate, Frank Matthew-Tyson, and some others, were struggling to make it outside the boat. Their fight was against time, gravity, and ultimately death.

Frank recalled that Budgeon climbed over him, while he (Frank) held on to the steering wheel. Fortunately, all three men had a will to live and survived the ordeal. There were the dead, the bleeding, and the horrified, dying everywhere around them. Instantly, the surrounding water had become a crowded flotsam and jetsam—with boxes, baskets, bodies, and struggling passengers all afloat on the surface. Helpless children, desperate men, and women, were all there—most of them dying. Unfortunately, many of those left alive in the water could not swim. Others had no will to try. They were too shocked and disoriented, even to attempt saving their own lives. Seemingly, the anticipated outcome of that mishap left many who dared to think, too dazed to be altruistic at that time. More than one hundred persons were clinging rigidly to the slowly sinking bow. It was a desperate search for safety and life as they saw overwhelming danger and death all around them. Their bewildered utterances were loud, desperate, and unforgettable. Some were prayerful, others blasphemous, but all very sad. The ongoing scene of confusion recreated the drama at the Tower of Babel—there was a need for calmness and communication, but the situation of desperation allowed neither. Nothing curbed the horror and terror of that afternoon—not the prayers, or the blasphemy. The helplessness, the fear, the struggle in the water, and the dying continued mercilessly. The bow of the ferry offered some of the people hope as it teetered for a while above the water. However, like a fleeting glimmer of sunshine on a stormy day, the bow of *Christena* soon disappeared into the sea. Many holding on for dear life sank with *Christena* to its watery grave. The ferry was gone in less than 15 minutes. By then, more people were struggling in the water. Some were flailing their arms in panic, others cried out in fear of death. Calm and cooperation might have saved more souls, but desperation and terror were the order of the day. None who witnessed that scene and survived it will ever forget what they saw. Ironically, some very good swimmers, including Orville Morton and Sam Sweeney, among them, were trapped in the captain's cabin and died at the onset of the disaster. When the boat made that first sinking plunge, the sudden oncoming water pressure had locked them inside. They were enjoying their goat-water. One month later, the divers sent down by the Commission of Inquiry saw five skeletons still locked inside the cabin.

Rescue

Some persons left alive read the situation quickly and fought to save others. One young man grabbed a piece of floating debris, drew a knife, and stuck it in the board. He warned others away with the comment: 'This is my life!" Livinstone Sargeant and some fourteen others stayed alive by clinging to an oil drum. It was a slow tedious process, but they maneuvered themselves to safety. Franklyn Browne, buoyed by skill and perseverance, helped his son Roger and another lad about Roger's age survive. However, others such as Carmen Joseph, who started the survival journey, were lost. According to reports, Carmen was seen floating on a crate. Later, some evil person grabbed the crate, knocked out Carmen and left her in the water. Then, that person used the crate to escape death. Carmen's body was among the first set of bodies brought to Nevis that Saturday afternoon. Rusty swimmers such as Victor Swanston swam, prayed, and hoped their muscles would not fail them. Expert swimmers such as Frank Matthew-Tyson, Arrington Browne, Clifford Browne, Wyclide Condell, and a number of others, moved around in the water, gave advice, and helped a number of stragglers stay alive. The calypsonian, King Barkey, could not swim. However, he was able to grab a roll of plastic that floated by. It kept him alive until one of the rescue boats came by and picked him up.

Reports, including the testimony of First Mate, Frank Matthew-Tyson and others, claimed that a number of swimmers sighted a ship passing by and did everything to attract the passing boat. It was identified as the *Hawthorne Enterprise,* on its way from St. Kitts. The ship came by shortly after the *Christena's* submersion. Initially the ship was sailing toward the area where the sinking occurred. A number of survivors actually started swimming to meet the oncoming ship. However, as if only teasing the people struggling in the water, the *Hawthorne Enterprise,* reportedly, changed course, lay-to for a while, then moved on. The captain and crew of the *Hawthorne Enterprise* later denied any awareness of the disaster, until they heard about it on the radio the next day. To this day, survivors who saw the ship approaching swear that its captain and crew lied. The matter became very political in the next few months and was woven into the islands' local politics. The government stuck to the position that captain and crew of the *Hawthorne Enterprise* did see the sinking *Christena* and its passengers struggling in the water, but they refused to answer a veritable SOS from the *Sea Hunter 1,* or worse, sailed away leaving scores to perish. A native Kittitian, Joshua Halliday, who served as harbor pilot, was aboard the *Hawthorne Enterprise* before it left St. Kitts, just behind the *Christena.* He stated later that they all looked at the ferry, "And we commented on its seeming in danger of sinking, as it passed by."

Election time was approaching and the opposition People's Action Movement (PAM) party on St. Kitts saw the ferry's sinking as good for opposition politics. The issue was later woven into the party politics of both St. Kitts and Nevis, like thread in cloth. Premier Bradshaw, leader of the Labor Party and government, accepted the reported statements that the *Hawthorne Enterprise* saw the swimmers, and that it was later contacted on radio by the *Sea Hunter 1.* These were serious accusations against Captain Wynter and the crew of *The Hawthorne Enterprise.* If the captain lost in court, he and his crew could be in big trouble. It would also relieve some of the political and psychological pressure on Bradshaw's government, that followed in the wake of the disaster. With about 250 citizens dead, families disrupted, citizens angry, and the government being blamed for everything, Premier Bradshaw would have given anything for a scapegoat, onto whom to shift some of the overwhelming blame. The government immediately banned Captain Wynter and his ship from operating in St. Kitts-Nevis waters. Not surprisingly, politicians of the PAM party, the opposition party on St. Kitts, disagreed with the government's action. They accepted the captain's denial and joined with its St. Kitts-based agent, S. L. Horsford, to defend and celebrate Captain Wynter, treating him like a hero.

In this matter, the politicians had a classic opportunity to unite on behalf of the citizenry of St. Kitts-Nevis and in the national interest. However, they yielded to party politics. The opposition leaders used every strategy to knock any crutch from Bradshaw's grasp. He, in an angry frustrated response, gave no quarter to his tormentors.

Whitman T. Browne, Ph.D.

Heroes

On the other hand, many ordinary citizens acted bravely during the disaster. None of them appeared to have thought about politics then. They saw the danger; understood the possible outcome, and acted to preserve life. Frank Matthew-Tyson, the first-mate, unselfishly assisted Budgeon to make it out of the sinking ferry on time. He was later picked up by the *Sea Hunter 1,* whose crew volunteered to get involved and saved as many lives as they could, when it was brought to their attention that the inter-island ferry, *Christena,* had sunk. Frank Tyson kept on assisting with the rescue, paying little attention to his own situation. Dulcita Browne lost five children, but she used a bag with about five breadfruit to help Edna Browne survive the accident. The two women were not related, but Edna could not swim and Dulcita noticed she was in danger of drowning. So, she shared her vehicle to survival, a floating bag with five breadfruit.

Wade and Parris

Ultimately though, the first heroes of the rescue operation were Rupert Wade and Earle Parris. Wade and Parris were there and rescued some of the first passengers who fell overboard. At the same time, since Wade sensed the magnitude of the ensuing disaster; he realized there was a need for help with such a rescue operation. His boat was small. Wade also knew he could not rely on its engine or his gasoline supply. Accordingly, the passengers Wade picked up were quickly put ashore at Nags Head. They were able to signal and warn Michael King of the disaster as he passed by later, taking his sister over to Nevis. Having put the passengers ashore, Wade headed for the Cockleshell Bay area where he expected to get help. However, no one was there. Undaunted by that initial failure to secure help, he headed for Cliff Dwellers on Nevis and hoped Captain Phillip Miller would be there with his very fast, deep-sea fishing boat, *Sea Hunter 1*. Luckily, *Sea*

Hunter 1 had just returned from one of its fishing trips and was putting up for the night. Captain Miller was already ashore, but his first-mate, Sonny Skeete, was still on the boat. Skeete did not hesitate once he heard Wade's story. Joined by Wade, he rushed *Sea Hunter 1*, to the scene of the sinking. Captain Miller joined the rescue action later, after the *Sea Hunter 1*, returned to Jones Bay, Nevis, with its cargo of survivors and corpses.

The Sea Hunter 1

The men aboard *Sea Hunter 1*, acted with urgency. They pulled both dead bodies and living persons from the water. Skeete also put his radio into action and attempted to call any ship that happened to be nearby. According to Moore, *Christena's* engineer, Frank Matthew-Tyson, and Skeete himself, the *Hawthorne Enterprise* was contacted by radio from *Sea Hunter 1*. The cargo ship left St. Kitts just after *Christena*. However, according to Skeete, the person who responded showed no interest in giving assistance. He talked about being on schedule to Guadeloupe and of not knowing the waters in the area. To that response, Skeete recalled he pleaded, "I am from here. I know the waters. I'll pilot you in." However, it was to no avail. The *Hawthorne Enterprise* left the area without offering the assistance requested. About ten or so years ago, Captain Wynter threatened to sue the author, because in the second book, he commented on the controversy related to survivors reportedly seeing the *Hawthorne Enterprise*, in the vicinity of the accident.

Michael King

Michael King came to the scene after Wade left to seek assistance. As soon as he could put his passengers ashore at Nags Head, King, too, joined the rescue action. By the time he was loaded with survivors, the *Sea Hunter 1*, was on the scene. King passed his cargo to the *Sea Hunter 1*. Then he continued his search and rescue effort. The query was later raised as to whether King had carefully selected whom he wanted to rescue. However, with so many persons struggling in the water that situation was perhaps unlikely. What really happened, according to Mr. King, was that he designed a rescue strategy for the moment. First, he rescued the people who seemed in most danger of dying. He left those swimming to be picked up later, because they seemed in less danger at that moment. With the arrival of *Sea Hunter 1,* everyone in sight was pulled from the water. The survivors rescued by King were not all people whom he knew.

Peter Maynard

Another controversial incident involved one of Desmond Tyson's boats from Jessup's Village. Contrary to what some believed, Tyson was not aboard, and he was very angry when he learned about what happened. The fishing boat was coming from St. Kitts and sailing to Jessup's Village on Nevis. When Captain Peter "Turkey" Maynard came on the disaster scene, he moved among the bodies and survivors, picked up a relative, some friends, and mainly people whom he knew. Ossie Tyson claimed that he was only rescued because he called out "Uncle Peter!" He knew Mr. Maynard. The boat then left for Nevis and did not return to give further help. Some time later, the said Captain Maynard died strangely in Jessup's Bay. He was very drunk. As if driven, he walked into the same bay and drowned himself. Some people saw it as a haunting retribution; others called it fate or karma. That was payment for his leaving so many adrift and dying in the ocean, off Nags Head, not very far from Jessup's Bay.

The News

The ferry's sinking caught the attention of every Nevisian that afternoon. However, for family, friends, and the entire community waiting ashore, nothing happened quickly, after the ferry sank. For all the people waiting for news about loved-ones that afternoon, there was a painful anguish. Seemingly, time stood still. Even as the rescue effort proceeded off Nags Head, few persons on land knew that *Christena* had sunk. It should have arrived in Nevis by 4:30 pm. People knew it left St. Kitts, but it had not arrived in Nevis at the anticipated time. However, there was no general anxiety. Those awaiting the arrival of the boat had no idea what had happened to it and its passengers. Suddenly, news of the disaster began to spread around the island communities. Very few Nevisians received that unexpected and dramatic news about what happened to Christena, without going into temporary shock.

Individually, and as a group, the people of Nevis and St. Kitts had a hard time accepting that the *Christena* had gone to the bottom of the sea, and was no more. Somehow, after its 11 years of fairly reliable service, many persons had come to believe the ferry unsinkable. The general alarm about the sinking sounded on both islands shortly after 5:00 pm. However, there was no urgent mobilization to deal with the disaster. No immediate, organized action was seen in Basseterre or Charlestown. Everybody, including government officials were too confused. Further, it took some time before tangible evidence of the disaster was visible in either town. As yet, no survivors had been seen; no corpse had arrived ashore! Rumored stories were the only reality. Hundreds of Nevisians gathered at Charlestown pier. Some still expected to see the *Christena* sail in, bringing their relatives, friends, and guests home. Despite the rumors, they expected to see the boat sail in, and passengers disembark, in a festive, happy atmosphere. Out there though, about 12 km from St. Kitts and about 8.5 km from Nevis was the evidence. *Sea Hunter 1*, was struggling to secure that evidence, and bring it to Nevis as quickly as possible.

The evidence of the disaster came slowly at first, but, eventually, it struck the societies with a vengeance! At first survivors and corpses were landed at Charlestown, Jessup's Bay,

15

Jones Bay, and Pinney's Beach. The British colonial experience undermined the islands' response to the disaster. An ineffective emergency preparedness machinery existed in St. Kitts-Nevis, during 1970. It was rust-bound, disorganized, and almost nonexistent. Accordingly, when an effort was made to get the communities in disaster mode, the machinery clanked, halted, then took a long time before it worked. Notwithstanding, the gravity of the moment demanded action. Official and unofficial telephone calls were made to inform the authorities on St. Kitts about what was happening on Nevis. Back then, however, poor communication between the islands and the insistence of government that every activity on Nevis be supervised from St. Kitts, served to undermine response to the disaster. By 7:00 pm that evening, other boats from Nevis and the police launch from St. Kitts had finally joined the rescue action. But, it was dark and there was no equipment on island for such an after-dark rescue. By that time, only dead bodies were being plucked from the water. The rescue boats had already taken on many survivors, or were picking up others from Nags Head, where they had swum.

The Hospital

Eventually the rescue boats took 38 bodies, most of them female, to Nevis. The crowd showed some initial hesitancy about handling so many dead people; but after some time the bodies were transported to Alexandra Hospital. Medical personnel treated most of the 93 survivors who visited the hospital. Some were required to stay overnight for observation. The authorities also used that opportunity to establish a list of survivors. Because the ferry was not available to return to St. Kitts, Dr. Kennedy Simmonds, who was stationed in Nevis for the day, was available to treat the first survivors that visited the hospital. Since he was an opposition politician on St. Kitts, Dr. Simmonds was probably assigned to work on Nevis, at that time considered a place to "banish" government workers from St. Kitts, who opposed the government, and who were thought to be deserving of punishment. It was fortunate that Dr. Simmonds had not yet returned to St. Kitts for the weekend. Nevis would have been without a doctor.

Later in the evening, Dr. Cutberth Sebastian, also from St. Kitts, took over from Simmonds. Sebastian and a team of nurses were sent from St. Kitts by the government to give assistance. An earlier attempt to land the medical team from St. Kitts at New Castle, by plane, almost ended in disaster. Efforts to light the Nevis airport by car light did not go well. Eventually, the *Sea Hunter 1,* was called to transport the medical personnel from St. Kitts to Nevis. Nurses from the Alexandra Hospital and a team of nurses that accompanied by Dr. Sebastian from St. Kitts, also assisted the doctors. Two nurses, Myrle Wattley and Louise Barker, reportedly, played outstanding supporting roles.

They placed the first 38 bodies on ice in an improvised morgue. One of the coroners later confessed shock at the grotesque manner in which it was done. The hospital on Nevis was simply not prepared to deal with such a sudden catastrophic event. Nevisians were not prepared culturally or ideologically either, for such a horrific event. However, it appears that both providence and negligence made Nevisians and Kittitians participate in what for them became a haunting, vicious nightmare. The circumstances were such, that both people could not avoid becoming actors in the drama which ensued. Despite their lack of prior experience, and having lived relatively sheltered lives, Nevisians and Kittitians were forced by the *Christena* event to reach within and beyond themselves, for survival strategies. The citizens of St. Kitts-Nevis learned that they needed new competencies to deal effectively with such tumult in their lives. They were suddenly thrust upon the Caribbean and world stage. However, only with additional props could they act and perform their roles effectively; a painful experience had come to overwhelm their lives and time.

External Assistance

Once darkness came, no locally owned equipment was available to continue the search. Fortunately, US Coast Guard vessels from Puerto Rico and the US Virgin Islands had rushed to the scene. The story about the disaster had spread across the Caribbean and to the wider world. Later, British and French naval vessels in the Caribbean also came to provide assistance. Without help from the US, French, and British ships, the search could not have continued that evening. Neither could it have gone on as successfully as it did, for another three days. The crews on the ships used helicopters, special nets, and body-bags, as they continued the grim search. Local seamen, the police, and some volunteer prisoners assisted them. The group managed to retrieve a number of drowned victims, some intact, others with severed body parts. The currents had moved some of the floating bodies away from the disaster area. Captain Ponteen's body was the last intact body to be pulled from the sea. Despite his work assignment on the sea, Mr. Ponteen could not swim. The clothes he wore, khaki shorts and a white shirt with epaulets, made his identification easily possible. Following that event, when no other intact bodies could be found for burial or identification, the French naval captain suggested the partial remains be left in the sea, as they would drift to the second of the deepest known sea-trenches—the one off Puerto Rico. Days later, people saw bodies and body parts drifting in the sea off St. Maarten, and toward Puerto Rico.

For four days Kittitians and Nevisians faced the gruesome task of identifying dead bodies, then burying them singly or en masse. After days in the water, identifying some the corpses became impossible. Many were without skin, eyes, arms, or legs. Because of the inability to identify some the bodies, many persons still hoped that by some miracle, relatives and friends who had vanished suddenly, made it ashore somewhere, and would turn up eventually to calm their fears. Unfortunately, for most families, that did not happen. However, because of the poor manner in which the records were created, there were persons listed as dead who were alive. There were also persons alive whose names were not listed anywhere. Years later, one was encountered on French St. Martin, and another on St. Thomas, US Virgin Islands.

Every country, island, and nation has happy and sad stories. That is the reality of human life. There are times of sunshine, but rain also falls into lives everywhere. The Caribbean area in general, or St. Kitts-Nevis, in particular, is no exception. Meanwhile, for such small communities, losing such a large number of citizens in one sweep of death, was no simple challenge to confront, surmount, and survive. Notwithstanding, wisdom and strength often come to human beings as products of difficult experiences. Kittitians and Nevisians had opportunities to learn, grow, and mature, as a result of the *Christena* nightmare. Coming from a colonial experience, they needed to study the event and comprehend how it affected their lives. As a postcolonial people search for identity, every experience, bitter or sweet, that occurs in their time and space, should be manipulated consciously to fashion what for them becomes destiny. Meanwhile, a number of the personal stories remind us that beyond the physical sphere lies the metaphysical.

Were efforts made by some beings to warn Kittitians and Nevisians of impending disaster? If so, why were the messages coded and some persons confused? As a result, the societies became easy targets, and were embroiled in death, emotional distress, and painful social disruptions. Could it be that some persons simply ignored their messages? Osmond Farrell's mother saved her son because she responded to what seemed puzzling, but became a protective message. Today, there is still need for more growth in people's consciousness on both islands. It is for the people that society exists. Political or social insensitivity to the people's needs should not allow another *Christena*-type disaster in St. Kitts-Nevis. Further, no political or social changes that come to St. Kitts-Nevis will be worth sacrificing another group of Kittitians and Nevisians. In that case, history will not absolve us. Colonialism and its dynamics have dominated Caribbean societies for too long. But creating new Caribbean awareness, including a better grasp of the link between culture and survival, can lead to a restructuring of Caribbean societies and the Caribbean reality. For the people of St. Kitts-Nevis, a critical time for change, renewal and for experiencing new beginnings can always be now. None can undo the mistakes from past experiences. But a people's approach to the future can be changed and made different. For Caribbean people, that change must make a difference. It must change from a past punctuated by painful tragedies, such as the *Christena* story, to a future characterized by critical awareness, improvement in the ability to survive challenges, and the fostering of an abundance of hope!

CHAPTER TWO

Of Dreams, Visions and Superstitions

On the night when St. Kitts-Nevis had the ceremony to mark its independence, September 19, 1983, rain fell—showers of blessing for some, an inauspicious occasion for others. Rain fell when the Prime Minister designate, Dr. Kennedy Simmonds, entered the park for the ceremony. Rain fell again when the Queen's representative to the ceremony, the late, Princess Margaret, entered the grounds. Rain fell again when the national flag was being raised. To some people there, the falling rain was an ominous sign. In many Caribbean islands, including St. Kitts-Nevis, there are persons who see signs and patterns in things and events that have no meaning to others. At times too, they can provide elaborate explanations to justify their view. Not surprisingly, many people connected the *Christena's* sinking to the supernatural. Indeed, the range and variety of strange stories that have been related to the ship's sinking, even now, do cause even normally rational people to speculate. Many people from both St. Kitts and Nevis claimed to have received signs and messages that warned them about the *Christena* tragedy. Some people talked about messages that came before the ferry sank. Others spoke of strange happenings after, but related to the *Christena* event. Another clearly mysterious factor connected to the sinking, was the way some passengers and

21

Whitman T. Browne, Ph.D.

would-be passengers, made last-minute decisions that led them to, or from the disaster. Thus, a seemingly obvious question:, Did fate select certain persons to participate in the event while it rejected others? This is a matter still being pondered.

Tokens of the Event

Stanley Franks of St. Kitts was aboard *Christena,* heading for Nevis, but he disembarked at the last minute. He opted to attend a cricket-related function on St. Kitts, instead of going across to Nevis. Sam Sweeney had a ticket to travel by plane to Nevis. But Sweeney chose to travel on *Christena* because he wanted to celebrate with his friend Orville Morton during the crossing. Unfortunately, they celebrated and died together. A man who was visiting from England escaped the disaster because the son with whom he traveled disappeared from the pier and went back to his grandmother's place, just before his daddy boarded. Initially, the father was angry that his son went off without his permission. He understood afterwards and forgave his son. Other strange incidents occurred on St. Kitts and Nevis before or after the boat sailed for Nevis and sank. Later many persons read such events as deliberate tokens and foreboding of the incident.

One such happening involved a number of pilot whales that came ashore on Nevis, close to Eden Brown Estate and Butler's Village, and died there. The school of seventeen whales grounded at Tri Piece Bay. One was 8 feet wide and 15 feet long. The others were smaller. Some people from the area made attempts to get the whales back into the sea, but the effort failed. The animals stayed on land in that general area and died there. To the people of St. Kitts-Nevis it was a very strange happening. It evoked much awe in both St. Kitts and Nevis, for a time too, that scene became quite an attraction. People from throughout the islands visited the area to see the sight. I still recall walking almost 10 miles, with a number of students from Combermere School, to see the dead whales.

At the time of the incident, there was no logical explanation given as to why it occurred. Interestingly, at first, no one associated it with *Christena*. Later, just as people came from throughout the islands to see the whales, in the same manner, people from everywhere flocked to see the victims claimed by the doomed vessel. There was hardly an area on St. Kitts or Nevis, that was untouched by the tragedy. There is still one superstitious notion about the disaster, that is still generally accepted. Time has not erased it. Some passengers who survived the sinking claimed they saw a strange man board the ferry. He was dressed in black. To them the man was an evil spirit and he caused the sinking. A few years ago, a well-known supporter of the PAM political party died at the hospital on St. Kitts. He was reputed to have "landed" (talked just before death of things that troubled his mind as he died). Some claimed that he admitted using obeah against *Christena*. An ongoing political quarrel existed between him and Captain Ponteen. The "death-trap" was for Ponteen only. However, even if such a confession was made, it seems to be suspect. Who knows whether the sick, dying man was really speaking truth? Another issue to be reconciled in that situation is whether a person could be so callous as to destroy the lives of so many people in a vendetta, when he really wanted to take the life of one man? Meanwhile, the circumstances surrounding the sinking seem to point away from such simplistic and mystical explanations. In reality, the total *Christena* story is much more complex. There are no such simple answers to explain why and when it happened. Notwithstanding, this section attempts to recapture the gist of the thinking, and to show how willing a bewildered people were to seek and create superstitious explanations for the *Christena* catastrophe. There were persons who discussed some of the experiences before the disaster. But, until the sinking occurred, few made any specific link between them and *Christena*. And, if the disaster had been avoided, none might have been made. Some of the people whose experiences are related here died in the disaster. They related their stories to relatives or friends who later passed them on to the author. All the stories recorded here actually occurred.

Personal Stories

Oretha Jones. Oretha Jones lived on St. Thomas, U.S.V.I. She came to Nevis to visit her parents and children at Fountain. One morning in July, Oretha awoke from a strange dream. She related the dream to her parents and kept talking about it for the week. Although she could not swim, Oretha had a very vivid dream that she was swimming in the ocean. She related how she saw both dead bodies and living people in the water. She also had another dream later. In her second dream, she saw that the ferry *Christena* had sunk and that St. Kitts and Nevis were in mourning. After relating her dreams, Oretha went as far as to suggest that she leave Nevis before such an incident could occur. However, at that time, no one in the family took her dreams seriously. Everything went on as usual. As she began to prepare for her return to St. Thomas, Oretha had to visit St. Kitts. For that trip she chose to wear a rose-pink dress. After the selection of her dress Oretha commented off-handedly, "This dress may be the one for my burial."

Despite her strange, seemingly warning dreams, and her parents' suggestion that travel to St. Kitts on August I, 1970, be avoided, Oretha made the trip. At that point in time, Nevisians could only get their tax clearance forms on St. Kitts, when they wanted to travel. Accordingly, Oretha and a friend went to secure the tax clearance certificate so that Oretha could return to St. Thomas. Her father remembered that as she dressed in the rose-pink dress that morning, Oretha danced wildly before the mirror. While she danced, one of the things Oretha said to her parents was, "Look how I am going to die on *Christena*." Later that day, Mr. Jones learned that some bodies were waiting to be identified at Alexandra Hospital on Nevis, so he went to see whether Oretha's body was there. For him, it was a short search.

He easily identified her in that rose-pink dress. How could he miss that rose-pink dress in which she had danced so wildly that morning? Oretha had also predicted correctly that it would be her burial dress.

Edna Browne. One month before the disaster, Edna Browne of Jessup's Village dreamt she was a passenger on *Christena.* In her dream, as the ferry came close to where some fishermen were pulling their seine. She accidentally fell overboard. She recalled that in her dream, Frank Tyson approached her in the water and said, "Look, Mrs. Browne, we will not let her drown." On the afternoon of August 1, 1970, Mrs. Browne remembered that as she struggled in the water, Frank Matthew-Tyson. the mate on *Christena,* grabbed her in the water saying, "Look, Mrs. Browne, we will not let her drown." Mrs. Browne did fall into the water from the *Christena* that fateful August afternoon. She had quite an unforgettable experience in the sea. It was Frank Tyson who pulled her out of the water. By then, he was aboard the *Sea Hunter 1,* helping to rescue persons still in the water. As Frank pulled her from the sea, Mrs. Browne recalled that he repeated the very words she had heard in her dream, one month before: "Look, Mrs. Browne, we will not let her drown!"

Gwendolyn Budgeon. Gwendolyn Budgeon was among the dead in the *Christena* accident. However, shortly before the accident, she had related a strange dream to her brother, Basil Bussue. In that dream, Gwendolyn saw her dead father at the Paradise Beach area on Nevis. Her father did not communicate verbally, he simply used the index finger of his right hand, and signaled her to be careful. Basil and Gwendolyn discussed the dream, but neither of them could agree on its significance. Despite her limited understanding of the phenomenon, Gwendolyn, a huckster from Jessup's, asked Basil to promise that if anything sudden and dreadful happen to her, he would remember to assist her children, should they be in need. Basil too, thought the matter quizzical, but he promised to be there. Not long after that conversation, Gwendolyn went to St. Kitts to do her usual trading, probably oblivious to the strange warning of danger she had received. Gwendolyn Budgeon was among those who died in the *Christena* accident. She kept her date with destiny. In a strange, mysterious way, Gwendolyn's death that afternoon, gave substance to her peculiar dream and the warning embedded in it.

Franklyn Browne. Franklyn Browne still lives at Camps Village on Nevis. He talked about how the dogs howled loudly and strangely throughout Friday night, July 31st. According to local folklore, that was a sure foreboding of lurking death. Consequently, he was hesitant about traveling to St. Kitts that Saturday morning. Mr. Browne felt that the pilot whales that came ashore and the howling dogs were signals, and bad omens. He had the feeling that something dreadful was about to happen. He could feel it. However, since his son Roger had to travel to St. Kitts for medical attention (another case of Nevis' overdependence on St. Kitts and its link to the death of so many Nevisians, that afternoon), Franklyn decided he should go along just in case something unexpected should happen. He also planned to buy some equipment he needed.

At the onset of the accident that afternoon, Mr. Browne found himself under water and separated from his son. By some strange miracle, and as if drawn by a mysterious genetic magnet, Browne surfaced beside Roger and another boy. All three were swimmers. The father carefully coaxed and coached the boys, and they worked together at survival—swimming toward Nags Head. One of the rescue boats eventually picked them up. Some time later when the investigating divers went down to *Christena,* they recovered some of the things Mr. Browne bought on St. Kitts. Even the receipt was intact and served to identify the owner. Franklyn Browne was also among the survivors of the *Lady Nisbett* and the *Enterprise* mishap. But that is another St. Kitts-Nevis sea story dating back to the early 1950s.

Wyclide Condell. As Wyclide Condell walked to his home, the smell that came to his nose told him that something good was cooking. He was coming home from his job at the sugar factory that Saturday afternoon. From the tantalizing smell of food, Wyclide knew instantly that his sister from Nevis was visiting and doing the cooking. Despite the fact that his mother always warned her children against traveling on holidays, the sister, and a nephew, had come to St. Kitts that morning. Now, the mother, Wyclide, and the others, were destined to travel back to Nevis on *Christena* that afternoon. Before the group left for the ferry, Wyclide recalled saying to his sister: "When the boat sinks, it will be so many of us from the same family." However, they got on the boat and like all the other passengers that afternoon, began dreaming about getting off in Nevis. It was thus, that the family's journey across to Nevis, began that afternoon.

When the ferry began to sink, Wyclide tried to reach his mother, but he did not make it. After the nightmare was all over, Wyclide stood alone. He was the only one in the group from his family who survived the tragedy. During the trip to Nevis, before disaster struck, Wyclide was involved in two interesting conversations. He teased a girl who had recently graduated from high school about how good she looked. They were neighbors on Nevis, so the two knew each other. Wyclide had also suggested that they start an intimate relationship. The girl's response was that she preferred to give herself to the fish than to Wyclide. As she spoke, she placed her hands on her crotch. Shortly afterwards the boat sank and the girl died.

Almost everyone aboard the ferry soon noticed it was sailing and rolling unsteadily that afternoon. Eventually, that concern was a matter for general comment among the passengers. One passenger jokingly suggested that the three nuns aboard were to be blamed and that the ferry would steady itself if they threw the nuns overboard. "I always notice that whenever such people travel with me, something unfortunate happens," he said. Condell's response to the suggestion was that he, too, was Roman Catholic. All three nuns died in the mishap. The young man who made the suggestion about them being thrown overboard, survived.

Victor Swanston. Victor Swanston had been selling a variety of goods at the market in St. Kitts for a long time. In 1970, he was one of the few men engaged in this form of trade, dominated by women. On Saturday, August 1st, Mr. Swanston's son, Hanschell, was with him as usual. Hanschell was 14 years old but quite mature and responsible. His father usually allowed Hanschell to keep the money for his day's sales until they returned to Nevis. After the selling was over that day, Daddy Swanston surprised Hanschell by asking for the money from his sales. When Hanschell asked his father about the new behavior, without thinking about the matter, the father replied, "I have to take the money." Later, as the ferry sailed toward Nevis, Mr. Swanston acted strangely again. Normally, he would travel in the mate's cabin and sleep throughout the journey to Nevis. That afternoon he did not go to the cabin, neither did he get the urge to sleep. Although he was tired from an early morning and a long day, Daddy Swanston remained on the outside with the other passengers and did not fall asleep. Actually, he was one of the first persons overboard and into the water when the boat started to sink. Later, one of the rescue boats picked him up. Hanschell's body was found after the accident. Unlike his father, Hanschell did not walk away alive from the incident.

Rose Hanley. Rose Hanley traveled to St. Kitts to visit her daughter, Gloria. As Rose ate and prepared for the return trip to Nevis, it was quite strange, but she turned to Gloria and said solemnly, "I am going to die and will never hold a child for you." She was so right. Rose died when the ferry sank, not long after that inauspicious conversation with her daughter. Later, in attempting to comfort her, Inspector Delsol suggested to Gloria that Rose might have swum some place from the ferry and could be safe. Gloria did not see the comment as understanding and sympathetic. She became very angry at Delsol. From the conversation mother and daughter shared before Rose left for Nevis, Gloria knew her mother was somewhere. But, she was dead.

Greta Salisbury. On that afternoon in 1970, Greta Salisbury lived in St. Kitts, but had just returned from Washington, DC. Greta was anxious to spend an August holiday weekend on Nevis. By midday that Saturday, Greta was dressed and waiting for her taxi to the ferry. When that taxi did not arrive at the appointed time, she decided to phone for another. However, her telephone had mysteriously gone dead. No matter what Greta tried, it did not work at that time. She rushed to a neighbor and tried using their phone. But the neighbor's phone would not work either. Greta tried a second neighbor and also had a problem with that phone. When she finally managed and made it to the pier, *Christena* was already at sea. Greta inquired whether there would be a second trip to Nevis. The response she received from one person nearby was that the ferry would not be coming back. It had left very heavily laden on its trip to Nevis. Greta felt miserable about missing the trip she needed to make so badly and had waited for so long, only to miss the ferry. At that time she could not see the misfortune of missing the boat as a blessing. Later, friends who knew of Greta's plans for Nevis phoned her home, intending to extend sympathy to the family, thinking she had died on the ferry. Greta sobbed as she began to understand the mystery of the toneless telephones. That experience helped Greta to develop a more positive attitude when disappointments come to her life. She even learned to adopt this approach, when the experience involved the delicate matter of love and the heart.

Lucilla Martineau. Lucilla Martineau's husband, Assistant Superintendent of Police Martineau, had asked her to send their daughter, Sheryl, over to Nevis, Friday afternoon, July 31st, accompanied by someone else. However, Mrs. Martineau did not send the daughter over. Instead of sending the daughter, Mrs. Martineau decided to take Sheryl to Nevis on Saturday afternoon, August 1st. Lucilla did purchase plane tickets so that they could make the trip by plane in five minutes instead of the hour by boat. However, it did not matter how she looked and searched the house, those tickets could not be found. Consequently, on that fateful afternoon, Mrs. Martineau and Sheryl joined the throng of passengers who took *Christena* to Nevis. Before she left for the ferry, Sheryl refused to lend a friend her bath suit. Sheryl promised the friend that she intended to bathe further than Pinney's Beach in the bath-suit. Both Sheryl and Lucilla died in the accident. Interestingly, Mrs. Martineau died close to the area on Nevis where her husband lost a ring she had presented him, only six months before. The plane tickets to Nevis were located quite easily, after the disaster.

Rose Martin. Rose Martin of Jessups had been a regular among Nevisians who traded in St. Kitts, 1970, the year *Christena* sank. Her usual trading pattern was to get to St. Kitts on Friday morning, sell all day on Friday and Saturday, then return to Nevis Saturday afternoon. She had done things that way for a long, long time, and could be expected to be among the throng for Nevis, every Saturday afternoon. To this day, Rose cannot explain logically why she made a sudden change and did what was done that Saturday when *Christena* sank. Mrs. Martin made the usual Friday morning trip to St. Kitts. By Friday afternoon, she had not sold half the goods she intended to sell, but Mrs. Martin left them with someone and returned to Nevis. Everyone in the family was surprised to see her come home on a Friday afternoon. Mrs. Martin could not explain the mystery to her family either. She just knew something impressed her to return to Nevis that Friday afternoon, instead of the usual Saturday afternoon. Mrs. Martin and her entire family came to understand the mystery of her sudden change of mind within twenty-four hours. They started to find meaning in the decision, when disaster struck and the ferry *Christena* went to the bottom of the sea, taking many passengers with it. Somehow, in that grand patterning of things, it was not intended that Rose Martin be present at that Saturday afternoon drama. By a mysterious shift in her decision making, she too was warned and kept away from a sudden unexpected death. She lived to share her mysterious story, and to mourn so many of her trading, huckster friends.

Hellen Bradley. Hellen Bradley was traveling to New York on August Monday. She intended to get her hair done on St. Kitts the morning of August 1st, then return to Nevis by ferry that afternoon. For some reason she could not explain, Hellen changed her mind about going to St. Kitts Saturday morning. She made the trip Friday afternoon instead and returned to Nevis the morning of August 1st. During the trip back to Nevis, she noticed the ferry's stern appeared to be sailing very low in the water. She drew the engineer's attention to the position of the stern in the water and suggested that the boat seemed to be sinking. The engineer responded, "Such a thing could never happen." Later that same day, the ferry sank stern first. When Hellen heard the news, she was horrified. Had she traveled to St. Kitts Saturday morning, she might have been a participant in the disaster. How it would have ended for her, she could not tell. Neither did she want to deal with such a traumatic question.

Edward Smith. Edward Smith lived at Zion in Nevis and was twelve years old when *Christena* sank. He was among the passengers and did not survive. Edward had gone to St. Kitts that Saturday morning because his mother was there spending time with an aunt and had asked him to come over. He had such a good time playing with sisters Debbie and Althea that Edward did not want to make the return trip to Nevis on that Saturday afternoon. However, his mother and his aunt kept insisting that he return home. Just about the time when *Christena* sank, his sister, Althea, awoke from a deep sleep. She smiled, called Edward's name; then Althea went back to a sound sleep. Why did Althea smile and say "Edward" while she slept, just about the time he was probably dying? Was it a dream, or did Althea experience some form of communication more vivid than a dream?

Orville Morton and Val Audain. The next two stories relate to Orville Morton of Nevis, and Val Audain of St. Kitts. Unfortunately, both men died on *Christena*. Beverly (not her real name) knew Orville and Val well. She spoke with them one week before the accident. In each conversation, reference was made to death. But none knew it would strike so soon, or with such cruelty. Saturday, July 25, one week before the disaster, Beverly was visiting St. Kitts from St. Thomas. She saw Orville talking with another girl. Beverly recalled that she asked Orville whether he still liked having so many girlfriends, despite his increasing age. She also remembered asking him, "Are you still such a whore, Orville; when are you going to stop messing around?" Beverly noted that Orville replied casually, "Not until I die." A week later, Beverly and her roommate, in St. Thomas, stood glued to their radio listening for news about *Christena's* sinking. Orville's name was among the first names called and given as missing. Instantly, Beverly began to cry, and kept crying as names were added to the list. Because of the number of her friends who died on *Christena,* Beverly reported that she cried, off and on, for a full two months.

Beverly's brother was a close friend of Val Audain. He was her friend, too. She knew he liked to drive his car very fast. On the Sunday before the ferry sank, it was Val who took Beverly to the airport, as she was returning to St. Thomas. Beverly remembers that as she walked toward the aircraft, a feeling she could not explain, suggested that she warned Val to be careful about his life. At that moment, Beverly turned, deliberately, went back to Val, and admonished him to be careful in his driving and with his life. A friend of hers on St. Thomas had been killed recently, in a car accident. She was in no mood to accept the death of another one of her friends by such an accident. Beverly reported that after the conversation with Val, she boarded the plane and for no known reason, cried all the way to St. Thomas. One of Beverly's friends from St. Kitts visited St. Thomas a day after the *Christena* tragedy. She was among the hundreds of persons at the St. Thomas Airport, hungering for news from St. Kitts and Nevis. When Beverly learned that Val was among those missing, she could only listen in horror and helplessness as her grief intensified.

Val's mother told close friends about his very strange behavior the whole week before he travelled on the *Christena* and died. Normally, Val was never home at dinner time. However, during the week preceding the accident, he was home on time and ate dinner every afternoon. As Val ate, he usually became very solemn and quietly stared into space. To his mother, it seemed that something was burdening Val's mind. Because of her concern about the patterning of Val's strange behavior, Mrs. Audain asked his father to question him. She wanted to find out whether Val had something on his mind that he needed to tell them. However, Val's answers to the questions were, "No, I do not have a girl pregnant." "No, nothing is bothering me." Whatever his dreams or his thoughts were, Val did not, or probably could not share them with his parents. However, Val caused those around him to become perplexed as he quietly contemplated his private thoughts.

Both Val and his friend James had girlfriends on Nevis, but James turned down Val's invitation to visit Nevis for the holiday weekend. Val's girlfriend also tried to discourage him from making that trip. However, nothing kept Val away from the *Christena* trip to Nevis that Saturday afternoon. He was destined to be there, to participate in the drama, and to die. No one has seen Val alive since the ferry sank. On two different occasions, however, Beverly remembers waking from dreams in which she had conversations with Val. Each time the conversation ended with Val saying, "I ain't dead you know. They just cannot find me." Beverly also remembered sitting up in bed without being fearful. Then one time, there was movement among the clothes in her wardrobe at the foot of her bed. It seemed as if someone was inside the wardrobe, moving among the clothes. During both of those occasions, Beverly was convinced Val had come back from wherever he was to pay her a friendly visit—she felt his presence in her room. Meanwhile, Val's best friend, James, had a different experience. He did not sleep in his bed for a long time. On many occasions, he saw Val's imprint in the bed. It looked just like old times when Val visited alive, visible and well. But for James, the relationship had evolved to another level, and beyond his sphere of comprehension. He was upset by those strange visits and the human shape he saw repeatedly in a bed where no human slept.

Roy Fortune. Roy Fortune is from Mt. Lily, Nevis, but in August, 1970, he lived in St. Thomas with his wife, Marlene. Two weeks before *Christena* sank, Roy woke from a strange dream. He shared its contents with his wife. In his dream, Roy was traveling from St. Thomas via an American Airlines airplane to Nevis. As the aircraft approached Nevis, it circled away from the island and crashed in the sea off Nags Head, in the same area where *Christena* sank. For Roy, the dream was very vivid. He kept wondering for days whether there was some meaning to it. He could not find an immediate explanation, but he remained curious. Quietly, he pondered whether there was any real-life association, in the future. Despite his dream, Roy was shocked when the ferry met its demise. He had not made an association with his dream. When the news came, like other Nevisians abroad, Roy listened and wondered who among his friends and relatives were victims. Eventually, Roy fitted the puzzle of his dream into place. He reasoned that the drama that was shared with him in a dream was a premonition of the *Christena* disaster. To this day, Roy believes he was shown in advance that something terrible was about to happen. But, like all those others, Roy could not fit the puzzle together. They were granted a preview of an event, but something was missing. It was only after the Christena tragedy that they could all decide what it was; also, how, where and when it happened.

Josiah Maynard. Josiah Maynard is no ready believer in superstitions or superstitious happenings. Should he have been asked to take a position on such phenomena before August, 1970, Maynard would probably have said such things do not happen. He and his family are Seventh Day Adventists and nonbelievers in such matters. Josiah, his wife and children were at church in Castries, St. Lucia, when *Christena* sank. None of them knew about the event then. When they got home from church that afternoon, *Christena* was far from their minds. The family was on the second floor of the house they lived in, when they heard loud sounds downstairs. A crashing sound was followed by a gushing, gurgling sound. It sounded like when rough waters are beating against rocks. The family rushed to see what was causing the unusual sound downstairs. However they saw nothing. Soon, curiosity was replaced by a sense of wonder. Why the mysterious sounds? The family became increasingly perplexed since they could see nothing to explain what they had heard. As the family's wonderment and curiosity heightened, their neighbor, Allan Smith, called to tell them about the *Christena's* sinking. Since the Maynards are from Nevis, but lived in St. Lucia, they quickly tuned their radio and were soon listening to *Christena's* sad story. However, the way the Maynards received the coded message left them with questions they had never asked before. Even today those questions remain unanswered. Despite his deep Christian beliefs, Dr. Josiah Maynard, a devoted Seventh Day Adventist Christian, has not been able to explain away his family's strange encounter with what appeared to have been a coded premonition about the *Christena* tragedy, of August 1, 1970.

CHAPTER THREE

First-Hand Accounts 1

When *Christena* sank, some unthinkable things happened as a distressed group of people searched for survival. One man tried swimming with a newly purchased car battery. Probably, he and his battery died together. One nurse rushed to the bathroom just as the boat started sinking. She died there. The dead body of an older lady was found bent over. She seemed cuddled in peaceful sleep. During the drama, a number of mothers tossed babies into the sea. They hoped that amidst the confusion someone would save them from the water. It did not matter whether anyone was in sight to carry out the rescue. In the darkness of that moment, the mothers simply hoped. Even if they died, they wanted their children to live beyond the *Christena*. That was the inspiration that drove bewildered and desperate mothers to toss helpless children blindly into the sea.

Meanwhile, in the midst of all that saga, there was one woman who became hope. She swam among the crowded stragglers offering encouragement to many persons in distress. Unfortunately, she was seen for a time, then she disappeared suddenly. Onlookers thought the woman was taken by a shark, or that she was overtaken by crippling cramps that caused her to die. Many people died unexpectedly that afternoon. Almost

250 children, women and men drowned. But some survived too, just under 100. They lived to tell their stories of struggle and distress. Included here are many of the first hand accounts of those experiences as they were remembered by survivors.

Ian Kelsick

Ian lived at Cayon Street on St. Kitts. At that time, he was a pilot with Leeward Islands Air Transport (L.I.A.T.). However, up to that time, Ian probably had more close encounters with death than most other persons on St. Kitts-Nevis. He lived through a plane crash, a motorcycle crash, and at that time, *Christena's* sinking. On the afternoon in question, Ian was aboard *Christena* traveling to Nevis for weekend fun. He had no thought that the "good times" waiting on Nevis would not be realized. After Ian boarded *Christena,* he noted the size of the crowd, but that did not bother him. Like other passengers, Ian soon settled down and expected to arrive at Charlestown in about an hour. The ferry left Basseterre pier, then went back and took on two other passengers. As it was doing that, Ian noticed that the ferry rocked ominously. Even as it headed out toward Nevis for the second time, *Christena* rolled unsteadily while passing the area where the barges were anchored. Many passengers stayed at the top level of the ferry, but Ian headed downstairs. He intended to lie there until the ferry crossed over to Nevis.

At about 4:10 pm., he heard loud shouts of both fear and anger. Some passengers were crying for the Lord to save them. Others queried the ferry's strange movements. Next, Ian recalled passengers being thrown violently against one side of the ferry while it continued to move full throttle forward. Then, as suddenly, passengers and cargo were tossed into the sea. In no time *Christena* disappeared from his sight. Fate was to determine destiny for the many persons still alive in the water. Ian saw many people panicking from shock. Others floated helplessly in the water, some dying, others already dead. All around people were swimming in the water. Many were swimming away in desperation. Ian remained sane and calm in the middle of all the confusion. Soon he found himself with a group of people swimming away toward land. For them, swimming together was company in distress. It made the desperation and sorrow less. They all found hope in being together. Ultimately, by cooperating, half of the group survived together.

Ian reflectively noted, that overall, more than one third of those who started to swim with his group did not survive. During the melee, Ian saw a side of human beings that was cold, vicious, and deadly. While some people who could swim assisted others, there were others who refused to give any help whatsoever. The drama before him, as he recalled it, was at the same time filled with scenes of both humaneness and callousness. In retrospect, Ian was not certain how it all began. He did not remember any sudden gale at the time of the sinking. The sea around was still quite calm. Ian felt that too much time elapsed before help came from shore. In addition, more people could have been saved if the communication system and the islands' disaster preparedness system were better organized.

It took two days for Ian to understand, accept and come to grip with his experiences on that final *Christena* trip to Nevis. He then sat down to write his thoughts. He wrote these thought provoking lines: "Between me and the next live person were people who lived a moment ago, but who, alas, had drifted to the great beyond . . . . In about ten minutes [the *Christena*] had gone completely, leaving dead and living behind in the wake of death."

Clifford Browne

"Look where *Christena* left people, way out to sea." That was how Clifford Browne reacted as he settled himself, after the ferry's sinking. Clifford's nickname is, "First Cock." He still lives in Nevis, but at one time worked for a number of years as a carpenter on St. Kitts. The afternoon when *Christena* sank, Clifford was aboard with Terrence Duzan, a friend from Brick Kiln. Clifford remembers that the sun was shining on a calm blue sea, as *Christena* left the pier in St. Kitts and set out toward Nevis. Despite an already crowded situation aboard, the ferry did turn back to the pier. It took on two late passengers. He also remembered that some persons took that opportunity to disembark from the ferry. Later, a speedboat brought a mysterious looking man in a brown suit and he too, boarded the ferry. In a short while, *Christena* was back on its way toward Nevis. The crowded condition and the ferry's rolling motion caused some passengers to vomit. At the same time, however, others nearby were eating and having a good time.

As Christena got further away from Basseterre, Captain Ponteen began to collect fares. He carried a brown leather bag over his shoulder as he moved among the passengers. At that time, Clifford recalled, the ferry, was in the hands of first mate, Frank Matthew-Tyson. As far as Clifford remembers, it did not appear that the boat was responding to the controls. It was sailing more southwest than southeast toward Nevis. The side-to-side roll had also become obvious to everyone.

The mishap it signaled came very quickly. The rolling motion and the water being collected inside the ferry were threatening and ominous signs. However, all on board still expected to arrive safely on Nevis. They had confidence in the safety of the ferry. In the midst of the calm, however, the stern plunged under water. The bow lingered above for about seven minutes or so. While the ferry was in that position a number of persons fell in the water. Some people also started to swim away while others started to swim back in the direction of the boat. Many in the water struggled and clung to whatever floating material they could find. It was a moment of grasping at straws. Survival was for the fittest, or for the luckiest. As the horror continued in the water, Clifford saw a large ship sailing from the direction of St. Kitts. Others in the water saw the ship too, and started to swim in its direction. However, shortly after, the ship changed course and sailed away from the area of the accident. Clifford also remembers seeing the three nuns from the Convent High School on St. Kitts. They were together in the water, linked in an embrace that in time became an embrace of death. The dead and dying were everywhere. One had to swim through or around them. Eventually, Clifford was picked up and taken to shore on Nevis. The question people ashore asked him most often was, "Did you see this person, or that person?" Most Nevisian had a friend or relative aboard. That evening everyone was hungry for news about what really happened. People wanted to know, why and how the *Christena* sank, and what happened to different persons who were there.

Clifford spent Saturday night and part of Sunday at the hospital before he could get home to Brick Kiln. It took him five days before he actually began to deal soberly, with the reality of that experience. Clifford is still convinced that he survived because of his grandfather's prayers for him.

Frank Morton

"The people of St. Kitts-Nevis needed to take stock of their lives." That statement was part of Frank Morton's response to the accident. Morton lives at the Chicken Stone area on Nevis, and at the time of the accident was a teacher. Frank does not like to recall his experiences that afternoon *Christena* sank, but he is not afraid to discuss the matter. Frank noted that unlike some other persons, he had no urgent reason to visit St. Kitts. All he wanted to do was to pass the day. It was holiday time and heading into August Monday weekend. When *Christena* started to sink, Frank saw many persons being tossed about. However, he had no problem getting outside, and into the water. Once there, he swam with two other persons for about one and a half hours before one of the rescue boats picked them up. Frank recalled that he shared a life jacket with a man from Cayon, St. Kitts, whom he did not know. The other person in his group was a, Trotman, from Rice's Village, Nevis. He also remembers swimming on an empty crate. Because Frank is a quiet person, a reflective and religious man, he saw the *Christena* disaster as a warning from God. The people of St. Kitts-Nevis needed to take stock of their lives. To him that was the ultimate meaning of the event.

Edna and Dulcita Browne

"Don't you see the boat is sinking?" "Lady, lady, please help me," were two of her comments, one before and one after the disaster. They lived with Edna forever. She was one of the regulars and traded in St. Kitts as a huckster, when *Christena* sank. Edna was on the ferry returning to Nevis and, through some miracle, survived the drama, and came away with her life. During the accident, she damaged one of her legs. It remained painful, but she was grateful for her survival. That accident in 1970, was Edna's second mishap on *Christena*. She was aboard the ferry in 1960, when it sprung a leak off White Horse Bay, and had to go ashore. That time they were rescued by another ferry, the *Silopana*, which was passing by.

The *Christena* accident ended Edna's days of trading regularly on St. Kitts. Meanwhile, her experiences, during and immediately after the tragedy, along with the injury she sustained, made her give it all up. After that accident, Edna traveled on a ferry only when she had to. However, when she did, her *Christena* saga always came to mind and filled her with fear. Like most of the other hucksters, Edna had come to feel very secure on the *Christena*. Despite the fact that it was travel on the ocean, she had no fear or thought, then, that the ferry would sink. On that fateful afternoon, however, something seemed amiss. Edna sensed early that *Christena* was not sailing right. As Captain Ponteen passed by her collecting the fares, Edna recalled asking, "Don't you see the boat is sinking?" Later, when the ferry sank, she was lucky to make it outside. It also happened that Edna had become adept at floating on her back, in the sea. Consequently, after the ferry sank she was not left totally helpless. As she lay in the water, she called out to everyone passing by for help. At first no one seemed to hear, and no one offered any assistance.

Eventually, a lady on a bag containing a few breadfruit came swimming by. The woman was Dulcita Browne. Dulcita was traveling to Nevis with five of her children. She was going to spend the weekend with her fiancé. The water that rushed inside *Christena* tore the youngest of her five children from her arms. The other four also disappeared. Even as she swam, Dulcita was certain they were all dead. When she encountered Edna in the water and offered her help, Dulcita did not have to. Another lady whom she met in the water had actually advised Dulcita against giving assistance to anyone, as it could cost her own life. Under such circumstances Dulcita should have acted selfishly, but she did not. Edna was fortunate that Dulcita was not a selfish person, even in a stressful situation. When she heard Edna's shout of desperation, "Lady, lady, please help me!," Dulcita refused to deal with her own loss and grief. She realized a fellow human being was in danger and went to help. It was a small matter that Edna and Dulcita did not really know each other before.

Dulcita promised Edna she would assist her, provided Edna held on to the bag and not on to her, Dulcita. The bag contained about five breadfruit. Edna probably realized if she held on to Dulcita and they both went under, that would be the end for them both. Such a strategy would be of no help. Accordingly, Edna agreed to hold only the bag. Soon, the two women were still in distress, but united on a bag with a few breadfruit as their hope to survival, in a cruel sea. Edna was still on her back as she held to the bag. Dulcita, meanwhile, was moving along in a normal swimming position. They moved along together, among the crowd in the water. Some were moving along at best they could. Others were struggling and dying. Many people in the water were already dead and beyond human help. On numerous occasions, Edna wanted to let go the bag and give up. But a determined Dulcita encouraged her to keep holding on. At one point, probably as she struggled with the matter of survival and the future, Edna told Dulcita about her concern as to whether she would ever see her grandchildren at Jessup's again. Dulcita, meanwhile, said nothing about the five children she had just lost. Instead, she kept encouraging Edna with the promise that they would be saved and everything would be well again. Eventually, Edna became very depressed and gave up hope. She asked Dulcita to leave her behind. Fortunately, the *Sea Hunter 1,* was already on the scene and busy making pick-ups from the sea. Both Dulcita and Edna were picked up shortly after they separated. However, for Dulcita things fell apart once she got into the rescue boat. Only then did she begin to reflect on the loss of her five children. By the time *Sea Hunter 1,* arrived at Jones Bay, Dulcita was a complete wreck. She remembered being lifted like a baby and taken to shore by Frank Matthew-Tyson. Her next stop was the hospital where she spent three days.

Dulcita met Premier Bradshaw when he visited the hospital on Sunday, August 2nd. Once he heard her story, the Premier complimented Dulcita on the fortitude and strength of will she exhibited. However, when she went downstairs for X-rays later, she was horrified to see the number of dead bodies at the hospital. One nurse actually advised Dulcita to close her eyes as she passed. That was how she managed to pass by the overcrowded morgue. During her stay at the hospital, Dulcita had to be given special medication to help her sleep. About one week after the disaster, she awoke one night and told her fiancé that they should go to Charlestown pier. Dulcita dreamt the five children she lost were there waiting for her. He had to restrain and remind her that it was only a dream. Dulcita now has four children, all alive. Every now and then, however, she still dreams of those five children she lost—Mavis, 9; Christena, 8; Joseph, 7; Carl, 3; and Verna, 2.

Edna also has many reasons to remember the *Christena* disaster. The event changed her life forever. She no longer went to trade in St. Kitts. However, she admired the courage and will of Dulcita. It was to her that she attributed her survival. Edna also holds vivid memories of that dream she had, and the words of Frank Matthew-Tyson, as he helped her from the sea. In the dream he had promised that they would not let her die. In real life he did not. Frank ensured that Mrs. Browne was rescued from the sea. She survived and lived to talk about it. Mrs. Browne was never her vibrant self again, although she lived for another 32 years. She eventually died in May, 2002.

Victor Swanston

Mr. Swanston was certain, "Only faith in God kept me holding on to life long enough to be rescued by *Sea Hunter 1*." Victor lived at River Path, in Gingerland, Nevis. When *Christena* sank he was still trading in St. Kitts, after doing so for about thirty years. That was how he made the money to raise fourteen children. That Saturday afternoon in 1970, Swanston was a passenger on *Christena* as it made its way toward Nevis. According to Mr. Swanston, he observed early in the journey that the ferry sailed unsteadily. As far as he recalled, Captain Ponteen did what he could to correct the imbalance, but nothing the captain tried worked. Eventually, Swanston became convinced that something would go wrong with the ferry. He tried to locate his 14 year old son, Hanschell, before the drama began, but his effort proved unsuccessful. When the ferry began to sink, Swanston looked for his son again, but could not find him. Because of the confusion and horror, Swanston could do little more than attempt to save himself. He knew how to swim. The fear Mr. Swanston had was how long he could last in a swim so far from land. He was fortunate to find an empty crate among the debris in the water. Mr. Swanston reasoned that with the aid of the crate, he could swim much further and maybe reach Nags Head. When he took a final look in the direction of the *Christena,* Swanston noticed the bow was in the air and out of the water. Desperate, frightened passengers, were still clinging to the section of the boat above the water. But, it was sinking slowly. Very soon, Mr. Swanston watched as the sea swallowed the entire ferry. What he experienced left Victor Swanston horrified. Thus, Mr. Swanston struggled in the water and kept wondering whether he could make the swim to Nags Head. Besides the grim, discouraging pictures of death around him, Swanston's arms soon started to become numb, heavy, and difficult to move. When darkness came, he found himself swimming alongside two female bodies that seemed to move with him. When the current shifted direction and moved toward Basseterre, that made the swim for Nags Head even more difficult. Swanston was experiencing tired arms and pain from his left leg, which was cut, as he left the ferry. Despite the fact that it lessened his chance for survival, Swanston yielded to the physical and mental challenges he faced. Eventually he was overwhelmed and let go of the crate. Now, Mr. Swanston found himself in an untenable situation in the water. As he moved, there was death around him and in his wake. But worst of all, death was on his mind.

When it was all over, Swanston reasoned, "Only faith in God kept me holding on to life long enough to be rescued by *Sea Hunter 1*." After that Saturday's experience, Victor Swanston refused to sell on August 1st. Instead he held open-air religious services. Swanston was among those convinced that the ferry sank because of carelessness on the part of management. The death of his son, at 14 years of age, and the loss of those other young Nevisians who died prematurely, was the worse aspect of the tragedy, according to Mr. Swanston. He talked of receiving one hundred dollars as compensatory aid. That in no way assuaged his physical and emotional pain. But, Victor Swanston held no grudges. He had lost a son. He came to the brink of his sanity and stared death in the face. And, all he got as compensation was $100.00. As much as was possible, Mr. Swanston continued faithfully to be part of the St. Kitts-Nevis trade. He also walked away from the *Christena* tragedy with a very deep sense that an omnipotent God exists.

Luella Budgeon

In describing her harrowing experience, Mrs. Budgeon said, "My husband assisted me again by pushing a floating bench toward me." After the experience Luella, continues to live at Jessup's Village. However, there were ten difficult years of change and uncertainty. A number of changes came to the huckster's trade between St. Kitts and Nevis, after *Christena*. For a number of years Mrs. Budgeon was forced to try the taxi business. After a time, she went back to trading in St. Kitts regularly. Before the *Christena* incident, Luella traded two days per week, on Tuesdays and Saturdays. She was very present that afternoon when the ferry sank. Her husband, Joseph, was there too. He had gone to St. Kitts on other business.

Following the day's sales, Luella boarded *Christena* as early as she could. Dozens of other passengers and much cargo came aboard after her. However, she had seen *Christena* under heavier loads before, and did not suspect it would have any difficulty making the journey across to Nevis. Long after Luella had an opportunity to review her position, she still held that the ferry sank under mysterious circumstances. Luella is among the persons who claimed to have seen the mysterious man in black, who came aboard and caused the disaster. She remembered that Captain Ponteen just joked about it. When Luella drew his attention to the strange looking man, the Captain's response was, "All of us are going to Nevis." The captain was among the many persons who did not make it to Nevis. He never reached beyond Nags Head that time.

Luella was seated beside Gwenneth Budgeon when the ferry left Basseterre. Both women noticed the unsteady movements of the boat. They discussed that matter among other matters. After a while, Gwenneth became very fearful, because, unlike Luella, she could not swim. Gwenneth died in the ensuing drama, but Luella managed to survive. When the ferry began to sink, Luella's husband was close to her. Both had initial difficulties getting outside, but Joseph helped to untangle his wife from some rope. Afterwards, he managed to climb out with the help of first mate Frank Matthew-Tyson. Once outside, Luella grabbed an oil drum. Other distressed passengers took that from her. Her husband assisted her again by pushing a floating bench toward her. This she maneuvered much more easily than the drum. Using the bench to help conserve energy and as a life raft, Luella moved herself around swimming, among crying, dying, and dead people, as she glided away from the disaster area. Not long after, a fishing boat heading for Paradise Beach near Jessup's Village, picked her up. About thirteen other survivors were in the boat. Among them were Diana Williams and Joe Martin of Charlestown. Her husband Joseph was there too.

The people rescued by that boat were taken to Pinney's Beach. From there, Luella walked about one mile to the pier at Charlestown. She was later taken to the hospital for examination. Years after the tragedy, Luella ceased to be as upset about the matter as she used to be. But many of her very good friends were still lost that fateful afternoon. Two years passed before she could find the courage and travel to St. Kitts again. One of her major concerns after the disaster was for children left without mothers. Luella knew of many cases. In one situation, a mother left six children behind. Luella, too, had seen the *Hawthorne Enterprise* come close by, as she and others struggled in the water. It was too unreal to think that the crew of that ship had not seen something was wrong with *Christena*. They must also have seen that crowd of struggling people in the water.

Arrington Browne

As he reflected on the ferry's sinking and recalled the drama, Arrington Browne said, "The last thing I expected was that my merino would be used to signal *Christena's* sinking." Arrington lives at Rawlins Pasture on Nevis. He is both a carpenter and a fisherman. Of the two, Arrington prefers fishing. He could easily make money in less time. On his way to St. Kitts the morning of August 1st, he noticed his merino (vest/undershirt) was on the wrong side. To him it was symbolic of some special event, but he did not change it around. Meanwhile, he waited curiously to see whether anything strange would happen that day. When the ferry left St. Kitts just before 3:30 pm, Arrington felt it was too heavily loaded at the top. He also noted its unsteady sailing. Off the point on St. Kitts called Red Cliff, water began to come into the lower section of the ferry faster than before. As the ferry approached Salt Pond, passengers drew the captain's attention to the danger of the water coming inside. There was discomfort from the water, and the unusual movement of the ferry.

Arrington remembers that the *Christena* sailed with a heavy list to one side from Green Point to Bug Hole. Both points are located on the elongated neck of St. Kitts. The strange sailing motions occurred just before the accident. Two sudden gushes of water entered the ferry, and stopped the engine. The passengers, meanwhile, responded to their predicament with confused, horrified shouts. In the midst of their terror, the stern dived into the sea, trapping many people downstairs. Arrington said he had little problem making it to the water. He had no fear of the water because he is an excellent swimmer. There, he too experienced that indelible scene of desperation and shock, of people crying helplessly. Many of them were young children and women who could not swim. They were all in fear and numbed by the terror staring at them. Death was inching its way to snuff out lives.

Meanwhile, despite the ferry's sinking, passengers such as Arrington Browne, experienced little fear. There was nothing unusual for him about being in the sea—at times much further out in the ocean too. But, there was something strange about that occasion. For Arrington, it was about the crowd, its composition, and its harrowing response to being in the water. Once he left the confusion and started to swim, Arrington found himself in the company of four other people. He offered encouragement to the others while he swam at a relaxed pace. The fact that he swam with a watch, radio and other articles in his hand reflects the nonchalance and defiance displayed in the situation. Fear and panic were far from Arrington Browne's mind. He and the other four swimmers in his group made it to Nags Head safely. Later, Arrington helped to pull other survivors from the water. Among those he assisted was a very tired Ian Kelsick. Arrington blames *Christena's* crew for the accident. Under the existing conditions aboard, they sailed too far from land. After that accident, he lost all fear of the sea. Very often, he enters the sea alone to fish long before the sun rises. In another sea incident, Arrington lost a physical battle against a shark, and had to be hospitalized because of bites. Again he walked away with his life. But, even that incident failed to increase Arrington's fear of the sea.

William Charles Demming

The statement that Demming heard, which eventually led to his rescue from the water was, "Lord, see one over there, let us help him." Demming, better known as King Barkey, was a popular calypsonian on St. Kitts in 1970. During the 1980s, Barkey lived at Irish Town, St. Kitts, and made a living as best he could. On August 1, 1970, while other persons were traveling to Nevis for fun, Barkey was on board on his way to Nevis to do serious, but strange business. He was on his way to see an obeah woman.

As St. Kitts-Nevis moved into the 1970s, Nevis was still reputed to produce the best of the lot in that type of business in the Leeward Islands. For that reason, many Kittitians paid frequent visits to Nevis and spent good money to fix their affairs. Barkey had a problem. He was convinced that a former girlfriend from Molineaux, in St. Kitts, was trying to hurt him physically and probably emotionally, too, through supernatural means. Sherwyn Bertie of Cayon and Barkey sat together as the ferry began the journey to Nevis. They were drinking from a bottle of rum when the terror erupted. *Christena* rocked violently, then it started to sink, stern first. Sherwyn, who was on his way to visit a girlfriend at Cotton Ground, has not been seen since. Barkey, however, came through the incident safely, even though he could not swim.

In the midst of the drama, Barkey found himself outside *Christena*. He lay in the water helplessly and cried to God for help. He remembered saying to himself, "I don't know if dat wha I come out here for." Then, as if by some miracle, a roll of plastic foam came floating toward him. It had been shipped from Coury's hardware store in St. Kitts to someone on Nevis. At that moment, however, survival was all that mattered to Barkey. He grabbed the plastic foam and held on for dear life. It did not matter that the plastic drifted with the current on its own course. The foam was taking him away from the struggling crowd.

That plastic foam did not reach its intended address on Nevis. Barkey floated on until rescued by one of the fishing boats that came to the scene, after the sinking. He remembered someone from the fishing boat saying, "Lord, see one over there, let us help him." Then, Barkey and the plastic foam were taken into the boat. They were then taken to Pinney's Beach on Nevis. From there Barkey traveled to the police station and the hospital. Later, Barkey was careful to visit Coury's store and thanked him for having put the foam aboard. The police returned the plastic foam to the hardware owner. For very special and sentimental reasons, Barkey later purchased the foam as a souvenir. Over time, however, the plastic brought back sad memories of his personal struggle and the of loss of friends. Eventually, Barkey did give the plastic away. Many years after the *Christena* incident, he would drift back in time and remember when he almost died in the sea. The mission Barkey set out to accomplish was designed to relieve himself of stress. However, because of what happened, the journey brought him quite close to death.

Oswald Tyson

"The boat will sink and I am going to drown." That was what Oswald Tyson was thinking, as he struggled in the ocean. That experience changed Oswald's life. He was a 14 year old student at St. Thomas' Primary School when *Christena sank*. His mother, Theodora Tyson; brothers, Dave and Kirsten Tyson; and sister, Anita Liburd were on the boat with him. Of the five, Oswald alone survived. That Saturday Oswald went to St. Kitts to sell genips. With the money, he intended to purchase school books for the new school year. His sister Anita, then a student at Combermere Primary School, went to sell coal, probably hoping to buy school books with the money, too. Their mother and younger brothers traveled to St. Kitts on Wednesday. Mother had to help dress and "turn out" a bride on Thursday, July 30th. That August Saturday the family boarded *Christena* and were heading for Nevis. They were all happy travelling together, and looked forward to being back home on Nevis.

Shortly after the family got aboard, however, out of nowhere, Anita said to Oswald, "The boat will sink and I am going to drown." She was so correct with her prediction, but at that time no one took those words seriously. Many passengers had come to think *Christena* was unsinkable. However, Oswald's attention was soon focused on how the boat was sailing. He too, noted the unsteady patterns in the movements of the ferry. However, Oswald, like all the other passengers, was shocked when *Christena* lurched suddenly towards its right and started to sink. Soon, Oswald found himself struggling in the water. People were thrashing about, crying, and dying all around him. He watched, unable to help, as his brother Kirsten drowned. Oswald attributes his survival that afternoon to four factors: learning to swim early in life, Psalm 107, a dead female body, and a mistaken identity.

At age 14, Oswald could swim but was not a very strong swimmer. However, he lived close to the sea at Cotton Ground and had learned basic swimming. On finding himself in the sea, Oswald began swimming for all he was worth. As he swam, Oswald repeated the words of Psalm 107 from memory: "They that go down to the sea in ships that do business in great waters; These see the works of the Lord, and his wonders in the deep . . ." When Oswald became tired, he rested on floating dead bodies. They were everywhere in the water. Meanwhile, the fishing boat from Jessup's was moving about in the area and the captain deliberately selected whom he wanted to rescue.

Oswald was perched on the dead body of a large female when the boat came by. He recognized and called the captain, known commonly as "Uncle Peter," and Uncle Peter rescued him. The captain knew he had a nephew aboard *Christena* so he moved in to rescue Oswald, once he heard the call, "Uncle Peter!" Later, Peter did find and rescue his nephew, Patrick. After his *Christena* experience and the loss of his mother, sister and brothers, Oswald's lost his zest for life. For a time he moved around Nevis, living with relatives and friends. He and his other four brothers have not lived together as a family since. For Oswald, those experiences have been tough, painful and psychologically damaging. Since the loss, he has had a vacuum in his life. Despite the time distance, it took a long wait before anything really filled it.

Malcolm Simmonds

As he reflected and thought about the events surrounding the *Christena* tragedy, Malcolm Simmonds' ready comment was, "I had many sleepless nights, and my dreams were re-runs of the *Christena* Disaster." Malcolm Simmonds lived at Low Street, Nevis, back in 1970. Presently he lives in Toronto, Canada. On the day of the disaster, six young men from Low Street, Charlestown, Nevis, found themselves traveling together. All six of those passengers survived. Their backyard was almost in the sea. Learning to swim, and how to do it well was an early challenge for each of them. One of those young men was Meridith Charles. He went on to become a senior officer with the police force on St. Kitts-Nevis. However, this section focuses on Malcolm's story. Back then, he was one of the many Nevisians who worked on St. Kitts. He taught at St. Johnston's Village School. It was the end of the school year and August holiday, so, Malcolm and some other friends from Nevis, who worked in St. Kitts, were on their way home. However, unlike others on the ferry, that was not the first time Malcolm had seen so many passengers on *Christena*. What he noted though, was that most of the passengers were in the upper section of the ferry. However, he was not disturbed. All Malcolm wanted to do was, get home to Nevis. So, like the majority of the people aboard, he settled down expecting to make it over to Nevis in safety. He had done this trip so many times before; further, since he was traveling with many friends, there was hardly any anxiety about the crowd or the lack of balance in the ferry's movements, as it glided along toward Nevis. Malcolm sat on the port side of the upper deck chatting with his friends. A few minutes before the ferry sank, he was invited to partake of the goat-water being shared in the cabin. However, Malcolm had delayed going to the cabin, since he was enjoying the conversation with his friends. He promised to be at the cabin in a few minutes.

Only one thing about the ferry bothered Malcolm. Some nuns were aboard, and his grandmother had warned him that having such persons around during travel, always spell danger. Superstition, yes, but one he still accepts. Further, the fact that *Christena* sank that afternoon has not changed that pattern of thinking. Malcolm did note that the rolling movements increased as *Christena* started to enter the channel. Also, more water started to enter the lower section of the ferry.

The captain was collecting fares and just about half an hour had passed since the boat left St. Kitts. Malcolm noticed many of the people were moving about. But, the passengers were urged to relax and keep calm. Shortly after, however, the ferry swayed and the passengers moved to the opposite side. Then, it swayed again, and again, as the people aboard responded fearfully to the sudden rolls. The third roll was the final one. With its motor still running at full forward, *Christena* swayed over to one side. Passengers were tossed overboard in the process. Then, suddenly, its stern section plunged beneath the water. Some of the struggling passengers caught in the ensuing whirlpool, caused by the sinking ferry, were pulled underwater. Meanwhile, Malcolm and the others who escaped that experience could only look on helplessly. Cries of desperation were heard everywhere. There were now so many people in the water, struggling, crying, dying, or already dead. Many in the water were simply responding uncontrollably to their predicament. There were utterances of prayers, blasphemy, and advice—all at the same time. Frightened, desperate passengers were clinging to blocks of ice, empty crates, other floating material, or to one another. Drowning people were seen bleeding, frothing from the nose and mouth, or simply depicting the stare of death. Meanwhile, others in shock and fear, swam in every direction—not choosing which was toward land. Many moved only in circles, and not to the nearest shore. Malcolm concluded, "During those first moments about half the passengers drowned. Some of those left alive and sane, soon began to head for the nearest shore at Nags Head.

Malcolm found himself in the company of about fourteen other swimmers. They all started the swim toward land, a little less than one mile away. Only about half of those who started survived the journey. Death was there on the entire route. Some of the swimmers died quietly. Others thrashed about in the water shouting, in a final and desperate grasp for life. There was also a third response to impending death. Some people held on to the person swimming next to them, pulling that person under water. Malcolm remembers advising Ian Kelsick to take off his clothes so that he could swim with more ease, rather than having the clothes slowing his progress. At that point Ian had started to slow down and to show signs that he was experiencing problems staying the journey. Eventually, a part of Malcolm's original group made it to a large rock in the sea off Nags Head. The *Sea Hunter 1,* picked them up later.

Later, Malcolm stayed aboard *Sea Hunter* and assisted with the rescue. He too, remembered that many persons were pulled aboard alive, but died later. Those engaged with the rescue lacked proper first aid skills. Like many of the others who survived and were in the water swimming for some time, Malcolm remembers seeing the *Hawthorne Enterprise* in the vicinity of the accident. He also recalled, sadly, the incident in which the fishing boat from Jessup's Village, gave only limited assistance to the many persons who needed help, then left the scene. Once he arrived ashore, like many others, Malcolm went to the hospital and had his name added to the list being gathered. He lingered there briefly, then returned home. It was some time after that Malcolm's whole being started reacting to the tragedy. He experienced many sleepless nights. Further, Malcolm noted, "And when I slept my dreams were always re-runs of the *Christena* drama." He approached Dr. Louisy for assistance and was advised to visit his relatives in Curacao. That was how he overcame that aspect of the tumult in his life, brought on by *Christena's* mishap.

Malcolm walked away from the tragedy convinced that a glaring lack of swimming skills, poor training on the part of the crew, and poor management from the government on St. Kitts, all contributed to the severity of the disaster. Although there is need for more people on the islands to learn how to swim, on Nevis, the *Christena* incident continued to be a psychological deterrent from learning how to swim for a long time.

Meanwhile, many suppressed memories of the *Christena* still haunt Nevisians and Kittitians. Most of those memories are sad ones. They are memories that can easily evoke uncontrolled emotions. Even as people seek to forget the experience, they do not escape the totality of its meaning and consequences. The loves, the hates, the stresses, the failures, and the successes in life, are all building blocks to a people's history and reality. The

Whitman T. Browne, Ph.D.

individual's mind, however, is a unique builder, which does
the ultimate fashioning from all those experiences. Through
the interpretation and use of such experiences, human beings
decide whether a community sinks into oblivion, or swim to life,
surviving into the future. After looking at the whole story and
its consequences, no one can say the *Christena* incident, and the
painful disaster that it became for Nevisians and Kittitians, did
not bring about a number of changes to the islands.

CHAPTER FOUR

First-Hand Accounts II

On the way to and from Nevis, Saturday, August 1, 1998, Captain Sonny Skeete deliberately steered his boat, *The Sea Hustler,* over the spot where the *Christena* lies. Then he did something unusual. Each of the four times he passed in the area that day, Captain Skeete stopped and dropped a wreath in memory of all those who perished on that fateful voyage 28 years ago—Saturday, August I, 1970. It was the anniversary of *Christena's* sinking, to the day. At the same time, the 24th anniversary celebration of Culturama was on its way. Nevisians and Kittitians were hustling back and forth, preparing for the calypso show and other Culturama activities. However, the weightiest matter on their minds that day was politics. In ten days time, Nevisians were to go back to the polls and decide their future relationship with St. Kitts. It was billed as a decisive 1998 referendum, to decide for, or against, secession from St. Kitts. Ironically, although the *Christena* incident helped to shape the direction of secession politics between the two islands, that vote eclipsed the *Christena* anniversary in importance.

The politics of *Christena* is always alive in St. Kitts-Nevis. But, during the summer of 1998, it was in deep competition with the politics of secession. The two matters, each with a dynamic history in the islands, were competing for attention at the time. Nevertheless, 1998, was still a good time to reflect on the *Christena* story with people who were in some way associated with the tragedy, in both St. Kitts and Nevis. After 28 years, it was appropriate to reflect on the event and have people tell how it affected their lives, or how they were seeing the event 28 years later. The names are of real persons. Their stories and reflections follow without embellishment. Many are still very painful to ponder.

Grenville Elliott

"Time flies. Twenty-eight years went by so quickly." As with many of the others who agreed to talk, Grenville did not have an easy time reflecting on those years of his life. That evening he sat up and waited for his dad, James Elliott, a headmaster of an elementary school, and a younger brother, Kennedy, to return home from their trip to St. Kitts. The boat normally came in early afternoon. It was 5:00 o'clock; they were late. Grenville only gave up on his vigil for his father as the night progressed and he heard the painful news, that so many people died on the *Christena*.

Mr. Elliott went to St. Kitts once every month. Always, he took one of the six children with him. On August 1, 1970, it was Kennedy's turn to go. He had done well on his end of the school year exams and dad was using the trip to St. Kitts as a reward. At the time, Grenville was ten years old. Kennedy was eight. Neither Grenville's father nor his brother made it back to Nevis alive. The authorities found Mr. Elliott's body the Sunday evening, and took it to St. Kitts. No one ever found Kennedy's body. As Glenville saw it, "Kennedy simply disappeared from the face of the earth." Someone recalled that during the melee in the water, Mr. Elliott was seen swimming toward the shore, then, apparently, he turned back to look for his son.

For Grenville and the rest of his family, it has been a rough and trying twenty-eight years, facing life after having lost his father and brother so suddenly. Most of the remaining family members have emigrated to Canada. Although Grenville visited them during 1995, he does not intend to leave Nevis. He loves the island and insists on making his contribution there. Grenville has been an accomplished joiner for the last 20 years. He really wanted to be a teacher. If his father had survived the tragedy, Grenville believes that he would have pushed him more toward an academic, than a vocational career.

Grenville summed up the effects of the *Christena* disaster on his life in this way: "My mother, Marion, suffered emotionally, spending many hours crying and hurting. My family became fragmented and struggled financially because my father was not there." His father was dead; the breadwinner was gone. August 1, 1998, did not hold any special significance for Grenville. He did not pay any special attention to the date. "There was much more talk about the disaster five to ten years after it happened," Grenville noted. However, that personal tragedy, which changed his life and the destiny of his whole family is never far from him. It is always there.

Clemontina Nisbett (Nevis)

Clemontina seemed very certain about this: "It was set to sink. A man willed it so." Clemontina also remembered dreaming that *Christena* sank on its way back to Nevis. Consequently, she advised her son Govin not to return to Nevis on the boat that Saturday afternoon. She suggested to him that he should return on Monday or Tuesday. While his mother spoke to him, Govin was eating a mango. He even commented, "It may be the last one I eat."

Govin was a mechanic. He had to visit St. Kitts to see the dentist and to purchase some car paint, so he ignored the advice from his mother and made the trip. He did not know that just as

his mother was saying, as she shared her premonition, the ferry was destined to sink that afternoon. Clemontina had also shared her strange dream about *Christena* with a neighbor, Inez, who was traveling to St. Kitts with two of her children. One of the children cried pitifully and in desperation. He resisted as best he could. At one point the child clung to a mango tree nearby trying to avoid traveling with his mother to St. Kitts that day. Venetta, one of Clemontina's daughters, even hid him under a bed. However, Inez demanded her child, and off they went to be there, and to die that afternoon.

When the boat sank, Govin, Inez, and the two children all perished. Someone told Clemontina that people saw Govin in the water and they were encouraging him to hold on to one of the bags with breadfruit floating by. He needed much more than encouragement though. Govin never made it. Some days later they found his lifeless body trapped among some rocks off Buckley's Estate in St. Kitts. According to Clemontina, there is belief that if one places a bucket of water in the yard early in the morning, a relative who disappeared, as Govin did, would make contact in some mysterious way. Early the Sunday morning, Clemontina decided to test that belief. At about 7: 00 a.m., she placed a bucket of water in her yard. According to Ms. Nisbett, Govin appeared to her in a dream, not long after. In her dream, Govin reportedly said to his mother "Thank you for placing the water in the yard. I was able to clean myself up. I did not want to go away as dirty as I was."

In 1970, Clemontina had five children. Govin, her second child, was 28 years old and her chief means of support. For a long time, Clemontina grieved remorsefully over the death of her son Govin. The help he gave her with the other children was missed so much. Consequently, with Govin being dead, Clemontina and her family, stared poverty in the face daily. In time, almost all of the other children dropped out of school. Life was too hard. They just could not shake the crippling grip of an enduring poverty. And, that situation continued for many years.

In time, however, her son Elmon, who was born in 1960 and who barely knew Govin, came of age. He had dropped out of school also. However, Elmon was able to become an apprentice to the contractor, Mr. S. Hunkins. For that, Ms. Nisbett was very grateful. She appreciated the fact that Mr. Hunkins gave her son a chance to make it in life. The apprenticeship Mr. Hunkins afforded Elmon contributed to changing his life and that of his mother. Deep poverty was one of the challenges the sinking of the ferry brought to Clemontina's life. She endured misery in a manner that she never dreamed of, before the *Christena* sank. Even her remaining children had their lives dwarfed by the misery that their mother's life had become. "Today," she says, "I am much better off."

Twenty-eight years after *Christena*, Clemontina still has eight of her thirteen children alive. She was very aware of August 1, 1998. Actually, as that day dawned, Clemontina asked her children and grandchildren living with her to, "Remember the *Christena* because of all the people who died on it." Like many other people in the twin islands, Clemontina Nisbett remained convinced that the *Christena* sank, killing her son and all those other passengers, because someone willed it, using obeah. She assured me knowingly, "It was set to sink by a man." But, as was asked before: How could one human being be so evil, and work with satanic forces to destroy the lives of so many people, just to be certain that one particular person was destroyed?

Iona and Lennox (Ted) Tross

"Whatever our lot, God knows best. We have been drawn closer to Him": These are the words of the Trosses, who lost a 21 year-old daughter, Marilyn, and a 17 year-old son, Alston, on the *Christena*. The daughter was a teacher. She had gone to St. Kitts to purchase clothes she intended to wear at her friend, Elmo Liburd's wedding. While Marilyn was a teacher, Alston was in high school. He went to see a dentist and have a tooth extracted.

"I was very shocked when we heard of the sinking," said Mr. Tross. "It was Sammy Elliott (the dreamer) who broke the news to us. I just came from the bay where I had some shoal pots. There was no wind. The sinking was quite a surprise to me." Mrs. Tross and her mother, Lillian Browne, were quickly on the way to Charlestown. However, there was no good news for anyone about the *Christena.* When Sunday came, nothing had changed. There were still many Nevisians who had not come home, after the *Christena* sank. The two children of the Trosses were included. They were still missing. They too had not come home. Marilyn's body was eventually found among some others that had been taken from the sea and landed at the pier in St. Kitts, the Tuesday after.

A sister, Yvonne, had rushed home from Canada to be with her parents during that difficult time. It was Yvonne who identified Marilyn's body in St. Kitts. Shortly after, the body was buried in one of the mass graves there. Mr. Tross thought that he had a strange premonition that indicated to him where his son's body was buried in a mass grave. One week after the disaster, Mr. Tross visited Springfield cemetery in St. Kitts with a brother-in-law, Leroy Dore. Tross remembered coming to an area in the cemetery, then strangely, he found himself riveted to one spot. He experienced a strange, overpowering feeling that his son was buried in that same area. Mr. Tross shared his conviction with Dore. Through the years, Mr. Tross held to the conviction that he found where his son was buried. Nothing changed his mind.

For the rest of the family, after those two sudden deaths, September 1970, was remembered as a very difficult month. Marilyn would no longer be working at Brown Pasture School. Alston would not reach fifth form in high school. Mrs. Tross remained quiet, but, inside, she was still struggling with her grief. At one point during the interview, Mr. Tross became so emotional, he was almost incoherent. He said, "Marilyn had been such a powerful influence on my life. She would have changed my life." The mother also said, "She always did things to help her father. Life would have been much better for us today."

After twenty-eight years of dealing with their loss, neither of the Trosses was angry with God. They jointly suggested, "Whatever our lot, God knows best. We have been drawn closer to Him." Mr. Tross further admitted that throughout those painful years, he often showed a pleasant face, so that his wife would not understand how much he was hurting inside. Twenty-eight years after, the parents were still aching and wondering about what could have been. Meanwhile, their son and their daughter were gone from them, forever, in this life!

Clifford Browne (Nevis)

"I came out of *Christena* without a scratch," said Clifford Browne, one of the fortunate passengers on the *Christena*. He was one of the persons who survived the disaster. He was age nineteen. Today, Clifford readily talks about his experience on *Christena*. His reasons for traveling to St. Kitts that day in 1970 were to visit his grandfather, and to purchase a bicycle tube. Luckily for Clifford he is a good swimmer, and increasingly, it has become obvious that he does possess a very powerful will to survive. This is how he reflected on the event twenty-eight years later. "The disaster helped me to expand myself more. It has not prevented me from traveling. I have become braver, but I was never a coward." To prove his point, Clifford related six different life-threatening incidents he has been part of, since the *Christena*. Any one of them could have caused the loss of his life.

The first was the amphi-car incident in 1971. This took place, of all dates, on August 1, exactly one year after *Christena*. A visitor to St. Kitts from England, Mr. Mills, brought an amphi-car, which he intended to use on a trip crossing over to Nevis. Since the *Christena* had sunk recently, Mr. Mills had a difficult time finding people to accompany him. To make matters worse, the water was rough that day. However, Clifford had traveled to St. Kitts, because he heard about it, and wanted to see that very car. Since Mr. Mills had problems finding riders, Clifford opted to give it a try. One other person from Old Road volunteered to make the trip across to Nevis. It took them four hours to make that crossing. The ride back to St. Kitts with the water much calmer took a mere thirty minutes.

Two years later, in 1973, Clifford had another life-threatening experience at sea. He went down to unfasten a fish-pot that was stuck between some rocks. But, it was a deep dive for a free diver. The depth of the water and the time spent unfastening the fish-pot caused Clifford to begin running out of oxygen. When he made it back to the surface, he was bleeding from the ears, mouth, and eyes. But, as with the *Christena* incident, Clifford made it back to land. Later, his doctor ordered a six-month lay-off from the sea. Clifford also had to consult an eye specialist before he could see well again. For him though, it was all a part of his great adventure in life.

Clifford's next encounter with death came ten years later, in 1983. One Friday afternoon, Clifford accidentally swallowed a bone while eating a goat's head. The bone stuck in his digestive system. According to Clifford, "It was longer than a match stick." The following Sunday. He felt an intense pain in his stomach, but the discomfort was ignored and treated as if it was just pain from gas. In a short time, what was thought to be gas pain became a severe pricking sensation. Without too much encouragement from anyone, Clifford decided to travel the nine miles to see a doctor at the hospital. He was fortunate that he did. Three doctors, Louisy, Dias, and the late Platza had to perform an emergency operation. They removed the bone from Clifford's stomach.

Three years later, in 1986, Clifford was daring death again. That time he and twelve other persons from the villages of Bricklin and Barnaby ate tainted barracuda. Perkins (Peas) had caught the fish. Clifford got food poisoning so badly that he could not wear his pants on the way to the hospital. His diarrhea was very severe. It did not allow him the privilege of normal dress and travel. He was hospitalized for nine days. For some time afterwards Clifford could not look at sunlight. Seemingly, the poison had also damaged his eyes. At times the itching was so severe that he scratched his skin with a grater. By the time Clifford left the hospital, the hair on his body had started to disappear.

As fate would have it, Clifford Browne just had to be one of the persons involved in that major vehicular accident on Nevis during Culturama 1989. A car driven by Patrick Hendrickson and a bus (van) driven by Carl Manners collided. One person, Sheldon (I-Terry) Walters, of New Town, St. Kitts, died on the spot. Clifford came close to dying too. He could not walk, but Clifford came away from that accident, too. Admittedly, he had to be lifted, but he was very much alive. He survived again! Both of his lower limbs were fractured. The left was broken at the instep, while the right broken at the instep and at the knee. Glass from one of the vehicles had also penetrated his body in many places. After one month at the hospital, Clifford decided he had stayed long enough so he begged to be released. He was given two crutches and allowed to go home. It took Clifford the next five months before he could walk again. Even now, some of the effects of that accident can be detected in the ungainly way he walks.

Two years later Clifford had his next mishap. He was doing a job in Charlestown that required him to cut a tree. In the process, a limb broke unexpectedly and again Clifford was injured. He had to visit the hospital in Nevis and one on St. Kitts for treatment. Clifford was hospitalized for almost eleven weeks because of that accident. Today, for someone who has experienced so many misfortunes and face-offs with death, Clifford is unbelievably calm, positive and serene. Of all his mishaps, it is the *Christena* incident that comes back to his mind most frequently. "So many persons died that afternoon," he reflected. However, as he puts it,

"I came out of *Christena* without a scratch." Clifford also appeared quite amused and very unconcerned. He reminded me, "I still do spear-fishing." His serenity suggested, whatever tomorrow brings, Clifford is willing to take it. He has been up the rough side of life's steep mountain many times. His near-death experience on the *Christena* was only one of many.

Annette Muriel Lewis (Nevis)

Annette Muriel Lewis, was one of the victims pushed to the brink of insanity, when the *Christena* sank. Her husband was aboard and died in the accident. In 1998, it was heartening to speak with Mrs. Lewis and note growing confidence and independence. She was quite assured when she said, "I look after myself. I also do gardening in the yard, look after my father's house, and from time to time, I sell fruits such as sugar apples, mangoes, pears, and golden apples."

She was 25 years old and had two children when the ferry sank and her husband died. Annette was also pregnant with her third child. That child was born October 13, 1970, barely two months after the *Christena* accident. She was named Ermine Oretha, but would be numbered among the many children of Nevis who grew up not knowing at least one parent, because he or she died on the *Christena*. Cora Alitha, and Paulette Rositta are the older sisters. While the older sisters had a chance to meet their father, they did not really know him well when he died. Meanwhile, the experience of such a sudden separation overwhelmed the mother. Mrs. Lewis' story is one that illustrates well how devastating the *Christena* tragedy became for some families.

It is a sad and haunting story. Her husband died suddenly and left her with three young children. Her sellable skills were limited and her mind too stressed to hold a job, in a society that might have cared, but did not really understand the terror she faced each day. That Mrs. Lewis persevered and made it through those twenty-eight years to 1998, was commendable. She also appeared to have outwitted the demons which plagued her mind. Mrs. Lewis seemed in much better control of her faculties. Meanwhile, the evidence was still there. Mrs. Lewis' story of pain, loneliness, and struggle with reality is ongoing. The story the *Christena* incident began to write for Annette Lewis is not over. It continues to be written and illustrated with the ugly, haunting, pictures crafted in depictions of her human frailties. Annette claimed that she and her husband were Baptists, but that their marriage was falling apart when he died. She had even warned him that if he went on the boat, it would sink. But if that was really what Mrs. Lewis wanted and wished for her husband, why did her life shatter and break into so many pieces, and needed to be put back together, after her husband died?

For the rest of 1970, and for quite some years after, Annette was incapable of caring for her children. Both of her parents helped. So, too, did the Nevis chapter of the *Christena* Disaster Fund, which was carefully supervised by the Anglican priest, Cannon Blant. They built her the house in which she still lives. Despite the efforts of the people from the disaster fund, and her parents, two of the children, Cora and Paulette, had to be placed in a foster home. As if ashamed that she was not always there for her children, Mrs. Lewis insists to this day, "I love my children and raised them nice. I used to visit and bake things for them. They came back home about 1972." Throughout the interview, it was amazing to see how Annette was so careful and very assured about dates. Her use of dates and the obvious search for accuracy were remarkable.

A seemingly quick twenty-eight years had gone by for everyone touched by the *Christena* tragedy. That included Annette Lewis and her children. None of the three children lives on Nevis anymore. Paulette is in St. Martin, while the other two sisters, Cora and Ermine, at the time of the interview, lived in Houston, Texas. During the conversation, their mother seemed to think it was important that I knew she, too, lived in Houston, at least during 1988. "I came out in 1989, to look after my father. He died May 23, I 992," she said. So that no one will conclude that her children have abandoned her, Annette made it clear that they are all in contact with her, but, as she explained it, "My children have their own lives. They write and send me cards Mother's Day, Easter, and Christmas. They send money, too. Cora visited me in 1993, Paulette did in 1994."

Annette still grieves for the many Nevisians who died on the boat. She knew a number of them personally. Mrs. Lewis also volunteered that since her husband's death she has not been romantically involved with another man. According to her, "I look after myself. I do gardening in the yard, look after my father's house and from time to time I sell fruits such as sugar apples, mangoes, pears and golden apples." What is interesting here, is that Mrs. Lewis' involvement with nature, may be a subtle strategy back to the vibrant, competent person she once was.

Ferdinand (Ferdie) Browne (Nevis) and Orlando Browne (St. Kitts)

Orlando Browne seemed very pained, as he spoke about his reflections on the *Christena*. "I lost the bosom of love. My family was broken up." Ferdie was the father, Orlando, the son. Both spoke of having their lives disrupted by the terror and disorganization that came into their lives. Orlando now lives in St. Kitts. His father died during March, 2011.

According to Orlando, he was just eight years old, when his mother made her last trip to St. Kitts. He remembers pleading with her to take him along but she did not. When the news of her death came, he was eating corn-meal and fish. Ferdie, on the other hand, remembered asking his wife not to make that trip to St. Kitts. He suggested that she sell her mangoes at the market in Nevis that Saturday morning. However, she seemed very determined to go down to St. Kitts.

When Josephine ("Nation") Browne, died on the *Christena*, she left her husband Ferdie to care for their five children. A sixth child, Valentine, died at home, some time before the *Christena* sank. Two of the other children were quite young and needed close supervisory care. According to Ferdie, "I had to learn how to wash, cook etc., and to spend time raising my children. I took their mother's passing very hard and had much difficulty coping. It was never easy trying to raise three girls and two boys." Orlando is still hurt, and still angry, that his mother left without him, and has not come back, because she died. However, his comments seem more philosophical than his father's. When his mother died Orlando commented, "I lost the bosom of love. My family was also broken up." Further, Orlando did admit that as time passed, and as he learned more about life and relationships, he understood better what caused the frequent conflicts between his mother and father. After they had all lived together for many years, the time came, he said, "When my other brother went to live with his real father." In time, his sisters and mother did help to raise the five children. Despite his claim of great success in raising his children, Ferdie just could not manage the children well on his own. Besides, he was hardly ever sober long enough.

Two of the girls, Ermine and Laurel, went to live with their aunt Iona Edgins, on St. Kitts. Jennifer, Will, and Orlando stayed with their father. They were really raised by their grandmother, Lillian Browne. Orlando suggested that with the death of his mother, the children lost most of the freedom they had. For example, he and his brother were often left alone in the house. However, on many of those occasions, he and Will would run away to their grandmother. She lived only a short distance away.

Orlando argued that his family did not receive any of the *Christena* Disaster Fund money. However, they did receive some of the food that was eventually shared. Four years after the *Christena* accident, Orlando left Nevis to live in St. Kitts. He was twelve years old. During all those years, Orland claimed, "1 have had to work very hard at making life." Presently he hangs around the ferry port in St. Kitts and seems to do anything that will provide food and his occasional high. That was where I met Orlando for the interview.

Orlando did remember August 1, in 1998. He celebrated by walking, talking, and by reminding himself, that it was the 28th anniversary of his mother's death. As he always does when he talks about his mother, before the interview was over, Orlando lost his buccaneering composure, broke down, and cried.

Frank (Matthew) Tyson (St. Kitts)

One of the things Frank Tyson said in his reflections, included, "I was not a professional seaman then. If I knew what I know about sailing now, maybe things would have gone differently . . . . There was a crew of six, plus the captain. Two of the crew were engineers. No one of the crew had any proper knowledge about boat work." Frank did remember it was August 1, in 1998. That day brought back many memories and he thanked God for sparing his life twenty-eight years before. In 1998, Frank also started having a new spiritual experience. He became convinced that after searching for all those years, he finally discovered why he did not die on the *Christena*. Frank said, "I became a Christian three months ago." He also explained, "I believe God spared my life so that I can tell others of his love. Many who died, including Sweeney, Parks and Orville Morton were good swimmers. But, they did not get a second chance."

Frank's experiences had been many and varied during the past twenty-eight years. Overall, Frank thought his life became richer and fuller during those years. He once worked at the seaport and piloted large ships in and out of the harbor. At that time his competence at the job was not in question. Frank was provided formal training in Jamaica during 1976. Since then, he has been among the first to agree with the author's suggestion as to the real reason why *Christena* sank.

The sinking of the *Christena* was due largely to the carelessness of its poorly trained crew. Frank admitted openly that as first-mate on the *Christena,* he was not prepared for the leadership role he played on the ferry. He said, "Two of the crew were engineers. No one had any proper knowledge about working on boats."

Some time after the disaster, Frank visited Barbados and was questioned about the bulkheads inside the *Christena,* that were to keep the ferry afloat. Although he had worked on the ferry, up to that time, Frank did not understand their function or purpose in the boat. One of *Christena's* builders from the firm of Proston's Ltd (Guyana) pointed out to Frank later that the bulkheads could not have been closed when the boat sank. If the bulkheads had been kept closed, the boat would have rolled but would not have sunk.

Frank and others who traveled frequently on the *Christena* talked about the time in 1965 when the Australian cricket team visited St. Kitts. A crowd larger than that of August 1, 1970, traveled to and from St. Kitts on the *Christena.* All it did then was to roll from side to side. There was no fear and no tragedy. No one died. The author remembers that trip very well. He was one of those passengers. Everybody still says it was the largest crowd ever to travel on *Christena.* The ferry's legal capacity was still 155. That time in 1965, it was loaded with almost 400 passengers.

There is one strange fact Frank noted that is worth mentioning here. He was surprised that neither the seats nor the other life-saving equipment on the boat floated out the afternoon in 1970. To the best of his recollection, Frank was certain nothing was fastened in place. There was also no particular reason he could give to explain the phenomenon. As he did in the early interviews, Frank stood behind his story that the crew of the *Hawthorne Enterprise* saw victims of the ferry's sinking struggling in the sea, and did nothing to help them. He said, "The *Hawthorne Enterprise* started coming towards us, then it turned away. Since that incident, I have seen Captain Wynter on different occasions, but he has always avoided a conversation." It was even alleged in certain quarters that the captain admitted he saw the mishap and was sorry about the outcome. However, he had to get to

Guadeloupe before Monday. Obviously, participating in the rescue would have cost him precious time. Frank said: "One has to have knowledge about the sea and boat work. If you do not, it can be very dangerous to work on the sea. Things do happen, which require knowledge and skill. That was what happened on *Christena* that afternoon. When the crew has knowledge and skill about boating, that tends to reduce the risk of losing property and lives." Frank continued, "Because so many people died, it made me feel very badly. At first, it was as if I went for a swim. Now, as a trained professional, I have a much better understanding of the leadership responsibility of a crew."

Charles (Brother) Freeman (Nevis)

Charles Freeman was a deeply religious man. It was not surprising that he made the following statement, "During the past 28 years, I have not been discouraged or set back. Through it all, God has been a real help to me. He has been very mindful and helpful." Charles Freeman was 85 going on 86 years old when he was interviewed. He noted that his first wife, Augusta, with two of her sisters, Miriam and Tamah, died on the *Christena*. His wife's body was never found. He remarried about one year later. His second wife died shortly before the interview.

Freeman, a well known and devoted Christian, still had only glowing things to say about his first wife. She was a diligent breadwinner. On a regular basis, she handled marketing the family's vegetable crops, including carrots, yams, potatoes and tannias. Above all, he said, "She was a dependable source of help. That was why I missed her so much when she died." Usually Mrs. Freeman went to market on Tuesdays and Saturdays. When things were very good, she sometimes did a third day. That Saturday, however, she did not go to St. Kitts to sell. She did her selling in Nevis that morning before she left for St. Kitts. According to Mr. Freeman, "Augusta went to St. Kitts that day to see our son Stanley off to St Croix. She was not selling."

News of the ferry's sinking came as a surprise to Brother Freeman. Its initial impact was devastating. They had eleven children alive. All of them came together from around the world, when they heard the news about their mother. Some came from St. Croix, Saba, England, and Barbados. The others were in Nevis. Brother Freeman noted, "She missed out on seeing our children come of age—all except Emmanuel who died early. Now, they are at the point where they could have returned some of her kindnesses to them."

His move to marry someone else in 1971, about one year after their mother's death, was not good news to Brother Freeman's children, particularly the younger ones. They were very negative toward the new wife. None of them took the time to fathom the depth of loneliness, or to understand the great need for companionship that their mother's sudden passing brought to his life. He also wanted the assistance of a woman in the home. However, the new wife, Cecita, handled the situation with much understanding and tact. The storm that threatened never came. During the period following the disaster and throughout the past twenty-eight years, Brother Freeman found Psalm 46, to be very assuring, a blessing to his life, and to others. Just like his dead wife, Brother Freeman, lost two sisters in the incident. But, he took the time to cheer-up others in distress. Another thing changed for Mr. Freeman. It was his place of abode. When Augusta was alive they resided at River Path. Mr. Freeman moved, and lived at Bucks Hill, with his new wife Ceceita.

In summation, Brother Freeman said, "During the past 28 years, I have not been discouraged or set back. Through it all, God has been a real help to me. He has been very mindful and helpful." (Freeman is one of the many persons impacted by the *Christena* tragedy, who died since the interview).

Whitman T. Browne, Ph.D.

Edna Browne (Nevis)

Mrs. Browne noted, "I can now tell my grandchildren about how I managed to survive on a floating crocus-bag with some breadfruit, 28 years ago." On Saturday, August 1, 1998, Mrs. Browne remembered August 1, 1970. She remembered talking to herself and saying, "This is the first of August." Reflecting on her close encounter with death on the *Christena* in 1970, she concluded, 'The Lord answered my prayers. He saved me." Besides surviving the ferry's sinking, she had another benefit coming out of the disaster. Her husband, Spencer, became much more thoughtful and kind toward her. He had worked at the sugar factory on St. Kitts for many years. For the rest of his life, they shared a very loving relationship.

Once the trauma, the pain, and the anger of *Christena* eased, some of the hucksters from Nevis returned to trading in St. Kitts. Mrs. Browne was one of them. She admitted, however, that fear often taunted her. Throughout the journey, her heart would race until she left the ferry and was standing on the land. To make things worse, on one of those trips the boat on which she traveled caught fire. Her friends advised her to stop taking the risk. They thought that the repeated experience was too demanding on her emotionally. Eventually, she gave it all up, during the 1980s. Those twenty-eight years have been bittersweet for her. In April 1998, death deprived her of the one person she came to love dearly and depend on, her husband. "After my husband died," she said, "I cried myself almost blind. I miss him so much." She lost her son, Clarence Newton, in December 1995, and, after 1996, she struggled with the onset of blindness. Mrs. Browne was also angry over the fact that she never received any money from the *Christena* Disaster Fund. It was not normal for her, but Mrs. Browne did admit she was 86 years old. Because Mrs. Browne was blind, she stayed in the house most of the time. Further, with her husband being dead, life was no longer attractive or easy for Mrs. Browne. She began to feel left out and bitter. That bitterness (not

74

toward anyone in particular) was apparent when I arrived for the interview. She talked with me, only after some negotiations. Mrs. Browne, too, passed since the second interview.

Her behavior for the first interview was different. Mrs. Browne was eager to tell her story then. Now, with her husband and son gone, she was largely dependent on her only daughter, Alitha. The grandchildren helped her, too. At least, had she not survived *Christena,* they would not have known their grandmother. She can also tell them in person: at times they asked her over and over about how she managed to survive on a floating crocus bag with some breadfruit, some twenty-eight years ago.

Joshua Guishard (St. Kitts)

"How can 1 ever forget that sickening sight of floating flesh, people I once knew, were floating in the water—dead? Joshua reflected. "I go for walks and attend church regularly, at the Salvation Army." He asserted. "I am not prepared to stay in the house and get crippled-up." Joshua always remembered August 1, 1970. He was involved directly and indirectly in the *Christena* affair. Joshua also remembered that he was preparing to celebrate his girlfriend's (later his wife) birthday on August 3rd. Consequently, he did not forget Saturday August 1, 1970, in 1998. During the early 1980s when Mr. Guishard was first interviewed, he insisted that, contrary to Captain Wynter's claim, there was a woman passenger aboard the *Hawthorne Enterprise* the afternoon of August 1, 1970. He saw her. Guishard also suggested that because Wynter needed to get that woman back to Guadeloupe by the Sunday evening, the *Hawthorne Enterprise* did not participate in the rescue effort. During the 1998 interview, Guishard stuck to his original story. "Captain Wynter lied. The *Hawthorne Enterprise* left Basseterre harbor shortly after *Christena* that afternoon. The boat left late because Captain Wynter was at the airport waiting the arrival of a woman who had come via Antigua to meet him in St. Kitts."

Because Joshua ran the agent's boat, *Corsair,* he ferried Wynter and the woman back to *The Hawthorne Enterprise.* On the way to the ship, Captain Wynter discussed his next scheduled stop with Guishard. Further, as the *Christena* passed by the *Hawthorne Enterprise,* Guishard remembered that the crew watching from the deck suggested *Christena* could not complete its journey to Nevis that afternoon. His counter comment was that as it always did, the boat would arrive safely. However, as fate would have it, Joshua was wrong that time. The crew of the *Hawthorne Enterprise* was right.

His occupation left Joshua to assist with the collection and removal of the dead bodies from the sea. He commented, "Some of the people I pulled out of the water, I knew them. One was the girl to whom someone had said, 'I wish the boat would sink and you alone drown.' . . . In one trip, 1 brought in about 100 bodies. When 1 came back to shore on Monday 1 drank a half bottle of whiskey in two gulps. The *Corsair* made six trips to collect bodies—three on Monday, two Tuesday, and one on Wednesday." Many of the bodies were in pieces, so they focused on collecting the whole ones. The human remains left in the water drifted with the current toward St. Eustatia. Joshua recalled that the St. Kitts Labor Administration banned Captain Wynter from visiting St. Kitts following the disaster. For Guishard, life got better during the years after the *Christena* mishap. He worked on a regular basis. He married his girlfriend in 1987, and held a seat on the Board of the Port Authority, since 1995. In 1996, Guishard's good fortune changed. He had an encounter with thrombosis—blood clotting in his leg. His sister, Claris Guishard and niece, Sylvia Dinzey, invited him to see a doctor on St. Thomas, but when he arrived, it was suggested that he go to Puerto Rico. There his left leg was amputated. He was billed $25,000 US. Luckily for Joshua, S. L. Horsford & Co. Ltd.—the company he had served for many years—paid the bill.

At age 68, Joshua looked almost the same as he appeared during the 1980s. That is, except for the prosthesis he wore from the left knee down. Joshua did not ride his bicycle anymore. Joshua recounted that on many occasions as he passed over the area where the tragedy occurred, he looked down and saw the *Christena*. He, too, concluded that the mishap occurred because of carelessness on the part of the crew. He said, "They were doing repairs the Thursday. The exhaust pipe was cut and the vacuum chamber left open." Joshua also suggested that it was another person, Aubrey Wilson, not Frank, who was at the helm when *Christena* sank. Frank did admit that it was he who took over from Captain Ponteen. Joshua stopped working in 1997. His son Joseph Greene, a qualified seaman, took over the captaincy and replaced him since 1987, the year Joshua got married.

Over the years, Joshua has continued to reflect on the *Christena* tragedy frequently. How can he ever forget that sickening sight of floating flesh—the bodies of people he once knew, floating around in the water? Mr. Guishard went for walks and attended church regularly at the Salvation Army. He asserted, "I am not prepared to stay in the house and get crippled up." (Mr. Guishard, too, died, since that 1998 interview).

Luella Budgeon (Nevis)

Mrs. Budgeon reflected, "I prayed quietly and loudly. I praised and thanked God for keeping me alive up to this time." Luella's initial reaction was that not much had changed for her over the years, except for the hard work. That was not all true. After further conversation, it became quite evident that life had been quite a rough ride for Luella, since the *Christena* disaster twenty-eight years ago. The tragedy interrupted her huckster trade from Nevis to St. Kitts, so she became a taxi driver for about 27 years. Eventually she gave that up, too. As her car aged and replacement parts became more expensive, it was harder for her to compete against taxi drivers with new vehicles. Passengers seemed to favor the newer vehicles.

Whitman T. Browne, Ph.D.

Luella's marriage ended in 1987. She and the husband who helped her get outside the *Christena,* walked away from each other. Since then, she has had to survive on her own. However, Mrs. Budgeon has not been daunted by the new challenges life has brought. After her effort as a taxi driver failed, Luella returned to what she knows best: the "turn-hand" or huckster trade. However, she laments the fact that the direction of the trade has shifted. Instead of Nevisians going to St. Kitts to sell vegetables, they now go there to buy them. When the *Christena* sank, Mrs. Budgeon's younger child (both were girls) was nine years old. She saw them both grow up. They hated to see her take the boat to St. Kitts. Despite the new safety precautions, the children remembered the *Christena* disaster and saw any form of sea travel between the islands as dangerous and a threat to their mother's well-being. Ironically, although she appreciated their interest in her safety, the travel did not bother her in the least. She became accustomed to it. However, Mrs. Budgeon did admit that she remembered the horrendous event each time she passed the area where it occurred, all of twenty-eight years ago.

There has never been an anniversary of the disaster when Mrs. Budgeon forgets to thank God for sparing her life. The twenty-eighth anniversary was not different. Even after so many years, talking about the *Christena* brought back to Mrs. Budgeon the events surrounding the disaster and her struggles to survive, in haunting and vivid colors. Somehow, for Mrs. Budgeon, as with many of the others who survived *Christena,* they cannot forget the event. It does not go away. It is permanently impressed on their minds. They still become very emotional about it.

Sonny Skeete (Nevis)

Mr. Skeete was certain, "I can never forget that ship's name, *Hawthorne Enterprise.* I saw the ship. I read its name. I called it so many times that afternoon, it was almost like a broken record." Captain Skeete still insists that the captain and crew

78

of the *Hawthorne Enterprise* were very much aware that the *Christena* sank. He remembers speaking to a crew member and then the captain by radio from the *Sea Hunter 1*. The *Hawthorne Enterprise* was told that the ferry from St. Kitts to Nevis had sunk and there was need for help. The response from the *Hawthorne Enterprise* was that they had to keep on schedule to Guadeloupe. Skeete is still upset that the *Hawthorne Enterprise* did not come back and help. "Many more people could have been saved," he said. According to Skeete, things would have been much easier for him in *Sea Hunter 1*. Instead of having to go all the way back to Nevis, he would have been able to shuttle bodies and people to the *Hawthorne Enterprise*. In between gathering corpses, the *Sea Hunter 1*, also made a trip to St. Kitts to bring doctors and nurses to Nevis. About four days after the incident, Skeete's body started a sudden uncontrollable trembling. Then he collapsed. Sleep shunned him for the next four days. The horror of the disaster, and his role in it, had finally caught up with him. Skeete played a very active role in the recovery, after the ferry sank. He, too, lost family members on the *Christena*; an aunt, some nephews, and some nieces. They, too, were there at that great calling home of Nevisians and Kittitians, August 1, 1970. More than twenty members of Skeete's family died in the disaster.

Today, Skeete is a businessman in the cargo and ferry service. Since he passes the area of the disaster frequently, it is very difficult for him to forget. At times he stops his boat and shows curious passengers aboard exactly where the mishap occurred. On Saturday August 1, 1998, he took the time to anchor and drop four wreaths at the spot. Each time there is an anniversary and he is in the area, Skeete does something to commemorate the incident. Sometimes it has been simply to stop and sound his horn. Wreaths were placed and anchored, and a memorial ceremony conducted on August 6, 2000, for the 30th anniversary, other than what happened to him four days after the accident, 1970, Skeete has taken the disaster in stride. At one point he became concerned that neither of the two islands, St. Kitts or

Nevis, had done much to preserve the memory of the people. To him, the government's attitude was, "They are just gone and forgotten like the donkeys which the police shoot on the golf course at the Four Seasons Hotel." (The government of Nevis has now built two monuments, which do serve as permanent memorials to the *Christena* tragedy).

Skeete thinks he has grown stronger during the past twenty-eight years. He has learned much more about boats, too. Many of the people who were saved still thank him for acting with haste to help them that afternoon. However, he will go to his grave believing that the *Hawthorne Enterprise's* captain made a conscious decision not to help the people of St. Kitts-Nevis, who were struggling and drowning in the water. As for himself, Captain Skeete said, "I did all I could to help."

Oswald Tyson (Nevis)

As much as possible, Oswald has put his difficulties of yesterday behind him. Now, it is his tomorrow that is haunting and calling him. He is convinced he escaped from dying in the *Christena* debacle that afternoon, because of prayers. On Saturday, August 1,1998, he went to work at the Four Seasons Hotel as usual. There he met another *Christena* survivor, Edmond Gumbs, from New Castle in Nevis. Together they spoke about the accident. They called it their rebirth, since, according to Oswald, "We both could have been gone 28 years ago."

That disaster changed Oswald's life. He barely escaped death; while his mother, two brothers, a sister, and some other relatives died. Oswald was to learn later that life without a mother, at age fourteen, can be very tough and unpleasant. There have been times when even his family members turned their backs on him. He lived with an uncle at Craddock Road for a while. When that did not work out, he returned to Cotton Ground to live on his own. His life has become a big hustle from then on. While still attending school, Oswald became a bartender at the then, Cliff Dwellers Hotel. In between school and work at the hotel, depending on what was in season, Oswald would go to the mountain, collect limes, mangoes, genips, or sugar apples to sell in St. Kitts. Oswald also helped the fishermen with their seines and at times tried his hand at farming. He did all those things so that he could feed and look out for himself. And, as he noted, "Keep from stealing and dealing drugs."

No one remembered Oswald when the disaster fund was being shared. He received nothing from the *Christena* Disaster Fund. However, he did get by, and unlike some others, Oswald persisted to complete high school, too. Even now, he boasts of having five CXC (Caribbean Examination Council) passes and claims that history and politics are still among his favorite subjects. Oswald is satisfied that his growing-up experiences made him strong, and taught him the art of survival. Those struggles also created a special place in his heart for people less fortunate than himself, particularly children.

At the time of the interview, Oswald worked as a bartender at the Four Seasons Hotel. He also found time to do missionary and charity work on Nevis and in St Croix. Older folks, shut-ins, desolate and needy children are usually the beneficiaries of his good work. Meanwhile, Oswald also helped to raise three children who were not his own, but who needed assistance. He got married in 1994 and now is the proud father of two girls, Leslie, then six, and Theodna, only months old. As much as is possible, Oswald has adopted a policy of putting his difficulties of yesterday behind him. Now, it is his tomorrow that is haunting and calling him. He dreams of studying at the University of the Virgin Islands for a degree in business administration, some time in the future. Oswald has also written a book detailing his personal experience the afternoon the *Christena* sank, bringing tragedy and grief to his life, and to the lives of many other Nevisians and Kittitians.

Arrington Browne (Nevis)

Actually, although he does thank God at times, Arrington is convinced that when *Christena* sank, the time had not come for him to die. They are not related, but Arrington's attitude toward the *Christena* accident is similar to that of Clifford Browne's. The experience seems to have toughened them. It served to harden them. Now, they appear to have the will to survive, no matter how life threatening the difficulty. At times, the two men have dared difficult circumstances with a certain abandon. Arrington did not have any special memory of the *Christena* disaster, Saturday, August 1, 1998. Thoughts about the sinking, did not challenge or bother him. Actually, although he does thank God at times, Arrington is convinced that when *Christena* sank, the time had not come for him to die. In a matter-of-fact, and deliberate manner, he dived out of the sinking ferry. He carried a radio in his pocket, and was fully dressed, with shoes on, as he swam away from the sinking ferry. There were people crying and struggling all around, but he swam the distance to land with ease. The task hardly bothered him physically or emotionally. Actually, in a distance swim in 1982, from Nags Head to Basseterre, about eight miles, both Arrington and the author participated. Arrington swam smoothly and almost effortlessly. He was the first man in. None of the other swimmers challenged him.

After the *Christena* incident, Arrington (who is a carpenter by trade) took to spear-fishing, alone, at times, even before the sun rises. One morning in 1974, he shot an eighty-pound shark that turned and attacked him. Arrington went to the hospital, but his stay was short. Today he continues to go fishing, but Arrington now takes company with him. Over the years, Arrington has been in search of a reason for his survival. Now he thinks he has found one. Some years after the accident his wife developed a mental illness. Arrington became convinced that God kept him alive so that he could look after the children, when their mother became incapacitated.

For a period of about ten months Arrington did emigrate from Nevis, and lived in St. Eustatia. There he worked as a carpenter and helped to build some houses. He does not work regularly as a carpenter anymore. However, now that Arrington has given up carpentry, he thinks that life has been going better for him. Arrington does continue his spear fishing, he sets fish pots, and builds boats. Although he does not particularly spend time focusing on Saturday, August 1, 1970, Arrington has not forgotten his *Christena* experience, or the events on the island related to the disaster. Occasionally, he also talks with his children about them. Arrington does not remember being in danger at any point, but he does give thanks to God for sparing his life that afternoon.

Wyclide Condell (St. Kitts)

Wyclide was among the swimmers who spotted the *Hawthorne Enterprise* coming toward them, as they struggled in the water. However, while the others started swimming toward the boat, Wyclide recalled James Weekes saying, "The ship has engine; let it come to us." He was very perceptive. The ship soon turned and left everyone in the water.

Wyclide was on the boat to Nevis the morning of August 1, 1998, when Captain Skeete stopped to lay one of the wreaths in the sea. There was no way he could have avoided the memory. It all came flooding back to him—three family members and numerous friends died in that very spot twenty-eight years earlier. A factor that made the recall even more potent was the fact that many other people who survived the *Christena* mishap were aboard Skeete's boat. Ironically, just as was the case with the original incident, they had not planned this. Fate simply brought them together again. That afternoon in 1970, Wyclide escaped death, but he lost his mother, a twelve year old sister, and an eleven-year-old cousin. He also lost good friends, including, Mrs. Martineau and Orville Morton. After the accident, two incidents stood out for Wyclide. As he swam with a group of about 30 persons, he saw a nun who swam well trying desperately to save another nun, who could not swim. There was also that moment when many from his group in the water thought the *Hawthorne Enterprise* was coming to rescue them. They turned and started to swim toward the ship instead of keeping on toward the shore.

Wyclide has given the best and most feasible reason for the ship's demise. It was not the obeah man, it was not simply that the ferry was overcrowded either, and it was not rough seas. Actually, it is the reason that has checked out and stood the test of time. Years later when the issue was discussed with Frank Tyson, he, too, agreed with Wyclide's conclusion as to the real reason why the ferry, *Christena* sank. He worked as a welder at the sugar factory and Wyclide remembers being assigned to do some welding on the boat's exhaust system on the Thursday before the sinking. Wyclide's theory is that after the work was done, no one noticed that the vacuum chambers of the ferry were not properly sealed or that the pump was not working properly. The lower section of the ship was gathering water. He said, "The second engineer, who also died, was downstairs trying to start the pump." Those oversights on the part of the untrained crew allowed water into the lower section of the ferry and that was the main factor leading to the conditions that made *Christena* sink. Years later, then speaking as a trained sea captain, Frank Tyson agreed that *Christena's* crew lack of training was a definite contributor to the accident.

These days, Wyclide has become very sober and reflective. The disaster changed his life in numerous ways. One is his attitude to life, death, and his spirituality. Going to Nevis for August Monday remains a ritual for him, but he is always committed to attending church there the Sunday before. Twenty-eight years after *Christena,* Wyclide was still working as a welder. He also continues to have vivid memories of that Saturday afternoon in 1970, when with friends and family members, he struggled in the sea off Nags' Head. He still thinks about the many other people whose lives were suddenly snatched from them at that unexpected moment. Quietly, as if expecting to see some of them, Wyclide paused, then stared into space and said, "My nephew would have been 39, and my sister 40 this year."

Dr. Kennedy Simmonds (St. Kitts)

The doctor noted, "I dealt with all except one of the survivors. There was a severe lack of equipment to handle such an emergency on Nevis. One person actually died at the hospital." Dr. Simmonds is among those who accept that the overcrowding on the ferry had the major role in its demise. To him, such an unfortunate event was very much an irony in time. He recalled that on occasions, when his political party, The People's Action Movement (PAM), hired the boat from the government to make campaign visits to Nevis; all types of precautions were taken to prevent overcrowding on the ferry, during those trips. While the ferry's official capacity was 155 passengers, on those occasions, the charters were limited to 100 passengers, and police officers were at the pier to enforce that rule. Many people wishing to travel to and from Nevis with the group, were left behind.

At the time of the tragedy, Dr. Louisy, then the resident physician on Nevis, was off-island on vacation. An itinerant doctor would come over from St. Kitts to fill the vacancy. That Saturday, it was Dr. Simmonds turn to work in Nevis. He was waiting in the afternoon for his return trip to St. Kitts, when news of the sinking came. Later other medical persons had to be brought over from St. Kitts. There was never such a tragic incident in any of the islands during contemporary times. The doctors, the nurses, the society, and the government, were all caught by surprise, and ill prepared, to deal with the accident sanely.

Throughout the 1970s, *Christena* haunted the lives of Nevisians and Kittitians. Meanwhile, a number of experiments were tried with different ferries to ensure safe, reliable travel between the islands. By the early 1980s, concern still existed about safe travel between the islands. The unstable situation remained until a change in the political guards occurred and the ferry, *Caribe Queen,* was brought to the islands by 1983. Dr. Simmonds still sees the *Caribe Queen* and the safety it brought to travel between the islands as a major achievement of his PAM-NRP coalition government (1980-1993). He also credited the late Ivor Stevens with setting a very high safety standard for the ferry service. According to Simmonds, "Ivor insisted that *Caribe Queen* be repaired and checked every six months. This strategy did enhance the safety of travel between the islands. The *Caribe Queen,* is undoubtedly a direct legacy of Ivor." Simmonds also suggested that the *Christena* experience helped to determine the operation of the *Caribe Queen.* The ferry was made to operate under all types of conditions at sea. It was also tested in high seas before it arrived in the State, and had been carefully equipped to take both passengers and luggage. One new safety factor was that the captain had the authority to decide whether the ferry needed to make more than one trip on any day. Another important factor was that the ship was being captained by a trained competent sea-captain.

Even when a second or third trip was not economical, the government encouraged and allowed it, in order to ensure the safety of travelers. No one reprimanded the captain for such decisions. In light of the *Christena's* physical and emotional costs to St. Kitts-Nevis, the PAM administration was very much against overcrowding on the ferry. They wanted to take every step that would avoid another painful, costly accident.

Arthur Evelyn (Nevis)

According to Mr. Evelyn, "At first the whole event had no immediate impact on me. The full realization came home about a week or two later. Gradually, all that I saw and did finally shocked me toward reality. It became very upsetting and I became very depressed."

Like many others who were around in 1970, Mr. Evelyn remembered the *Christena* tragedy on August 1, 1998. He was there on land and saw quite a bit of what happened afterward. According to Evelyn, he was visiting Government House on Nevis that afternoon. He had been invited to an event there for the afternoon of August 1, 1970. Mr. Evelyn remembers looking toward St. Kitts from that vantage point and seeing the *Christena* making its way to Nevis. Later everyone was quite shocked to learn that the ferry disappeared and had not arrived in Nevis. Once the news got around, Nevisians began to head for Tamarind Bay (Jones' Bay) where the *Sea Hunter 1,* was bringing survivors and bodies ashore. Mr. Evelyn headed there, too, and met Ivor Stevens among others. He remembers helping to revive four people with the use of artificial respiration.

All the survivors, along with those already dead, were sent to the hospital. Not too long afterward, Evelyn helped to off-load some other bodies. Then, his next task was to make contact with the cable office on St. Kitts, to give the sad, breaking news to the rest of the world. At that time in our history, there was no cable office on Nevis. There were also very few privately owned telephones on the island and Mr. Evelyn, a businessman, owned one of those phones. Soon Evelyn was using the telephone in his office, to create a communication system for the island. He sent and received messages there for many days. It was all done at his own expense. Evelyn pointed out that Attorney, Henry Browne, then a student at the University of the West Indies, St. Augustine campus in Trinidad and Tobago, proved to be a very able assistant. Evelyn's role did not end there. He had to help deal with other related problems and emergencies. They included, working with the government's disaster team to bury the dead.

Mr. Evelyn went on to say, "That whole experience is riveted in my memory. I just can't forget it." He also noted, "The scene comes back to me every August 1st, and I find myself talking about it frequently." Evelyn lived at Government Road, Nevis, at that time. He still remembers trying to prevent his children from staring at so many dead bodies sprawled on trucks, on the way to the morgue at the hospital. Despite the pivotal role he played in dealing with that sudden, unprecedented disaster on Nevis, Mr. Evelyn is not aware that he suffered any long-term physical or emotional damage. However, he does agree that the disaster brought home to Nevisians, the need for a new politics with St. Kitts, including greater autonomy for Nevis. They had to find alternatives to the existing system that required them to travel to St. Kitts for job promotions, for the purchase of simple merchandise, to visit a dentist, and to sell their agricultural products.

Like other Nevisians, Evelyn remembers that the people of Nevis became very angry at the human loss on the *Christena*. They blamed Premier Bradshaw for the disaster and for their grief. However, Evelyn recalls that Mr. Bradshaw acted as quickly and as efficiently as he could, under the existing circumstances. He repeatedly showed a sense of pain and genuine sorrow for all the trauma that had come to the lives of people in St. Kitts and Nevis. Some people recalled that Bradshaw, too, did shed tears, because of the human and other costs the sinking of the ferry brought to the islands.

Arthur Anslyn (Nevis)

For Anslyn, "The memory still lingers as if it were yesterday. Families and survivors are still haunted and suffering from the mishap. So little has been done to preserve the memory of so many people lost." After 28 years, Anslyn was still angry at the authorities in St. Kitts-Nevis. His gripe, like that of some other people, has been that not enough had been done to preserve the memory of those who perished on the *Christena*. On August 1, 1998, as Captain Skeete had done, Anslyn, too, was careful to sail over the spot where the ill-fated ferry lies. However, even as he did that, Captain Anslyn wondered whether there would be an official memorial service to mark the twenty-eighth anniversary of the mishap. Unfortunately, time did confirm his fear. The government forgot the twenty-eighth anniversary. Nothing was done in 1998, to mark the occasion. Anslyn is one of those who believe the area where the *Christena* sank should not be a dive-site for anyone, including tourists. The area, the event, and the memories should be considered too sacred to citizens of St. Kitts and Nevis, to be visited and disturbed at will, by disinterested persons. Anslyn suggested that the area should be declared off limit to casual visits, and strictly monitored as a memorial site. Unlike the public, Anslyn disagreed with the notion that overcrowding was the chief cause of the ferry's sinking. He accepts the other explanation that blames the disaster on damaged exhaust pipes and vacuum chambers, left open accidentally, in the ferry's lower section.

Captain Anslyn is not convinced that the traveling public learned much from the *Christena* disaster. He said, "They would sink the present ferry at the pier with no regard for their own safety. They should be more conscious and careful." When the *Christena* sank in 1970, Captain Anslyn ran a business as a commercial fisherman. He was one of the professional divers engaged by the government to dive down to the ferry in search of evidence and the cargo owned by the passengers. Anslyn captained the government's ferry *Caribe Queen,* for some 19 years. To prevent another *Christena*-like disaster, Anslyn suggested selling all tickets at the dock, before anyone boarded the boat. He insisted that there be strict effort to regulate the number of passengers that came aboard. The ferry could have taken 180 passengers, but that number was restricted to 150. Anslyn also suggested that there be systematic training for the crew on the boat. It should include having the crew trained and prepared to deal with situations such as man over board, fire, and abandon ship. Meanwhile, there was another requirement, that a regular, semi-annual overhaul of the ferry be done. It is also mandatory that ferries meet Standard Safety of Lives At Sea (SSLAS) requirements.

Lee L Moore (St. Kitts)

Mr. Moore seemed certain about how the sinking of the ferry impacted both St. Kitts and Nevis societies. He said, "It did not weld us as a people. It intensified the hate. But, good people on both sides, were lost." Mr. Moore, who is now deceased, was the public relations officer for Bradshaw's Labor government in 1970. I interviewed him on May 2, 1999, for this project.

Moore remembered that it was about twilight when news reached St. Kitts, stating that the *Christena* had disappeared. Once it became clear that a tragedy was on hand, Premier Bradshaw, he recalled, became very active. The *Christena* sinking was the biggest event of a tragic nature in St Kitts-Nevis. It was bigger than the Brimstone Hill tragedy, on Easter Monday, April 10, 1950, when according to Bertram Gilfillan, twelve persons died suddenly in a human stampede, ten at the scene of the incident, two some time later. Interestingly, in that accident too, the victims were from both St. Kitts and Nevis. In time, the U. S. Coast Guard in Puerto Rico was contacted, to report *Christena's* sinking, and to seek assistance. A helicopter was rushed to St. Kitts-Nevis as quickly as possible. On its arrival, Bradshaw, Moore and some other people travelled to Nevis. However, by that time, there was hardly anyone left alive in the water. The rescue effort was continued, but it consisted largely of taking dead bodies from the sea. Relatives of the dead people claimed some the remains gathered in both St. Kitts and Nevis. Mass graves for burying large numbers of bodies were created on both islands. At that time, some of the families were too grieved, too poor, and too angry, to conduct such a sudden funeral.

According to Mr. Moore, the government introduced two important initiatives because of the disaster. It established a disaster fund designed to assist the relatives of those who died, and a commission of inquiry was set up to determine what really took place that afternoon. The commission was also expected to establish rules that would govern future operations of a government-owned ferry. Mr. Moore noted that because of the *Christena* incident, he came to establish an enduring friendship with Captain Sonny Skeete. From time to time, Skeete, too, has referred to his friendship with Mr. Moore, and what it has meant for him. Ironically, while the *Christena* tragedy helped to shape Skeete's politics; his friendship with Moore also helped to fashion the glasses through which he views the secession debate between the two islands.

Years after the sinking, the popular movie, *Titanic,* forced Moore to revisit the *Christena* incident. As he viewed the film with his children, the incidents of carelessness, neglect, and callousness, Moore saw there, brought the *Christena* matter back to life for him. He reflected philosophically on what he saw and, once again grappled with the magnitude of the economic, political, and social impact, the disaster had on the ongoing, and on the emerging relations, between St. Kitts and Nevis. He commented:

> Firstly, the size of the disaster overwhelmed the
> communities. They were ill prepared for the numbers
> of persons involved. Secondly, the politics that
> emerged exacerbated the age-old tensions and mistrust
> between the two islands. For Nevisians, their personal
> loss provided concrete meaning to their sense of
> other-ness. Again, hatred for Bradshaw and the Labor
> Party became an endemic feature of Nevisian society.

Moore recalled "coming close to being lynched" on occasions when he and Fitzroy Bryant attempted to hold Labor Party political meetings on Nevis during the 1970s. Thirdly, recommendations came out of the inquiry that set the stage for improving the safety measures taken during future inter-island travel. It was also suggested that the ferry receive regular inspections, and the crew had to be professionally trained and qualified. Strict rules were put in place about boarding procedures, and the number of people set as the ferry's passenger limit was to be enforced.

The intent of the government was to ensure that a new-look ferry service was created. According to Moore, one idea discussed was a proposal for a wharf to be built at the closest tip of Nevis that faces St. Kitts. The government also had plans to construct a road on St. Kitts to accommodate the land portion of the new travel route from Nevis to St. Kitts. It was hoped that the government could develop a new and full-fledged ferry service to transport people, regular inter-island cargo, and vehicles. "All was intended to improve and encourage travel between the two islands," he said. Interestingly, Moore stressed that the introduction of the *Caribe Queen* to St. Kitts-Nevis killed the evolution and development of the proposed roll-on, roll-off service between the two islands.

> While he lived, Premier Bradshaw always recognized and lauded the oneness shared by Kittitians and Nevisians. He wanted to improve communication between them. At one point too, he even proposed the building of a bridge connecting the islands. However, the cost and the antagonism of Nevisians were two difficult problems he did not resolve in his lifetime

Moore concluded that there should still be rethinking about the idea of having terminals at Salt Pond on St. Kitts and at the Round Hill area on Nevis. For Moore, "The road that exists in the Salt Pond area, The Dr. Kennedy Simmonds' Highway, was constructed poorly." However, he thought that government should continue its development with the intent of enhancing travel between the islands, and to facilitate the development of tourism.

Doris Richards (Nevis)

Ms. Richards remembered well. She commented on her pre-*Christena* years this way: "I met it hellish. I met it bitching, but I wanted my children to become something. I did not want my friends or my enemies back in Sandy Point to laugh at me. I had a hell of a big mind in my poverty state."

Doris Richards came to Nevis from Sandy Point in 1938. She was 27 years old. When I interviewed her in 1998 Ms. Richards was 88, but, a warm, vibrant, and charming old lady, totally gray. Her memory was phenomenal. We spoke about her son Sam Sweeney who died on the Christena. She also told me about his father William Sweeney who worked at the sugar factory, but never helped to raise his son. Ms. Richards still laughed about her mother's superstition that led to her migrating to Nevis, pregnant, and at her mother's expense, but with her mother not knowing about the pregnancy. For Ms. Richards, the trip to Nevis was really a camouflage to hide her pregnancy from an unsuspecting mother. Even her mother had agreed that the many dreams family members and friends were having about her were ominous. To avoid the impending doom, it was agreed that her daughter should "cross the sea," and she did! But no one suspected Doris was pregnant when she made that trip.

From that pregnancy was born Sam Sweeney, her only son, a child whom she adored, and raised without a father. Lyra, one of her daughters, admitted, with a tinge of jealousy, that there was a sense of mutual adoration between her mother and brother. All of the mother's dreams for Sam were good ones. She saw him as successful, wealthy, having the world at his feet, always being there for her and the girls, throughout the rest of their lives. However, that was a mere dream. On the afternoon of August 1, 1970, there was a sudden twist of fate when Sam died on the *Christena*.

Commenting on her reaction to the news of the sinking, Ms. Richards said, "That Saturday I was cooking souse for my son. I was also preparing clothes for two grandchildren, Denise and Greg, and me to go to church the Sunday. But God is a good God. I would have died if I did not have God." About one year later, July, 1971, Ms. Richards also lost another child, her daughter, Govanne "Baby", who was a nurse in St. Kitts.

Lyra and her mother both agreed that an opportunity to save Sam's life did present itself, but nobody unraveled the coded message. On the evening of July 31, Lyra had a serious accident in Antigua. But she chose not to inform her family back on Nevis. At the time, Lyra was on her way to attend a Girls' Guide Jamboree in Jamaica, and she did not want them to worry about her unnecessarily. Neither mother nor daughter doubted that Sam would have travelled to Antigua that fateful Saturday, had he known of Lyra's illness. For him, Lyra's well-being would have taken precedence over his usual weekend visit to Nevis to be with his mother and sisters. But Sam did not have that information, so he was travelling to Nevis to be with his mother.

Ms. Richards continued to mourn the loss of her son. His departure was sudden, untimely, and very painful to her. However, over the years, she had also fallen in love with what he became in his short lifetime. During the conversation, Ms. Richards made general comments about her son, her other children, and the youths of these times. She continued to read Sam's diaries on a regular basis. There was one of his white drill shirts, with epaulets, that she treasured and kept as a special souvenir for years.

Sam did dramatic performances in the shirt, and she always liked to see him wearing it. After some time she noted the shirt had developed a stain. Probably, only a still doting and grieving mother, would have noticed and cared about the stain in a shirt that no one had worn for the past twenty-eight years. According to Ms. Richards, Sam and his sisters shared a deep, loving relationship. There was always mutual respect, although he had to scold them every now and then. One would hardly argue with Ms. Richards's conclusion, "If Sam was alive, more of his friends would have been around." She admitted that

Sam's friends have generally been kind to her. Ms. Richards also commented on how the society changed from the time when she grew up. Parents did not tell children much back then, Ms. Richards noted. "I was a big old woman and still stupid." She recalled someone asking her, "Are you a young woman yet?" Ms. Richards neither knew her age, nor understood the expression then. She was about sixteen years old. That question was a coded way of asking whether a young girl had reached puberty. Doris recalled that when she asked her mother whether she, Doris, had become a young woman yet; her mother was very annoyed about the question. She never answered it. Ms. Richards had this to say about Nevis, and young Nevisians today:

> Nevis used to be called the Queen of the Caribbean.
> Today the children do not even tell you good morning.
> They know everything. They do not have any morals.
> They are not into that type of thing. They do not
> want the old people anymore. I wish God will change
> the children and bring our island back. They are like
> leggo-goats [untied goats]. Parents need to go back
> to the old time religion—the living, the morals, the
> respect, the behavior, the manners and the courtesy.
> I wish God would change the children and bring our
> island back.

Ms. Richards remembered the *Christena* incident constantly. She said, "Sometimes I sit down and everything comes back to me. Yes, I did remember it on August 1, 1998." Her real concern was, that a time had come, when Nevisians, too, needed to remember the *Christena*. "In a short 28 years, much of the island appeared to have forgotten what happened that afternoon. For me, I cannot forget. That was when my son and oldest child died. The pain from that loss continues to hurt!"

Dulcina Wallace (Nevis)

Dulcina lost her only child Lorna and her only grandchild, Candida, on the *Christena*. They were two of a total of seven family members who died in that tragedy. The daughter was in her early 30s, the granddaughter about 4. Both of them were traveling to Nevis to attend Elmo Liburd's wedding. The shocking news reached Dulcina in England, by that evening. She lived there with her husband, Neville. Immediately, they rushed to Nevis, in order to mourn with family, and all other Nevisians, victims of the great tragedy on the island. As she reflected on that time, Dulcina commented, "I could not cry."

Today, almost all of Dulcina's behaviors have become abnormal. Some think it was the impact of her pent-up emotions interacting with her mind, following the tragedy. Others believe it was probably more related to her love-hate relationship with her daughter Lorna, before she died. Whatever the cause was, Mrs. Wallace started to depict unusual behaviors in England, after she returned from that painful visit to Nevis, on learning that her daughter had died suddenly in the *Christena*. It was also reported that during the height of her stress, Mrs. Wallace fell, striking her head severely. She spoke repeatedly about having headaches, ever since that fall. Further, Lorna was Mrs. Wallace's only child; then her husband died, too, shortly after their return to live on Nevis, during the 1980s. In Mrs. Wallace's words, "I try to avoid thinking about them. So I pray a lot to Father God, but I do look at their pictures."

Despite some tries at probing into her present world, Dulcina did not say very much in her answers. But she lived alone in a darkened house and world. Dulcina was noted to smile and laugh inappropriately. She also seemed very much alone and somewhat afraid. When she was located, I did not know what to expect. Seemingly, Dulcina soon started to live in a strange, peculiar world. There she found solace and escape from the tumult that had come to her life. Two other strange things about Mrs.

Wallace were her constant making of lists, and the nonchalance with which she handled money. According to her sister, "There is a list of money for church, there is one for buses to town, and others for other things. However, when Dulcina used her lists to explain how she spent her money, it never added up."

Just about ten years after she lost her daughter and granddaughter, Dulcina returned to Nevis from England. Shortly after, her husband also died. Suddenly, the people she considered closest and dearest to her went and left Mrs. Wallace behind—all alone! In a period of just about ten years, her life had become bare and almost worthless, so, Dulcina was living in the dark physically and ideologically. During the afternoons, she closed her house early so she could sit in the dark. She did not take care of the house, or of herself anymore. And when she spoke, her conversation seemed weighted with sensuous suggestions. Despite sincere efforts to share with and care for their sister, Millicent, Priscilla, Agnes, and Nathan, felt locked out and existing beyond her changing reality. In the process, and over time, Mrs. Wallace seemed to have entered a strange world. One that was eerie, convoluted, and different. She marched to unusual drums, and only Mrs. Wallace heard the beat. She alone understood the rhythm.

Alfred Romeo Parris (St. Kitts)

"I have to go home to look after my children," was among the last words that Romeo Parris' mother spoke during that fateful afternoon. Later, on that journey back to her children, his mother, Hannah Parris, died an untimely death on the ferry *Christena*. Alfred Romeo Parris is one of those children left behind. By the time he was interviewed in 1998, Romeo had become a successful businessman and entrepreneur in the prescription drugs and health food business on St. Kitts. Despite the early challenges in his life, Romeo has taken a very positive, "Yes I can do it," approach to life.

His story is fascinating. It is about how Romeo became successful, after the experience of having debilitating tumult in his life, coming from the tragic loss of his mother at about age two. Romeo's mother, Hannah Parris, had traveled to St. Kitts to do her usual turn-hand, or huckster business. That was how she made a living for herself and her eight children—five boys and three girls, all of whom she left behind. Romeo does not remember his mother very well. However, he admits that he might have inherited some of her entrepreneurial skills. At the death of their mother, Romeo and Steve were first placed in the home for orphans on Nevis. Later, they were adopted by Mr. and Mrs. John and Catherine Douglas, of Tabernacle, St. Kitts. He remembers that life there was not easy and the discipline was very severe. Mrs. Douglas, in particular, was very tough on her two adopted sons. Of his other brothers and sisters, Romeo said, "They were scattered around Nevis among friends and family." When Romeo was about 10 years old, he went to live with his father's sister, Sandra Huggins, in Jamaica. There was much more freedom in Jamaica, and Romeo liked the experience. But he returned to St. Kitts at age fourteen. There he attended Cayon High School. Meanwhile, the Douglases were careful to ensure that the two boys made no contact with their brothers and sisters on Nevis.

On one occasion when Romeo received a letter from a pen pal in Canada addressing him as Romeo Parris, Mrs. Douglas slapped him. She made sure that both Romeo and Steve were christened at the Moravian church in the Tabernacle area, and given the last name Douglas. Romeo recalled that Mrs. Douglas dabbled with obeah. She received her special material from a Professor Cabellero. Supposedly, it provided her with special protection beyond the ordinary. Accordingly, Mrs. Douglas believed and acted as if she possessed powers her neighbors and friends could not access. As a result of her dabbling with obeah, Mrs. Douglas tended to live dangerously. In order to provide for her family, Mrs. Douglas grew sugar cane and manufactured illegal rum (Hammond) for retail. The family got no assistance from the government for the two boys.

Once, when the police raided the area in search for illegal rum, neighbors clandestinely passed the news on to the Douglases. However, Mrs. Douglas took very little precaution. Instead, she pulled out one of her special handkerchiefs, waved it in the air while saying, "I am protected, I am protected." It did not work. The police located the rum-still in the yard. She and Romeo were arrested and had to spend that Sunday under arrest. He laughs about it now, but Romeo remembers crying that morning, on waking up in jail, "Me want me cocoa tea. Me want me cocoa tea." The Douglases were charged $2,000 by the court. At age 14, the authorities accepted that Romeo worked in the business, and might have been a partner, but he was not in charge of the family's production and distribution business.

Eventually, Romeo met his brothers Samuel and Calvin on St. Kitts. Later, he challenged himself and dared to make the trip to Nevis. It was almost a providential experience for Romeo, but that was the day he met his three sisters. One day in 1980, Romeo was walking back to school after lunch. He noted that a young man, who was selling fish nearby, kept staring at him. Romeo looked back once, twice, three times, four times. At that point the young man beckoned to Romeo, then started to question him. "What is your mother's name? Do you have brothers and sisters? Can you name them?" By then Romeo had become very curious. He too wanted to ask some questions. However, he proceeded to answer the questions that had been asked of him. Romeo gave his mother's name, then he started to call the names of his brothers and sisters. When he got to the name Samuel, the young man responded, "That's me." Later, he offered Romeo some fish, but Romeo had become very emotional and so afraid; he said to Samuel, "No I do not eat fish." It was a big lie. He was overcome with strange feelings. Romeo just did not know how to handle the situation that confronted him. He was meeting a brother he knew he had, but had not seen for a number of years.

When Romeo got home from school he was excited about having met a new brother. He gave a report to Mrs. Douglas about the encounter, and Romeo also included his refusal to accept the fish. Hardly a surprise to Romeo, Mrs. Douglas reprimanded him and asked, "How come you do not eat fish?" She added, "Even so, you could have brought the fish for the rest of us." Some time after that encounter with Samuel, Romeo and Steve were told if they worked hard to help reap the Douglases' private plot of cane, they would be allowed to travel to Nevis to see their family. Romeo remembered that they worked extra hard. The cane was reaped in a timely fashion. They wanted to visit Nevis more than anything else they could think of. But, after the crop was reaped, nothing was said about the promised trip again. The Douglases did not let the boys go over to Nevis. Seemingly, Mr. and Mrs. Douglas had come to fear that if the boys went to Nevis they would not come back to St. Kitts.

Actually, such thinking was more an unreasoned fear of losing the two boys who had become their virtual slaves. However, the boys' desire was to make contact, meet and know their biological family. They had no intention of running away and remaining in Nevis, despite the severity of the lives they lived with Mr. and Mrs. Douglas on St. Kitts. Further, the brothers and sisters on Nevis were too scattered and living with different families. The glue that once bound them together—their mother Hannah was gone. Up to that time, the eight children had not been together as a family in one place since their mother's death. Calvin had come to Tabernacle once, during 1980, to look for his brothers. Steve and Romeo were with a group of boys when Calvin came asking for them. They were able to share a short time together. Calvin also promised to come back and see them at school the next day. However, once Mrs. Douglas was told of the encounter and the promise, she did not send the boys to school that next day. She seemed afraid that Calvin would have taken the boys to Nevis.

Despite Mrs. Douglas' effort to limit Steve and Romeo's contact with Nevis, Romeo, in particular, was determined to establish and build his contact with his brothers and sisters there. One day, still in 1980, Cayon High School was having a special sports program and the students were given the option to come to school out of uniform. Romeo left for school, as usual, but there, he explained to his teacher that he was going over to Nevis to look for his sisters.

When he left for school that morning, despite the fact that he was out of uniform, no one at home suspected Romeo was on the way to Nevis to search for his family and reconnect with his roots there. The $2.50, a one way trip to Nevis by ferry was all the money Romeo had. He reasoned that if he connected with his family on Nevis, they would have to pay his fare back to St. Kitts. So, Romeo left St. Kitts for Nevis that day, without knowing where he was going.

Since he knew the names of his sisters, Romeo began to ask on the street of Nevis how he could find where they lived. All the people he encountered and questioned were very helpful. As he was walking about, Romeo noticed that a girl just about his age, was looking at him quite intensely. He was about 16 then. So, Romeo started to think the girl might have had romantic interest in him. Despite such thoughts, Romeo had more important business on his mind. He made his way to Craddock Road where he had been told his sisters lived. On his arrival at the house Romeo introduced himself, then began to meet his sisters one by one. When he met Thelma, emotion overwhelmed him. Romeo recalled, "I started to cry. She was the baby when our mother died." He met Lavonne, too. Then, he was introduced to the third sister, Jasmine. She turned out to be the girl he saw on the street, and whom he thought was interested in him. And sure, she was interested in him. When Romeo inquired, "Why didn't you call me?" Jasmine responded, "I noticed you look like Othniel and I was curious about who you are, but I did not know you are my brother!"

Romeo had a happy and very memorable reunion with his sisters. But, unfortunately, the happy reunion had to be kept a secret. He could not dare let the Douglases know he had been to Nevis. Today, that clandestine trip to Nevis is still among the few treasured memories Romeo holds of Nevis and his divided family. In 1981, the Douglases proposed to Romeo that he stop school to help them work. They claimed that they could not keep him in school any longer. Apparently they had already arranged for his apprenticeship to a Mr. Bell, a contractor. However, Romeo was about to be promoted from the fourth form to the fifth and he intended to finish school. It was not a difficult decision for Romeo. He left the Douglases and moved to Molyneaux to live with another young man, Gene Herbert, who was then a police officer. They knew each other at school and during the days of their Hammond exploits. Besides sharing his apartment with Romeo, Gene also ensured that Romeo was fed. As fate would have it, other people including Mr. Douglas, Mac Parris, a cousin; Joe Hull, the school bus driver; and a Mrs. Dorsey who provided Romeo lunch free of charge, came to his assistance. They all helped him and made school attendance less burdensome for Romeo than it could have been. Romeo felt that God was there with him all the time, too. He admitted,

> Everything always seemed to work out so perfectly
> and so much on time. Books and clothes were always
> provided. When it was time for my exams I did not
> have the money. So I prayed to God about that need.

Romeo explained that in good time, a woman from the Social Welfare Department contacted him and gave him $1,000. The government had come up with a sum of money to aid victims of the *Christena* disaster.

All Romeo had to do was to ensure that $300 of the money went to the Douglases. The gift from the government was a very timely answer to Romeo's prayers. There was no longer a problem with finding money for his exam fee. Looking back over his life, Romeo is almost certain that Mrs. Douglas never wanted him and Steve to experience success in school. Whenever it was exam time, she always wanted them to "go and weed the land, or do something else." There were times when Romeo was torn between what Mrs. Douglas seemed to wish for him and what he wished for himself. He did not want to be ungrateful. There were two persons to whom Romeo often turned for counsel and guidance. One was the preacher at his church and the other a policeman who worked in the area.

On leaving school, Romeo received a number of job offers. First, he worked at Skerritt's Drug Store briefly. Then, he taught at the Basseterre Junior High School, and the Tabernacle Primary School. Later, Romeo worked in the laboratory at J. N. France Hospital. In 1985, he received a government scholarship to study pharmacology at the Community College in Barbados. He graduated in 1989. After graduating from the school in Barbados, Romeo returned to St. Kitts. He worked full time for the government, and part-time at Skerritt's Drug Store. In time he aspired to take over and supervise the operations at Skerritt's Drug Store. However, the deal fell through. Consequently, he started to take the suggestion of a friend, Bucknell Thompson, seriously. The suggestion was that he go into the prescription drug business on his own. Eventually Romeo did just that. He teamed up with his cousin Mac Parris and at one time they owned two drug stores in St. Kitts, one on Nevis. They also owned a health food store at Fort Street in St. Kitts.

Romeo credits his initial launching out into business back in July 1992, to the assistance, the patience and understanding given, and expressed by friends, and by other people who trusted him. The group included John Caldwell of Scotia Bank, Bucknell Thompson, and Austin Matthew, who willingly put up property as collateral to support his venture. There were also those persons who invested in shares. Then, of course, there was cousin Mac, too, who lost his job at the City Drug Store because he supported Romeo's stepping out on his own. In time, Mac also brought his skills and his friends to the new business.

Despite his entrepreneurial and other successes, Romeo still experiences pain over the untimely death of his mother. It also bothers him, the way his brothers and sisters grew up apart from one another. According to sister Thelma, who once worked as a librarian, at the public library in Nevis, "Samuel virtually grew up on his own. For a time he sold newspapers, did gardening, and eventually became a fisherman. Samuel still lived on Nevis. Calvin, the oldest brother, sang with a band and worked for the Ju-C soft drink company for a time. Later he migrated to Puerto Rico, then to the U.S." At the time of the interview, Othniel, worked at the Charlestown Secondary School on Nevis. He had been adopted by Hellen Daly; Thelma, Jasmine and Lavonne were adopted by Elvina Maynard. They grew up together in the same home, with Elvina and her two daughters, Claris and Norah.

According to Thelma, the discipline was firm, and life was not always a bed of roses. But the three girls did grow up together, and that meant a lot to them. In time, Jasmine did migrate to St Martin. Steve, who grew up with Romeo, migrated to the U.S.A. Lavonne is still living in Nevis. Romeo stays in touch with the others through email and telephone. Thelma did learn that her mother had missed the ferry, initially. She managed to get on when it returned to the pier to take on someone else. Thelma was told her mother, Hannah Parris, got into the *Christena* and insisted, "I have to go home to look after my children." Little did Hannah know she was destined to be part of that mass going home drama, off Nags' Head, that fateful afternoon.

Thelma still wonders, as do Romeo and all the others, "What would life have been like, if we grew up together, and with our mother?" Thelma reported that in the process of doing her work at the library, she read and reread the newspapers and the books about the *Christena* incident. "It was very touching to read the story," she said. "My mother died there, when I was only nine months old." It has been a long forty-two years, since the *Christena*, for Romeo, his brothers and his sisters. Their lives have had some very low ebbs. But there have been some flows, for them, too. The ebbs came first!

Despite the loss of his mother early in life, Romeo survived the challenges of being raised without his mother. Through the years, he has also come to enjoy and experience a wide measure of success. However, Romeo has never forgotten where he comes from and the past experiences that shaped his present. When the call came, Romeo took the responsibility without a murmur. He buried both Mr. Douglas and Mrs. Douglas. From time to time, old friends from that harsh past do stop by. Not all have been successful in life; some know what it means to have been "down and out" in this life. However, those friends can always count on Romeo to help them. Sometimes Romeo voluntarily goes out searching for such people. They shared their blessings with him in the past; it is now his turn to give back. For example, he still remembers Gene Herbert. Romeo gave him a job to manage the drugstore on Nevis. He was the person who helped Romeo when the Douglases forced him out. Romeo agrees, he did come up the rough side of the mountain. But he readily admits that perseverance, good friends, and God brought him to the top.

Devon Liburd (St. Kitts)

It was all a shocking experience for Devon. He noted, "Although I was only 12 years old, I was a very good swimmer. I was also able to help some other people survive." Devon Liburd is better known on St. Kitts by his calypso name, Lord Kut. Probably, very fewer persons are aware that Lord Kut, who likes to perform in dark clothing, and with a peculiar calypso style, at times mirroring the Mighty Shadow, is a *Christena* survivor. Devon was merely 12 years old when the *Christena* tragedy occurred, in 1970. He was on his way from St. Kitts to Nevis to take food and messages from his mother on St. Kitts to his grandmother in Nevis.

Although he was born at Cole Hill on Nevis, Devon lived alternately in St. Kitts and Nevis during the early years of his life. His mother had moved to St. Kitts to, "Look work." Devon said. "I traveled between St. Kitts and Nevis on my own from the time I was nine years old. Every weekend I had to take food over to Nevis for my grandmother." In August, 1970, Devon had just moved back to Nevis for about a period of six months. That afternoon when the ferry sank, the sail to Nevis was a normal one for Devon. However, it was very crowded aboard. Many people wanted to attend the August Monday horse race on Nevis. Devon was sitting at the back of the *Christena,* just in case of an emergency situation.

To the best of Devon's recollection, there was a brief drizzle and the passengers started to shift from one side of the boat to the other. He remembers quite clearly that just before the boat danced and began to sink, stern first, someone was heard asking, "Do you think the boat will make it." The truth was, no one thought it would not. Even as the boat began to sink Devon and the mass of passengers failed to anticipate the worse. But as the boat continued to sink he swam away from the boat and around the crowd in the water. The screams of a helpless, drowning crowd in the water can still be heard. Every now and then his mind does take him back to the incident. It comes back fresh to his mind. Devon recalled seeing a group of persons swimming away. Some of the stragglers slowed down and were struggling with death. Devon saw the floating drum with people such as Livinstone Sargeant and James ("Frayco") Weekes holding on for dear life. Devon was also pushing someone along on a floating bench as he neared the group swimming around the drum. He left the bench passenger on his own and moved to join the group around the drum. They insisted that he continue to help the passenger on the bench and not leave him behind. "Go back for him," they told Devon. He did not hesitate. Devon did just that. He still boasts, "Although I was only 12 years old, I was a very good swimmer. I was able to help some others survive." The drum was leaking, but according to Devon, "The group on the drum was trying to make it into Nags Head." Before they could make it in, however, the *Sea Hunter 1,* came along and picked them up. The swimmers were taken to Nevis and dropped off at Jones Bay.

Devon did not go to the hospital as did many of the other passengers. Instead, he went home to his grandmother, whom he met crying. She had a son and a grandson on the ferry. She thought they were both dead. There was much relief for the grandmother when she saw him. When she heard the announcement about the ferry's sinking, grandmother thought that everyone, including Devon, had died.

Two days later, on the Monday, Fitzroy Bryant, a member of the government, took Devon to the hospital to be examined. Since the *Christena* incident, Devon believes he has become a more independent person. He is convinced the experience worked to make him a better decision maker. At times, when he is in deep reflection, Devon weighs and recognizes the drama and the true meaning of the *Christena* event. By the following week, Devon was back on the sea between St. Kitts and Nevis. Devon is still certain that the official count for passengers on *Christena* was wrong. He stated, "There was at least one person whom I knew, and whom I saw on the boat. But I have never seen that person since. The initial number given as the list of passengers on the *Christena* was not correct." It has been adjusted since 1970. Devon claims, "Every time I travel between St. Kitts and Nevis, since the *Christena* incident, I am prepared to swim. These days I travel to Nevis very often. I work for a heavy equipment company there." Devon is without personal remorse over the way the *Christena* matter was handled by government. "Now that I am older, I understand that such things do happen in life. But these days, the event comes to my mind quite frequently," Devon said. He does continue to harbor two criticisms though. "The people who suffered from the *Christena* accident should have been given more assistance by the government." "And, today, one can hardly find the spots where the mass of the bodies were buried in the cemeteries. Nobody seems to care about them anymore," Devon said solemnly.

James "Frayco" Weeks (St. Kitts)

It was almost thirty years after *Christena*. James (Frayco) Weekes served as a deck hand on the ferry. He was there that memorable afternoon, but now seemed resigned to destiny. Meanwhile, he is happily married to a former shipmate, Ruth Lynch of St. Vincent. They work their backyard garden together, and they still exchange stories about when they worked on the vessel, *River Tar,* and were courting each other. One's first impression of Frayco is that he is a quiet, reserved and cautious man. But, he took on the role of a leader that afternoon in 1970. Many of the other people who were there, and were interviewed, named Frayco as one of the heroes, during the *Christena* tragedy. Frayco kept his wits about him, helped to keep a group of people together and eventually ensured their survival on that legendary oil drum. In the group was Nevis' then greatest cricketer, Livinstone Sargeant. He barely survived the accident. "From time to time," said Frayco, "Sargeant still pushes something into my hand to show his appreciation. He never passes me."

Although he now calls St. Kitts home, Frayco is a native of Montserrat. He came to St. Kitts-Nevis and has lived on one or the other island since 1962. Frayco does not recall anything abnormal about the sea or weather condition, on August 1, 1970. There was no rough water. However, as the ferry made its way toward Nevis, just about the area called Green Point, the boat started to dance abnormally. Then, suddenly, it began to sink—starboard and stern first. According to Frayco, "It did linger, bow toward the heavens, for a brief fifteen minutes." He also remembers that "the man-hole was open." That was one of the openings that allowed water into the ship's tightly closed vacuum chamber area. Like most of the other survivors, Frayco can still see pictures of desperate people struggling in the water. "I can still hear them screaming too; many were crying, Help me! Help me!" he said. "I saw Mrs. Mills and Mrs. Martineau, after I had dived into the water and came upon a small group of people crowded around, and clinging to a floating drum." Frayco distinctly remembers Livinstone Sargeant being on the drum. For the others, he can still see the faces but the names escape him. In a relatively short period after being in the water, the *Sea Hunter 1,* came by, and all who stayed with the drum were taken out of the water.

Later, Frayco reported to the hospital, but he did not stay. The night after the accident, he experienced nightmares, however, he has not done so again, since that time. Further, the very next day, Frayco reported for duty on one of the recovery boats. He stated that when a military ship involved with the recovery operation rocked the *Christena* at the bottom of the sea, a number of bodies floated up from the ill-fated boat. Many sharks were also seen swimming around in the area snatching and tearing bodies apart as they floated up from the ferry-boat. At times, Frayco would suddenly remember the date August 1, 1970, and the horror it brought to the people of St. Kitts and Nevis.

Before he settled down to a life on shore, accepting a job with the Electricity Department, Frayco had three other close calls at sea. In 1972 or 1973, Frayco and two other persons were on a boat called *Blue Bird.* They were traveling from New Castle in Nevis to St. Kitts. That boat sank off Everland and Frayco with his friends, had to swim ashore. Some time later, Frayco was traveling on the *Lady Christian* from Basseterre to Salt Pond. That boat, too, sank off Guana Hill. That time it was Captain Reuben James and Frayco who had to swim ashore. Frayco's fourth, and he hopes his last sea-related incident, came in 1989. He and the cook were aboard the vessel *River Tar.* Frayco was on as night watchman. When Hurricane Hugo came, it forced the ship to pull its anchor, then it slammed into the pier at Basseterre and sank. Frayco and the cook, Ruth Lynch were able to escape without any injury.

Ten years later, in 1999, Frayco and Ruth Lynch were joined in matrimony. Their shared experiences on the *River Tar* appeared to have bound them together in special ways. After the *River*

Whitman T. Browne, Ph.D.

Tar incident, Frayco accepted a position as a laborer with the Electricity Department on St. Kitts. This job was quite a change from what he did at sea. He planted posts, pulled wire and other related tasks. With time, Frayco has made the work-patterning shift and likes what he does for a living now. When asked, Frayco was quick to respond, "No, I do not miss the sea. I done with that. I wash my skin under pipes. I do not even go to the sea to swim anymore. I have not gone to Nevis for years." At age 62, Frayco seemed calm, assured, and was quite reflective. He agreed that his mishaps on the sea have worked to affect his life. "I have become a better person." He continued,

> During the *Christena* time I was young and strong. I am an old and weak man now. What I could have done before, I cannot do now. I feel good, but I have sugar. I go to church now, and I try to keep from trouble. The times when I think about *Christena,* I see the accident all over again. It is still fresh in my memory after all those years.

Charles "Spin" Chapman (St. Kitts)

Mr. Chapman observed, "It was sad to see all those turn-hand women die. Since that incident, that business still has not caught itself." Despite his being on the *Christena* that afternoon, up to 1998, the name Charles Chapman did not appear on any of the *Christena* passenger lists, created after the incident. However, Charles "Spin" Chapman was 14 years old in 1970, and he too, was aboard the *Christena* that afternoon. Further, he was among the list of passengers who defied death that afternoon. Charles looked death in the face, as he too was thrown into the waiting sea. But as fate had it, he stayed alive. After the incident, Charles learned that his sister Sharon (age 10) and brother Granville age (20), were also on the *Christena*. They did not know that Charles was there, too. For Sharon, that was her last sail from St. Kitts to

110

Nevis. She died in the accident. Charles was very surprised when he met Granville aboard the *Sea Hunter 1,* after being rescued. Charles claimed that once he learned Sharon was on the ferry, he wanted to go back and search for her. As Charles remembers it, the ferry was heavily loaded and everyone was trying to get the best seats. Other than a brief drizzle, it was a good afternoon for sailing. It was just off Nags Head, that the ferry danced briefly, then suddenly began to sink, stern first. Since he was sitting at the stern, Charles was quickly in the water. However, like scores of others that afternoon, Charles, too, expected the *Christena* to right itself, as it had done time and time again in the past. So, with that expectation in mind, Chapman began to climb up on the lettering in the ferry's steel frame. However, since he was outside the boat already, it dawned on Charles that it could be really sinking. It was then that he started to swim away.

Chapman went back to the scene, and noted, "There was a lot of crying. I heard Victor Swanston calling his son: Shelly! Shelly! Shelly! Others in the water were praying, swearing, shouting desperately, "Save me, save me, save me!" Charles recalled seeing teacher, Frank Morton, and another male sharing a life jacket between them as they swam toward land. He remembers seeing Devon Liburd (Lord Kut), help a fellow swimmer onto a floating bag with some breadfruit. He saw young Alston Tross, who could swim, hugging his older sister Marilyn Tross, who could not swim. And since no one has seen them alive again, Charles assumed that they must have died an untimely death, in that embrace.

Charles recalled, too, that "Sammy, the dreamer, had warned both of the Tross' children that they would die young." There were other people whom Charles saw, that could not swim. Some were grabbing onto those who could swim and showing their desperation to survive. In time, Charles, did come upon the group that was holding on to the drum. He remembered that they kept talking and encouraging one another throughout the ordeal. Charles also remembered that Devon Liburd gave some assistance to Livinstone Sargeant along the way. For Charles, however, if there was one hero that stood out that afternoon, it was Sonny Skeete, whom he saw at the helm of *Sea Hunter 1.* "He saved a lot of people," Charles said.

Before he was rescued from the water, Charles, like many of the other people thrown in the water, started to doubt whether he could swim the almost one mile distance to shore. However, Charles found the will and kept on swimming. He was determined to stay alive, no matter what happened that afternoon. Some time later, one of Charles' older brothers said to him, "If one person survived that sinking, I expected that person to be you." After they were swimming in the water for about half an hour, the *Sea Hunter 1,* picked up the group holding onto the drum. Someone in the group had managed to wave a shirt and attracted attention to their plight. On boarding, the *Sea Hunter 1,* Charles remembers seeing Victor Simmonds, Frank Morton, Livinstone Sargeant, Meridith Charles, and other people aboard. The boat went into Jones' Bay, bow first, and the passengers got off before it dashed back to the rescue again!

Once he was on the land, Charles experienced a strange melancholy feeling. It overwhelmed his whole being. However, as he and everyone else began to grapple with the magnitude of the human loss to St. Kitts and Nevis, Charles became happy and relieved that he was alive. But, that sad melancholy feeling would not leave him for a time. His sister was dead, and they had been very good friends. Other people he knew well, died that afternoon too. Sharon went to St. Kitts that Saturday because, Mellie Williams, the lady with whom she lived, sent her with some messages for her daughter. Charles did not bother to visit the hospital for any check-up. His brother Granville did. During the next few days, many Nevisians and Kittitians abroad came home to St. Kitts-Nevis. Both populations were caught-up in the drama of collecting bodies, identifying them for single or mass burials, and to mourn their losses. Many people were also involved with moving around the islands to extend condolences, comfort family and friends. Everyone felt some pain caused by the tragic sinking of *Christena.* The loss was sensed by Nevisians and Kittitians at home and around the world. Among the Nevisians, who came home was Charles's father, who visited from St. Martin.

Since Charles had forgotten his passport in St. Kitts, his father insisted that Charles travel back to St. Kitts, soon after the *Christena,* to fetch it. Since his mother agreed with his father, Charles had to dare the St. Kitts-Nevis crossing again, much too soon, after the recent tragedy. Although he hated the idea of traveling to St. Kitts, so soon after the *Christena's* sinking, Charles obeyed his parents and made the trip. Notwithstanding, the whole experience made him very angry. He thought his parents, particularly his father, was very insensitive to his situation. As a result, Charles did not speak with his father for the next five years. However, today, Charles sees that matter differently. He admitted that it was probably his father's way of teaching him to be tough and resilient during stormy situations in his life.

Since the ferry's sinking, Charles tries to cross the waters every year. Usually, it is on or close to the date, when the *Christena* sank. That is how he quietly brings the event back to mind and commemorates it. Victor Swanston did something different. Charles remembered that he would hold a memorial thanksgiving service at Market Shop, on Nevis. Once, when Mr. Swanston invited Charles to attend the service, Charles was on his way to his quiet personal, memorial event, off Nags Head. There the *Christena* continues to rest in its watery grave, still with many dead passengers aboard—never to see St. Kitts-Nevis or their families again.

On August 1, 1998, twenty-eight years after the tragedy, when Captain Sonny Skeete paused on the *Sea Hustler,* to drop wreaths over the spot where *Christena* sank, Charles was very much present. Today, he is one of the thousands of Nevisians who left Nevis to live on St. Kitts, for one reason or another. Charles laughs about it today, but he left Nevis because he had a silly dispute with his brother, Teddy. They both worked at the Zetland's Hotel. Teddy was Charles' supervisor. However, Charles claimed that he just could not handle that situation. He had an argument with Teddy, then he left for St. Kitts. That was in 1975, five years after the *Christena* tragedy. On his arrival in St. Kitts, Charles lived with McKenzie Peters. They were together for some two years until Charles experienced a consciousness awakening. He became a practicing Rastafarian. Charles noted, "One Christmas-eve, I moved out and went to live with Gertie Clark. By that time I had become much more conscious about life."

Generally, Charles avoided speaking with the authorities in St. Kitts-Nevis about his experience on *Christena* . . . Actually he is still upset over the fact that no one cared enough to search for him and to get his name on the list of survivors. Up until 1998, his name had not been listed officially as a survivor of the accident. On August 1, 1998, the government owned media sought to do a special program on the *Christena* incident. Charles admitted to them that he was there, but he refused to be interviewed. He was still bitter and angry over the manner in which the matter was handled by the government.

Like many of the others people who survived *Christena,* Charles thinks about the incident and its aftermath frequently. However, he seems to be the only person involved in the accident who suggests that *Christena* be resurfaced and put back on its run, as a ferry, between the islands. "1 will be glad to travel on it again," Charles said. Unfortunately, things have not always gone well for Charles since the disaster. At one time he had a real struggle maintaining himself and his six children. One time he was out of a job for a while. In time, however, things did change for Charles. He is now a grandfather. In 1998, Charles had a steady job with Cable and Wireless as a handyman rigger. At times, he also works on special assignments with Z.I.Z. Radio Station on St. Kitts, and V.O.N. Radio Stations on Nevis. One of the dreams that Charles wishes to have realized is that one day he can sit with all his grandchildren and relate to them, live and direct, his personal drama and survival story, as he recalls it, about the *Christena* experience, August 1, 1970.

When asked to give his final word and reaction to the loss of lives on the ferry that afternoon, Charles was quite blunt. He said, "Who were to go, went. Who were to survive, survived." As far as Charles saw it, the *Christena* incident mirrored that of the *Titanic* in a number of ways. He watched the film frequently. "Each time I see that movie, it brings back memories of the *Christena*," he said. "But the only time I cried, back in 1970, was when I got home. I did cry about my sister."

There is no doubt. Charles is happy he survived the Christena and is still alive. "I am happy to be alive," he kept saying. "Thanks, Jah. I would like to see a reunion of all the survivors one day. But the number was never correct. There was always at least one left out—me!" Charles also said quite pensively, "It was sad to see all those turn-hand women die. Since the accident, that business still has not caught itself as yet." He continued, 'I would like to see *Christena* come up. If I had the money I would pay to bring it up." In his comments about his life in general, since the *Christena* incident, Charles noted, "My years have not been wasted. I am proud to be living the life of a Rasta. Thanks to Jah Rastafari."

However, despite his claim of personal satisfaction and contentment, from some of his comments Charles does appear to be searching for something. "I want the *Christena* to come up. I want to have a reunion." Meanwhile, there have been suggestions that there may be some psychological gap, something missing in lives such as that of Charles. There is the still submerged *Christena*. The government's action was inept and inadequate; it provided limited, and in some circumstances, no support for the victims. There was also the community's failure to act as a body in ensuring that the *Christena's* memory be preserved on both islands, in tangible and meaningful ways. Seemingly, these poorly handled and unfinished events left some people searching for closure. In the interview, that was what Charles appeared to be reaching for. Probably, he was also making suggestions to others, by the dreams he continues to hold.

Ultimately, although some people moved on physically with time, there is still a psychological uncertainty about how to move forward from such an overwhelming and haunting past. Like Charles Chapman, many survivors and other people associated with the tragedy keep reaching back to, and down for the *Christena*. That horrific experience continues to present itself as a forever force impacting their lives. For many Nevisians and Kittitians, the *Christena* tragedy left some kind of scars on their lives. As it were, a part of every Nevisian and Kittitian died there that afternoon in August, 1970. The afternoon changed suddenly into night on Nevis—a night when everyone cried. Even at the present time, a number of survivors, their families and friends, have not experienced a complete expunging of their *Christena* memories.

To date, Nevis has tried, but St. Kitts has not done enough to memorialize the citizens of St. Kitts and Nevis who died tragically on the government-owned ferry, *Christena*. An effort should also be made to honor people such as Sonny Skeete, Earl Parris, Rupert Wade, and others, who were among the rescuers. They are also forgotten heroes of St. Kitts-Nevis. Meanwhile, the people of both Nevis and St. Kitts still need to evaluate and come to grip with what they lost and how they changed, since the afternoon of August 1, 1970. The event was so invasive and traumatic for St. Kitts-Nevis, that it caused changes in the islands' social and political cultures. However, not all that change was in a negative direction.

Francis "Mellon" Griffin (Nevis)

Winifred Sutton was commenting on how her mother, Francis Griffin reacted to the death of her daughter Lorraine "Gertie" Griffin: "She kept a picture of Gertie and stared at it regularly." After receiving the news of her daughter's death, Mrs.

Griffin was never again the vibrant person that she used to be in Butler's Village. She appeared to give up hope, as slowly, over time, her body deteriorated.

Mrs. Griffin eventually died June 2, 1998 at age 92. For her, those last twenty-eight years of her life were years of personal turmoil. The experience of losing her daughter brought a slow, enveloping darkness to her life. After Lorraine died, on *Christena,* Mrs. Griffin was never the pleasant church-going person, she had been before. Seemingly, her total life became focused and riveted on one fact: her Lorraine was gone. She died on the *Christena.*

From August 1, 1970, until shortly before she died, no one visited Mellon, as she was affectionately called, without receiving an earful about Lorraine. Of her five children, Mellon became very attached to Gertie, and seemed to have loved her most. Consequently, her sudden, untimely departure, in the *Christena* was too traumatic an event for the doting mother to accept. She withdrew from society, as her mirth disappeared, and her normal life ended. The rest of her years seemed plagued with turmoil beyond her control. Mellon kept a picture of Gertie and stared at it regularly, as if wishing her back to life. She also spoke often about how devastating and shocking the experience became, on hearing the news about her daughter's death. After the incident, Mrs. Griffin would tell people, who visited, that she was losing blood from her brain. According to another daughter, Mrs. Winifred Sutton, Mellon did use a tonic for a while, then stopped. Mrs. Griffin also admitted that the sudden unexpected news of her daughter's death was so traumatic that from time to time, as she moved about, she would lose her balance and fall. Also, on one occasion when Mrs. Griffin fell, a stick struck her in the eye. She gradually lost sight in that eye, and was never able to see well again.

In 1997, Winifred discovered that her mother was blind. It was a condition that Mellon hid from everyone. She did not share the truth about her growing darkness with anyone, including her daughter. For Mrs. Griffin, the next twenty-seven years were filled with difficult personal challenges—dealing with the loss of Gertie, a progressive diming of her eyes, and those recurring headaches. She was often heard saying, "The *Christena* put it on me." Throughout those years, there was one incident that Mrs. Griffin claimed brought some consolation to her life. It was the hug she received from Premier Bradshaw, when he visited Nevis, shortly after the accident.

Dulcita Browne-David (St. Kitts-Georgia)

Mrs. David lost five of her children, but she survived the accident and was happy to be alive. Despite her great loss, a very grateful Dulcita Browne-David found the courage to say, "Thank God that He spared my life."

Of all the personal stories highlighted in the book, that about Dulcita Browne-David is one of the most fascinating. After losing five children, and at the risk of losing her own life in the open sea, Mrs. David accepted the challenge to help save someone else she saw struggling in the water. This, was despite the awful fact that fate had just dealt her a very painful blow. Five of her children were taken from her arms unexpectedly when the waves flooded the boat. Then, she was thrown to the mercy of the sea, with only a crocus bag with five breadfruit to cling to, as a floating device.

I met Mrs. David for the first time in St. Kitts, about 1982. It was 12 years after *Christena,* her life was coming back together, but there was a question that bothered her. "I am certain there is some special purpose why I survived the *Christena,*" she said to me. Through the years Mrs. David kept searching for that answer, but she did not find it on demand.

The next time I saw Mrs. David was in St. Thomas, U.S.V.I., ten years later, in 1992. She told me she had found the answer to why she was saved from the *Christena,* while five of her children and over 200 other people perished. Mrs. David was convinced the reason was that, "God led me to become a Seventh Day Adventist Christian. My new found life of faith has brought me a new level of happiness and a spiritual security that I never experienced before." In December 1999, Mrs. David wrote me from Atlanta, Georgia. She asserted in her letter, "Thank God that he spared my life. Although it is over 29 years now since my life has been spared, I am still holding on to Jesus as Jacob of old and will not let him go." She continued,

> He is so good to me that I don't have tongue to give Him thanks. From the many things that are happening in the world today, we know that they are messages of warning to us to be prepared to meet our Lord, without a spot of sin in our lives. So brother, let us remain faithful and stay faithful in Jesus' name.

At the present time, Mrs. David lives with one of her children in Georgia. She moved there after her husband died in the mid 1990s. Most of her time is spent traveling with church groups, visiting senior citizens, and doing other missionary activities. Despite a move to the U. S., during such a late stage in her life, Mrs. David seems quite assured and contented there. Her life also appears to have found a new purpose. Mrs. David spoke as if she is focused on what Seventh Day Adventists call, "The Blessed Hope." It is a belief in a physical, Second Coming of Jesus Christ, to redeem from this world all those who have been faithful to His teachings and commands.

Mrs. David lost five children in 1970, then she lost her husband in 1995. However, those misfortunes have acted together to take Mrs. David from what she had known in the Caribbean area, to strange new places and a different world, far beyond where she once called home. Probably, Mrs. David should be long-faced, grumpy, and sorry for herself. But she is not. To her, she now has purpose and meaning for living her life. Mrs. David is now living to help others. She joins with others to bring joy to her fellow human beings. Mrs. David had been there. She witnessed that unforgettable drama in the cruel, unfeeling sea on

August 1, 1970. A number of able swimmers died that afternoon. But she was allowed to escape with her life. That was a miracle from God—one for which Mrs. David is eternally grateful. Now that she can put the pieces of he life's puzzle together, she is very thankful to God. However, at times she still pauses to ask the question, "Why me Lord?"

Camella Dore-Caines (Nevis)

Camella Caines' mother died on the *Christena*. She was 11 years old, so, Camella missed her mother throughout most of her life. But, from what she has heard through the years about the *Christena* story, and about what her dear mother was like, Camella developed a special appreciation for the mother she hardly knew. Despite the time distance, Camella continues to remember her mother with positive, good thoughts, "May your soul rest in peace. God bless you always" is a statement that reflects Camella's sentiment toward the memory of her mother.

On Sunday August 6, 2000, a group of Nevisians, through a determined effort, conducted a thirtieth anniversary memorial service to honor the people who died on *Christena*. Among the organizers were Hensley Daniel, his wife Sonita, Sonny Skeete, and Thelma Parris. Skeete volunteered his boat, *Sea Hustler,* to transport participants to the spot off Nags Head where *Christena* rests. With its anchor resting at the bottom of the sea, the *Sea Hustler* danced, as to a solemn rhythm, while the special memorial service was conducted there, in a calm Caribbean Sea. The ceremony began about 2:30 pm., and lasted a little more than an hour. Dave Morton, a young, dynamic Nevisian preacher presented the homily.

Thelma Parris and Camella Dore-Caines were among the 50 or so people present. In the matter of the *Christena*, Camella and Thelma share some common experiences. Each lost her mother when the ferry sank. Each of them is one of eight children left behind by that mother. And, as a result of such a tragedy during early life, persons other than the two women who were their biological mothers, raised and nurtured both Thelma and Camella to adulthood.

Reference was made to Thelma's mother, Hanna Parris before. In this section the focus is on Camella's mother, Claristine Dore. Apparently, that Saturday Claristine went to St. Kitts to visit her lover and father of her children, James Byron. Claristine intended to take her two boys on the trip, but Elvette's foot was injured, and Calbert was not interested, so he hid himself.

Ultimately, Calbert and Elvette were two of the many people for whom fate intervened and shielded from a horrible *Christena* experience. When the ferry sank with Claristine on board, she left eight children to mourn. They were Angella 2, Ilet 5, Laurel 7, Calbert 9, Elvette 10, Camella 11, Yvette 12, and Cynthia the oldest 13. By 1998, they were in their 30s or 40s. All were still alive and well. At that thirtieth anniversary memorial service, in August, 2000, Camella presented a heart-wrenching letter, in tribute to the memory of her mother. To me, though, Camella's letter was more than a tribute. It was a letter interspersed with memories of her mother, the pain of losing her, the special yearning for her presence, admiration for what she has come to mean to Camella, and unbounded love for having been mother to them all. There were questions too. In that love letter and message to a mother whose breasts eight children once knew and shared, but whom fate wrenched mercilessly apart, at a time in their lives, when they needed her most. She was the mother they have been yearning for—all their lives. But she went down with the *Christena,* making it impossible for them to see and know her, to touch her, to talk with her. Now, that could happen only in their dreams. It has been the case, since she left them for St. Kitts, early one morning in August, 1970.

As I read the letter and reflected on its message, I felt tears flowing. In my mind's eye I saw eight children yearning for the touch, the assurance, and unconditional nurturing from a caring, biological mother. Further, it was a time when the struggle to live and survive on Nevis was not easy. Those difficult economic and political years of the 1970s, challenged one's very will to survive. Nevisians who lived through that time, may still remember the horror, the uncertainty, the great loss, and the pain, the entire island experienced.

The Letter

For my dear beloved mother Claristine Dore from your eight loving children, 30 grand children and 3 great grand children.

Mom,

> *You only lived but a short while. God took you home for a purpose. You were so dear and sweet to your 8 loving children, 6 girls and 2 boys. You didn't even live to see us become young men and women. We struggled in our young life. Since you are gone, our grandmother Ida Morton and sister Cynthia Dore continued the task as mother. Now, our grandmother is gone also, but she will never be forgotten. You both now have grand and great-grand. Mom, I always think of you and wish you were here to enjoy life a little longer, and to direct each of us in life and talk to us when we needed advice about life, but, anyway God knows best.*
>
> *You only lived to see 32 years of age and now 7 of us are over that age, only your last is heading towards it. Mom, I only wish you were here. We don't have any idea of how you struggled and perished on that boat, the Christena. Anyway, may your soul rest in peace. God bless you always.*

> *Your daughter*
> *Camella Caines.*

CHAPTER FIVE

Newspaper Reports

After the tragedy, a wide range of views about the incident appeared in the two local newspapers: *The Labor Spokesman,* and *The Democrat.* The government also published the report on the accident prepared by the Commission of Inquiry. Both newspapers in St. Kitts support political parties; consequently, each publication then, as now, interprets events according to its party's views on the politics. The *Democrat,* which supports the views of the People's Action Movement, published articles that were largely critical of the actions taken by the Labor Government. Alternately, the *Labor Spokesman,* mouthpiece of the Labor Party, took a more sympathetic pro-government view on the issues. Both newspapers published articles on the *Christena* catastrophe. They also allowed ready access to, and public use of the documents. Some of those columns that appeared in *The Labor Spokesman,* during the period, are reprinted in the first section of this chapter. Newspaper columns from *The Democrat* are in section two of the chapter.

Whitman T. Browne, Ph.D.

Section 1

The Labor Spokesman, **Saturday, August 1, 1970,**

Government Press Release

On Saturday, I August, 1970, the *M. V. Christena* capsized and sank off Nag's Head while she was making her scheduled afternoon run between St. Kitts and Nevis. The *M. V. Christena* is a government owned and operated boat which is used on a regular ferry service between the two islands and provided an inexpensive means of travel and communication. Fares on the boat for the twelve sea miles from Basseterre to Charlestown are $1.00 first class, and $.50 second class.

The *Christena* was ordered in 1958 and was built by Sprostons Limited of Georgetown, Guyana, and delivered, and put into service in June of 1959. The boat was equipped with compass mooring and heaving lines, and equipment for safe landing and navigation. It contained five buoyant seats as well as life 'jackets which were equivalent to a life saving capacity of 180 persons. There has been no structural modification of the boat since it was purchased new here, but it was regularly sent to dry dock for overhaul and repairs. The boat returned from its most recent docking in Barbados only two months ago, ie., 17 May, 1970. The cost of these latest repairs was about $42,000. There was a crew of nine aboard the boat. Captain James Ponteen, and Assistant Engineer Conrad Pinney were among those who lost their lives. Seven members of the crew survived. The boat left St. Kitts at 3:30 pm. News of the disaster reached St. Kitts at about 5:50 pm, local time. An early arrival on the scene was a fiberglass fishing boat, *Sea Hunter 1,* owned by the West Indies Industrial Development Company Limited, and captained by Phillip Miller. This played a major part in the rescue operations . . . Z.LZ. has featured coverage since the first news on Saturday.

Sunday, August 2, 1970.

Citizens and friends of the State of St. Kitts, Nevis, and Anguilla: It is with the profoundest sorrow that I speak to you at the moment of our national, tragic experience in the sinking of the *Christena,* when everybody was preparing to celebrate the historic occasion of our emancipation 136 years ago. But alas! the hand of fate has chilled what would have been the exuberance of our spirit, and today we are depressed by yesterday's tragedy.

Let us not lose hope, but bind up our national wounds and continue the battle of life, singly and collectively. My wife joins in extending our deepest sympathy to the many families and friends who are saddened today at home and abroad.
Acting Governor, Mr. Milton P Allen

Deputy Premier, Hon. CA. Paul Southwell

. . . extended his sympathy and that of his family to the bereaved. He paid tribute to the Medical Service, the Police and Defense Forces, the Permanent Secretaries, who took charge of certain Departments, the Prison, Z.1.Z., the Christian Council, the Jaycees, the Rotarians, the undertakers, and all those persons who gave voluntary assistance. He announced the establishment of a Christena Disaster Fund and asked for generous contributions to that fund so that substantial relief could be given to bereaved and needy families.

Since it was acquired, the boat made several hundred runs between the islands and is said to have carried an estimated one million passengers over more than 30,000 miles before tragedy struck on Saturday.

Tuesday, August 4, 1970

August Monday, always a day of rejoicing and celebrating the anniversary of release from slavery, will never be the same again in St. Kitts, Nevis, Anguilla. Many of us buried large numbers of friends and loved ones that day as body after body was recovered from the waves in the wake of the *Christena* disaster . . . . To all those who are bereft of father, mother, husband, wife, son, daughter, and other relatives, the *Spokesman* tenders deepest sympathy . . . . May the departed be embraced in the infinite Mercy of God, and may their Souls Rest In Peace. Ironically, those in St. Kitts were buried not far from the spot in the cemetery where there stands a monument to the 231 souls who perished in the flood that struck Basseterre in 1881. The new graves form three long rows at the southeastern part of the cemetery.

Wednesday, August 5, 1970

The Premier, the Hon. R. L. Bradshaw, in a broadcast delivered last Saturday evening, August 1st, after news was received of the tragic disaster which had overtaken the *M. V. Christena,* expressed his shock and sorrow. He extended his sympathy, the sympathy of the government and all the people of this state to the bereaved families. He asked for a period of national mourning starting on Sunday, August 2nd. He also asked that the celebrations which were planned for the August holiday be cancelled. "Naturally all of us are shocked, terribly saddened, and grieved beyond words," said the Premier. He asked that we should not panic and that we bear our great loss with fortitude. He asked everyone to lend every possible assistance, and solicited the cooperation of all. "In comforting the bereaved, we can know that there is a God who knows what is best for each of us," concluded the Premier.

Thursday, August 6, 1970

House Passes Sympathy Resolution

We are through an hour of deep travail in the State in which all of our people are now companions in distress, travelling a common road of grief. I can only hope that what has brought us together will serve to generate a spirit of unity in another sphere, and help to keep us together. This is no time for apportioning blame or finding culprits. This is a time when all of us should rise above ourselves and give expression to the sadness that is in our hearts. The sinking of the *Christena* has left children without their parents, wives without their husbands, husbands without their wives, brothers without their sisters, sisters without brothers, cousins without cousins. It has touched all three islands of this State. It has touched the high and the low . . . . The Premier went on to say that all would be put on record when a Commission of Inquiry sat in the next few days to investigate the sinking of the *Christena*. The Premier also told of a ship, *Hawthorne Enterprise*. which buried itself in shame because it refused to render assistance when called upon to do so by Randolph Skeete and two members of the crew of *Christena*. who spoke to the ship over the radio. "At one stage," said the Premier, "the boat headed in the direction of *the Christena* then turned away. Of this shameful crew, one offered an obscenity and said they were on schedule, and couldn't be bothered. The captain, a man called Stanley L. Wynter, will be reported to the maritime authorities in the United Kingdom, and to the Cayman Islands where the boat was registered. That boat will be banned from here," said the Premier.

Thursday, August 13, 1970

Premier Condemns Two Christena Incidents

"The *Christena* had been built to the order of this government," added the Premier, "and not as reported in Nevis, been a river boat. Nor was it a second-hand boat. A national tragedy was being reported to suit the political purposes of some persons," said the Premier. Such persons were despicable creatures who by opening their mouths in that fashion placed themselves beneath contempt. The facts would be brought out by the Commission of Inquiry." The Premier revealed that the British Government made a contribution of $24,000 in respect of the *Christena* disaster. The British Development Division in Barbados took steps to secure the charter of a motor vessel by which a limited service of passenger and cargo between St. Kitts and Nevis could be resumed. The Premier hoped it would soon be possible, with expert advice, to obtain a suitable replacement for the *Christena*.

The *Christena* Inquiry

The Commission appointed by His Excellency, the Acting Governor to hold an inquiry to investigate the circumstances surrounding the sinking of the *Motor Vessel Christena* intends to hear evidence in both Nevis and St. Kitts. Sitting in Nevis will commence at the Court House, Charlestown, on Monday, 7 August, 1970, at 9:30 o'clock in the forenoon, and the sitting in St. Kitts on Monday, 24 August 1970, at the Court House, Basseterre at 9:30 am. Persons desirous of giving evidence in Nevis or St. Kitts should submit their name and address to the Secretary to the Commission, Crown Council Chambers, Government Headquarters, Basseterre, (or to the Government Secretary's Office, Charlestown, Nevis, in the case of persons in Nevis) before 3:00 pm on Friday, 14 August 1970.

Friday, August 14, 1970

It was in bad taste for anyone to try to make personal and political capital out of the tragedy, asserted the minister. "All of us must grieve because death knows no political loyalty; death has no political affinity." "As we view this tragedy, which has differences, and rise to the challenge which this tragedy has set us," declared Mr. Bryant . . . . Mr. Bryant urged that we weather the catastrophe; that we realize the sinking of the *Christena* was a challenge to us; that we rise to meet that challenge so that those of our relatives who perished in the disaster would not have perished in vain. Bryant calling for a Time for Unity in the *House* on August 6th.

Saturday, August 22, 1970

Christena Disaster Inquiry Opens

On Monday, 17 August at about 9:50 am, His Lordship, Mr. Justice D. Barry Renwick, Resident Puisne Judge, walked into the Court House in Nevis and the Commission of Inquiry into the *Christena* disaster had begun. By Commission from His Excellency, the Acting Governor, His Lordship had been appointed a one man Commission of Inquiry to obtain full information and to examine the circumstances surrounding the sinking of the *M. V. Christena* on Saturday, 1 August, 1970, and to make such recommendations as he should think fit. The Commission was to commence its business before 31st August, and to report by 15 September; and the judge was directed to hold hearings in public . . . . The first of 14 witnesses at the Commission of Inquiry into the *Christena* disaster on Monday was Mr. J.B. Cox, Permanent Secretary to the Minister of Communication, Works and Transport. Mr. Cox, who was led by Lee Moore, said that he was responsible for the administration and maintenance of the *Christena* . . . . Mr. Cox said that the builders had advised the carrying capacity of the boat to be 155 passengers made of 25 on the upper deck and 130 on the lower deck. He himself had never received any formal reports about overloading of the boat; but according to the records, Mr. Maguire, then Warden of Nevis, had written to the Harbor Master on the subject, on 1 July, 1959. On 26 January 1960, a letter from Mr. King of Delisle Walwyn and Co., the insurer, raised the subject of overloading. Mr. King's letter, he said, referred to a report in the *Labor Spokesman* of the 26 January 1960 *that Christena* had on board 192 passengers. (This was at the time when she had sprung a leak and had to be put in at Ballast Bay) . . . . When *Christena's* mate, Matthew Tyson, gave evidence on Tuesday, he said it was his opinion that the boat had been overloaded on 12 July. He knew of the interview between Mr. Cox and the Captain because the Captain had told him that Mr. Cox had called him and spoken to him about the overloading.

Saturday, August 22, 1970

Commission Visits Location of Christena

At about ten minutes past twelve on Tuesday, the Honorable Mr. Justice Renwick, the one man Commission appointed to probe the *Christena* disaster, stood on the deck, peered over at the spot where the *M. V. Christena* lies at the bottom of the sea. The Commissioner, who had asked to see the spot, was taken there by Captain Phillip Miller aboard the *Sea Hunter 1,* a fiberglass fishing boat, owned by the West Indies Industrial Development Company Ltd.

Monday, August 24, 1970

Bradshaw Thanks Those Who Helped

The House of Assembly, at an Emergency Meeting on August 6th, passed a Resolution of Sympathy to the relatives of the victims of the *Christena* disaster. The Resolution was moved by the Premier, Hon. R. L. Bradshaw. Speaking on the Resolution, the Premier expressed sincere thanks to everyone who, when the *Christena* sank on August 1st, gave ready and willing help in the rescue of survivors, in the recovery of bodies of dead from the sea and in the burial of those bodies, both in Nevis and in St. Kitts. The Premier paid tribute to our Radio Station, Z I.Z., which throughout the entire period sent out messages of all description, relative to the disaster, and so kept people informed, and kept them together. "Z.I.Z.," said the Premier, "performed a very wonderful job." . . . Among those who came in for special mention by the Premier were some prisoners who, on Tuesday morning, 4 August, volunteered to assist, went out on the Customs Launch, and helped in recovering bodies from the sea.

The Premier learned that one of these prisoners, Charles Cozier of Nevis, has lost his mother, whose body he identified at sea. Cozier was subsequently released after being granted extra remission in respect of the remaining period of his prison term. Consideration will be given to partial remission of sentence to the other prisoners who willingly volunteered. The Premier said that high among the list of all those who assisted, mention must be made of His Worship, Mr. Arrindell and his jurors who helped both in Nevis and St. Kitts. "Theirs had been a very disagreeable task," he said, but it was a necessary one . . . . Referring to the statement made in the House by Mr. Parris—"Sufficient to the day is the evil thereof"—The Premier said it was not a statement which he took lightly, nor which the government of the country should take lightly. "If the statement was meant to be a threat," continued the Premier, "it would be viewed against the background of the *San Juan Star* newspaper of Monday, August 3, I 970, in which Parris was reported to have said certain things." As Mr. Parris did not elaborate in his statement in the House, the Premier dealt no further with it. The Premier ended his comments by advising that we should be considerate, we must continue to be forgiving, and make greater efforts to love one another.

Thursday, August 27, 1970

The arrangements for Nevis vegetables, etc. to be taken over by the Marketing Depot is a good way to keep the food line to St. Kitts running. With the tragedy which overtook some fifty Nevis peddlers who lost their lives on the *Christena* on August first, the regular stream of trade in peasant products has been interrupted. The effect of this has been felt to no small degree by consumers in Basseterre particularly. The Agricultural Department now steps in to fill the gap. By establishing buying centers at various places in Nevis, the business of getting the foodstuff from peasant to the final market place becomes a simplified and convenient service.

Saturday, August 29, 1970

Chief of Police Wade pointed out in the hearing that he received the first notice of the disaster at about 1745 hours. [*Authors Note: The Commission invited* Mr. Wade to discuss his role in, and reflections on, the disaster, but he declined].

Monday, August 31, 1970

Mr. Wentworth Nicholls of Penneys Beach Hotel realized that something had gone wrong with the ferry at about 4:20 pm. He notified the police by 4:45 pm.

Tuesday, September 1, 1970

It was noted that Captain Wynter was sailing to Guadeloupe.

Friday, September 11, 1970

The Honourable Commissioner, Mr. Justice J.D.B. Renwick, said he had been informed that divers had gone down to the *Christena* and would give evidence before the Commission. The divers were Philip Miller, Mr. Yearwood, and Mr. Anslyn . . . . During their last dive, said Mr. Miller, they brought up the Government Accountant General satchel, among other things. In the cargo hatch were woven baskets, ropes, etc. *[Author's· note:* There was also a fourth diver, Desmond Sargeant.]

Saturday, September 12, 1970

Anslyn

On closer. inspection, he turned one of the propellers by hand and it turned pretty easily. He went inside the engine room and found that the throttle was on in full power position. The cushion seats in the first class section were loose. He saw bodies in the captain's room but did not venture to move them. They brought up several articles which they delivered to the Treasury. Still on the *Christena* were about 30 bodies, including children. He saw nothing wrong with the hull . . . . Saturday, November 7, 1970. In so far as the report on the "Circumstances Surrounding the Sinking of the *M. V. Christena*" is concerned, the House should be advised that Government is giving effect to all the recommendations.

[*Author's Note:* (i) The Commission of Inquiry Report was tabled in the House of Assembly on November 6, 1970. But government refused to comment on it, or discuss any aspect of the report. (ii) About that time it was also announced that the Disaster Fund had passed the $100,000 mark, in terms of funds raised].

Saturday, November 28, 1970

An article was carried pointing out that in a public meeting at Warner Park, Sunday, November 15th, Lee Moore, a member of the Labor Government, stated that a lady came to St. Kitts from Antigua on July 31st, and gave the *Hawthorne Enterprise* as her address.

[*Author's note:* Attempts to locate that document have so far been unsuccessful. However, a woman did join the *Hawthorne Enterprise in St. Kitts,* as a passenger, on the afternoon of August 1, 1970.]

Section 11

The Democrat, Saturday, August 8, 1970

May Their Souls Rest In Peace

The darkness of death has closed over the bodies of many of our loved ones. We have been tragically plunged from the festive atmosphere of the August holiday to the depths of gloom and sorrow. After the first misleading news had been issued that some two hundred persons were aboard the ill-fated *Christena,* we were compelled to face the harsh reality that many more persons went down on a boat that was not supposed to take over one hundred and fifty-five passengers. No AMOUNT OF SYMPATHY OR CONDOLENCE will comfort those who have been so tragically bereaved. No amount of propaganda will wipe away the ugly facts which caused so many of our brothers and sisters to meet such a violent and gruesome death. We can only pray for the souls of all those departed and trust that grief will one day fade away. The *Democrat* wishes to express its most profound sympathy and its grief to the people of our stricken islands.

IN MEMORIAM: The People's Action Movement realizes that for decades to come the tragedy of the *Christena* will stamp its painful mark upon the history of these islands. The tragic loss of our people cannot be minimized and we sincerely hope that all attempts will be made to bring to justice the parties responsible for the waste of human lives. This State owes it to the dependents of victims to compensate them for the loss suffered and we expect this to be speedily done. To all the people of this State and abroad who suffered, we extend our Deepest Sympathy.

William V Herbert President, People's Action Movement

August 8, 1970, *Christena* Sinks:

Great Loss Of Life—123 Bodies Recovered, 91 Rescued

Teachers, nurses, civil servants, market vendors, holiday makers, and many, many other citizens of St. Kitts-Nevis are today lying in mass graves and on the sea bed. The catastrophe that brought about this great loss of life occurred when the *M. V Christena,* the government-owned ferry boat, sank last Saturday afternoon in the Narrows—a channel between St. Kitts and Nevis. The vessel was registered to carry 155 passengers—125 on the lower deck, and 30, on the deck. Crowded with passengers, it was on one of its regular trips to Nevis and had left the Treasury Pier at 3:30 pm, in a comparatively calm sea. Forty minutes later near Nags Head, according to a survivor, it dipped to the right, then sank from the stern within three minutes. Motor vessel *Sea Hunter Number One,* owned by the West Indies Industrial Development Company Ltd. in Nevis and captained by Phil Miller, sped to the sea. In the first instance 63 persons, some of whom were swimming, were picked up and carried to Charlestown, Nevis. Another number was rescued on a second trip. Many of the survivors were taken to the Alexandra Hospital where Dr. Kennedy Simmonds and nurses attended them. Other private boats also took part in the rescue operations. A total of 38 bodies were plucked from the sea and taken to the mortuary a the hospital. Included in this number were three Catholic nuns—Sister Amelia and Sister Marie from Canada, and Sister Patricia from England. The facial "expressions of all the victims still bore the anguish and bewilderment that these unfortunate people underwent before drowning. News of the tragedy reached St. Kitts at 5:50 pm, according to a government release published elsewhere in this paper. And when the news was first announced over Radio Z.I.Z., some minutes after 6 pm, thousands congregated along the Bay Front and the pier and stared across the sea. From that Saturday night until Tuesday morning, recovery of bodies was undertaken by three helicopters and a ship from the U.S. Coast Guard, *H.M.S. Sirius,* which sailed to the disaster area on Sunday from Carriacou, a French Minesweeper and local boats. Placed into plastic bags and covered with blankets, the bodies were brought in batches to the Treasury Pier by the Police and Customs launches. There they were examined for identification and viewed by a coroner, Magistrate Arrindell, and a five man jury; being put in hurriedly made coffins and transported to Springfield Cemetery for mass burial in long trenches. Ministers of the Christian Council were at hand to perform the last rites. On Tuesday morning 30 bodies were brought ashore. These were the last batch as it was decided that owing to their condition no more should be recovered. There are 91 survivors. Dead are 123 persons. Of these, 89 were buried in St. Kitts, 34 in Nevis. Many could not be identified. It is believed that some 135 were not recovered. This great loss of life has resulted in pitiful cries everywhere in this small community in which almost each person knows the other, and in fact, is related in some way. It is a tragedy which will continue to haunt the minds of many throughout the years. It is one that should never have happened in St. Kitts-Nevis.

[*Author's note:* The most recent count suggests that 236 passengers died on *Christena*, while 99 survived.]

August 8, 1970

Queen Sends Condolences

Her Majesty the Queen has sent the following telegram to the Acting Governor the Honorable M.P. Allen: I am much distressed to learn of the sinking of the *Christena with* the loss of many lives. Please convey an expression of my sincere sympathy and that of the Duke of Edinburgh to the relatives of those who are drowned.

Elizabeth R.

Whitman T. Browne, Ph.D.

August 8, 1970

Memorial Service At St. George's Anglican Church

Hundreds of people from all walks of life and from almost every religious persuasion in St. Kitts crowded into St. George's Anglican Church Thursday night {August 6, 1970}, to attend a memorial service for those persons lost in the *Christena* disaster last Saturday. The service, held under the auspices of the St. Kitts Christian Council, was conducted by Rev. Bernard Hodge, and the address was given by Rev. Robert Buttalph, parish priest of St. Peter's. Reverend Buttalph said that we are looking through a mirror darkly and that for some years the reflection of the tragedy will be a very dark one. He showed the back of a tapestry with its confused colored silks forming a blurred picture, then turned it around revealing the clearness of the other side. This he did to illustrate the unhappy and happy sides of life. He pointed out that God sees life as a whole from beginning right through. He said that those who believe in intercession for the dead should pray for the peace and happiness of the departed souls. Those who did not believe should turn their prayerful energies in practical prayer for the bereaved families. "We should give our love to the bereaved," he said, and he admonished them to cease from being despondent and to go to their homes "bursting" with joy for in spite of all the calamities in the world, and the sinking of the *Christena,* God reigns. Maybe out of this tragedy we may emerge a stronger people.

Official Memorial Service

(Figure 0-1 The Order of the Service)

Hymn .... Pleasant Are Thy Courts Above
Prayers......................... God Is Our Hope and Our Strength

Scripture Reading...................................Matthew 8: 18-27
Remarks .... His Excellency, M.P. Allen O.B.E.,
Acting Governor
Hymn .... Oh God of Jacob
Scripture Reading........Revelations 21 Hon. R.L. Bradshaw,
Premier
Hymn ....Tell Me the Old, Old Story
List of Names ....Archdeacon G. P. J. Walker
one minute of silence Intercessions
Hymn .... The King of Love My Shepherd Is
Address...Father R. Buttolph
Hymn .... Rejoice the Lord is King
Offerings
Benediction ....The Bishop of the Roman
Catholic Church

August 8, 1970

Calypsonian Returns Thanks to Coury

Calypsonian King Barky (William Demming) of Molyneaux,
St. Kitts, a survivor of the *Christena* tragedy, returned thanks
to the firm of Messrs. David Coury and Co. Ltd., when he
arrived from Nevis earlier this week after spending a night at
the Alexandra Hospital in that island. Barky felt it was his
duty to do so for he owed his life to two sheets of plastic from
that firm. Last Saturday, Mr. Peter Coury, Director of Messrs.
David Coury and Company and manager of the hardware
department, gave instructions to one of his employees to
roll, tie and address two sheets of plastic foam and to put
them aboard the *Christena* for shipment to Nevis. When the
Christena sank, the sheets, two inches thick and measuring
77 inches by 55 inches, floated free and Barky caught hold
of one which served as a life belt until he was picked up by
a boat. Mr. Coury said in an interview with the *Democrat*

that Barky had told him that the sheet of plastic foam had saved his life and that he had come to return thanks to him for he could not swim. "It seems as though I was given those sheets. I cannot explain how I got them. Perhaps it was a miracle," he said. Mr. Coury has confirmed that the police have returned the plastic foam to him. Now Barky wants to buy them as souvenirs.

August 8, 1970

There Was No "Sudden" to This Disaster

Opposition member, Mr. Fred Parris of Nevis, called for an amendment to a resolution moved by Premier Robert Bradshaw in the House of Assembly on Thursday morning. The resolution expressed "deepest sympathy to those bereaved, in the sudden national disaster caused by the sinking of the *Christena,*" and returned thanks to all those who assisted or sent messages of condolence. Mr. Parris supported the expressions of sympathy and thanks, but emphatically pointed out that there was no "sudden", to the disaster caused by the sinking of the *Christena,* and consequently that word should be deleted. "We have had our warnings; we must blame ourselves," he said and reminded the House that Attorney General Eugene Walwyn had made the last statement earlier. He said the suffering of Nevis in the disaster exceeded that of any of the other islands of the State because so many Nevisians were travelling on the boat. "If we must blame ourselves, we must do so for something." And he thought he should look deeper in the wording of the resolution. Apart from the deletion of the word "sudden," he said that the resolution should say that a special Board of Inquiry including members of the Opposition should be set up to investigate the disaster. And that the dependents of the victims should be fully compensated. He went on to say that the boat was made to carry a certain number of passengers but on the last occasion it had been carrying about twice that number. It was so overloaded that one man jumped back off on the Treasury Pier. (At this stage he was interrupted.) No Serious Action: He further said that when the *Christena* was no longer seen at 4:30 on the fateful afternoon, Mr. Nicholls, of Nevis, reported the matter to the Charlestown Police Station. He said no serious action was taken and suggested that the House was aware of it . . . . All through his speech, Mr. Parris was repeatedly interrupted. "Nobody allows me peace of mind to make my contribution," Mr. Parris stormed. "I am always interrupted by members of the other side. If my contribution suits them I am allowed to speak; if not, the wrath of the whole House falls on me. Anyhow, Mr. Speaker, I am going to say this: that sufficient unto the day is the evil thereof." He said that there have been a lot of flowery speeches from time to time, but he reminded the House that there are distressed families in Nevis. There is one such family—eight children without parents. The Social Welfare Officer went to the home and left food without asking who could cook it. The eldest of the children is 14 years old. Mr. Parris said that since the disaster there has been no addition to the Welfare Department in Nevis. "I am saying this: though we speak with the tongues of men and of angels and have not charity; we are becoming like sounding brass or tinkling cymbals," he declared. Mr. Parris refuted a charge against Mr. Ivor Stevens, of Charlestown, by Premier Bradshaw, that Mr. Stevens had refused to supply a government owned truck with gasoline on Monday. He said that to incriminate Mr. Stevens, who had done so much the day before, was "very bad."

Saturday, August 15, 1970

Mass Destruction

It is possible that the first baleful words to be uttered by anyone scanning the list of dead persons published in this paper will be "Mass Destruction." The sinking of the *Christena* has caused untold grief among the people of St. Kitts-Nevis and compels us to look below the surface of the disaster.

IT IS ESTABLISHED THAT ON ITS FATAL JOURNEY to Nevis two weeks ago in fair weather, the boat was carrying well over three hundred passengers not to mention cargo—although it was built to transport only one hundred and fifty-five. The obvious conclusion must therefore be that the *Christena* was overloaded as it had been on many occasions. The government had to be long aware of this from the fares collected and paid into the Treasury, yet no action was instituted to restrict the number of passengers and thereby safeguard their lives. If this was done, this mass destruction by drowning would never have occurred.

WITH ALL THE GLOWING INFORMATION contained in a government press release as to the condition of the boat and its equipment, there was an obvious omission of the number of passengers it was supposed to carry. We find that over the years, not only did people question the suitability of the *Christena* to provide a proper ferry service between the two islands, but they felt it was being mismanaged. Indeed, the Attorney General, a government minister, must have had some definite and fundamental reason when he got up in the House of Assembly last week Thursday and pointed out that "We must blame ourselves."

IF THE *CHRISTENA* HAD BEEN PRIVATELY owned, one might have heard the government saying that the person or persons liable for this great waste of humanity in our small community would be brought to swift justice.

Saturday, August 15, 1970

Nevisians Praise Dr. Simmonds

A group of six Nevisians sat by the roadside in Charlestown, Nevis on Tuesday night talking among themselves. Their conversation? The *Christena* Disaster. Said one to another: "It is a happening that I will never forget. I was at the hospital when the 38 dead bodies were put in the mortuary. Never before did I see so many at one time and I believe this goes for the hundreds of Nevisians who were there. It was a pitiful sight to see . . . ." "But yes," interrupted another. "And there was no permanent doctor in Nevis—only Dr. Kennedy Simmonds, who was here for a short while to hold clinic.

He was in Gingerland." In reply to a question, all six persons—two women and four men recalled that they had seen Dr. Simmonds, "working busily among the dead and living at the Alexandra Hospital, assisted by some nurses," until a medical team arrived from St. Kitts. "He should be praised for his work, but some people do not want to acknowledge it," said one of the men. Dr. Simmonds, a medical practitioner in St. Kitts, was temporarily appointed to work in Gingerland, Nevis, in the absence of Dr. Louisy, who, since the sea disaster, has cut short his vacation and returned to the island.

The Democrat is reliably informed that on Saturday, August 1st, Dr. Simmonds had a clinic of 47 persons ill on Nevis that day. Knowing that there was no other doctor in the island at the time, he made himself available for any emergency at the hospital. When the *Christena* sank that afternoon and the recovered bodies and survivors were taken to the hospital, he was contacted by telephone at the hotel in which he was staying. He raced by car from Gingerland to the hospital where he met the nurses already at work. He examined 63 survivors and gave advice where necessary to the nursing staff. Out of the number of persons who passed through the hospital, some 14 were detained. Dr. Simmonds recorded his findings in a book at the hospital. He left Nevis the following day, Sunday, and returned on Monday to give any necessary assistance.

August 15, 1970

239 Die On Christena

A new list of the unfortunate persons who perished on the ill-fated *Christena* has been compiled, as other names have been added to those published in last week's issue of the *Democrat* The number known to be dead has now risen to 239. And according to an official list, 91 persons were rescued, bring the total number aboard the boat to 330. The vessel was registered to carry 155. Of the number dead, only 123 bodies have been recovered and buried, both here and in Nevis.

August 15, 1970

C.F. Charles Writes:

. . . It is my sincere hope that those bereaved will turn to the Supreme Being in this, their hour of grief, because He is the great burden bearer. I do not share the view expressed by many persons that this was the Will of God; it has been the policy of human beings to look for a scapegoat to put any mistakes on. This seems to be a case of culpable negligence to put it mildly, a boat whose capacity is about 150 persons had on it at least 100 more than that amount. The people of St. Kitts-Nevis have been handcuffed and muzzled for too long, by irresponsible people in responsible positions. I have not included Anguilla because they were wise enough to cut the millstone from around their necks before it was too late. The time has come, and it is long overdue, when the government should get out of commercial enterprise. I suggest that responsible Nevisians and Kittitians form a corporation and acquire two boats to ply between St. Kitts and Nevis; this corporation should be given Pioneer Status for at least five years. Had the *Christena* been a private boat this might not have happened. I imagine seeing two or three helpless policemen on the Basseterre pier, watching the boat being overloaded, but afraid to do their duty, because they may eventually lose their jobs. One of the fundamental objectives of the policeman is "the safeguarding of persons and property," and if this was implemented on Saturday afternoon this tragedy might have been averted. St. Kitts and Nevis are the only two islands in the world in which the word progress is not in their leaders' vocabularies. If the government machine had not been in reverse gear, several boats would have been plying between the two islands instead of the river boat on which, according to a local radio station, there was no control over the number of people who went on it. This statement sounds queer but it is true. Whenever the Board's report is completed, copies should be sold to the public. It is our business and we should know. I have no malice against individuals but I hate injustice, and this disaster has caused so much distress that I would consider myself a felon if I remain silent.

C.F. Charles

Whitman T. Browne, Ph.D.

August 15, 1970

Sympathy from West Africa

Please allow me space in your paper to offer, on behalf of my wife and myself, belated condolences to those of our people in St. Kitts and Nevis who have been bereaved as a result of the tragic loss of the *M. V. Christena*. The news of this appalling loss of life has stunned us and our hearts reach out to all those who have lost relatives and/or friends in this disaster. We know that mere words cannot assuage the grief they must feel, but we would like them to know that their grief is our sorrow: that we too mourn their loss. It is our earnest prayer that time, though not erasing the memory of their loved ones, will nevertheless gradually ease the pain they now feel, and dull the poignancy of their sorrow. Since such a tragedy cuts across all political and other sectionalism and functionalism, I am sure that all other sons and daughters of St. Kitts-Nevis abroad will like to join us in once more extending sincerest sympathy to the bereaved. May the dead rest in peace!

Yours faithfully, Rupert Neville Herbert (Kittitian)

St. Andrew's Secondary School Bo, Sierra Leone, West Africa 2/8170

August 15, 1970

What Really Caused This Sea Tragedy

After the mourning let us have an investigation: let us find out why 184 people lost their lives by taking a ferry from St. Kitts to Nevis. We want to see evidence, after the investigation, that the loss of life in the future will not be due to man's negligence but to what we call acts of God. There is too much in reports from St. Kitts at the moment to suggest that negligence on the part of authorities and operators of the ferry was the cause of the disaster. It must be understood that an investigation and government action against negligence at sea is owed not only to the bereaved relatives of those who drowned, and those who live in St. Kitts-Nevis, but to the people of this entire region. For the free movement of people for pleasure as well as for business will in time become as essential in the existence of a Caribbean Free Trade Area as the exchange of goods, services, and currencies. And a Trinidadian leaving home to go to St. Kitts would like to think that the government there has taken as much trouble to protect his life as his own government has done. Too strong is the suggestion that there is a disregard for lives at sea around the smaller islands. More than sixty persons traveling home to St. Vincent from the Grenadines for Christmas in 1968 met their death. Reports said that the *Federal Queen,* on which they were travelling, overturned when passengers dashed from one side of the vessel to the other to avoid being wet by spray. This does not suggest that the *Federal Queen* was the sea worthiness of passenger vessels. Then, St. Vincent's Chief of Police, Commissioner Sydney Anderson, described the tragedy as the worst sea disaster in the region for 15 years. But what have the authorities done since to prevent another such accident? Again, with the overturning of the ferry boat on Saturday while it was crossing with holiday passengers from St. Kitts to Nevis, the question of the seaworthiness of the vessel comes up. Worse than that, however, is the report that the vessel might have been carrying about 100 passengers above its capacity. Survivors of the disaster say the bow of the vessel at regular intervals dipped under water, and at one stage the ship listed heavily, then in righting itself shipped water. Just as disturbing is an official explanation that it is difficult to compile a list of passengers because people just bought tickets and boarded the ferry. We are afraid this does not give the impression that the ferry service was efficiently run. It might suggest even that less attention was given to the safety of passengers than minimum standards would require.

(Extract from Trinidad Express)

August 15, 1970

Prisoner Charles Cozier Released

Prisoner Charles Cozier of Cotton Ground, Nevis, who was committed to H.M. Prison for one month hard labor on 18 July, 1970, was today granted extra remission in respect of the remaining period of his prison term, by His Excellency, the Acting Governor, and released from the prison in accordance with the prison rules. Prisoner Cozier willingly assisted with the recovery of bodies from the *M. V. Christena* and he suffered the misfortune of losing his mother, whose body was identified by him at sea. As was intimated by the Premier in the House on Thursday, the Cabinet will be asked to consider partial remission of sentence to other prisoners who willingly volunteered their assistance following the *Christena* disaster.

(Press Release from Premier's Dept. Gov. Headquarters 8 August, 1970)

Saturday, August 22, 1970

Nevisians Must be Vigilant

The people of Nevis bluntly refused to repose their confidence in the St. Kitts government at the last general elections and at the subsequent local council polls. As never before there is now a desperate attempt to woo them to the Labor Party by playing on their sensibilities. Even at a time like this when the Nevisians: hearts are sore with grief, certain members of government have not relaxed their behavior but have intensified it. Compensation resulting from the *Christena* tragedy may now be used as opportunistic imposition on the minds of the people.

NEVISIANS HAVE A GREAT DEAL TO REMEMBER and ought not to allow themselves to be hoodwinked by political force, misrepresentation or propaganda. These ill-conceived tactics are void of sincerity and can only constitute an outrageous disgrace and deception. This disagreeable atmosphere is not conducive to the clear thinking of the people and should be made to disappear.

IT APPEARS THAT MEMBERS OF GOVERNMENT leave their offices in St. Kitts merely to parade idly through Nevis in a concerted effort to exploit the gullibility of certain people. In some cases, too, to generate intimidation among the more intelligent who dare to oppose them.

VIGILANCE HAS AN IMPORTANT ROLE IN THE safeguarding of a people's priceless virtue and joy. If Nevisians desire to retain their pride and to preserve their freedom of thought and choice, they must set at nought the deceptive efforts of the Labor Party.

August 22, 1970

Deep Sympathy from Vietnam

I hesitate to put into words the deep feeling of sympathy which I hold for the families, relatives and friends of those who perished when the *M. V. Christena* went down recently. Hesitation is necessary because I know no one can ever return the love, and maybe someone's all in all sank with the *Christena* at the bottom of the sea on that black day. Although I am in

149

this war-torn land, and should be accustomed to seeing and hearing the worst, news such as this which occurs among the people with whom you lived, worked, and played over the years will always find a soft spot way down deep, and leave you with a lost feeling that is in-explainable. I would like to suggest, if government has not done so already, that a day of mourning be proclaimed on an annual basis to pray for the souls of our loved ones who were victims of this unfortunate fate. I feel that this is no time to say who did what wrong, but that each member of the community in St. Kitts and Nevis should take time out to pray for those who did not make it back to the land of the living. It is impractical to write each family, as much as I would like to, but through this medium I express my heartfelt grief, and convey my deepest condolences to them all, as I mourn their loss with them.

MAY THEY REST IN PEACE.

Ira A.C. Peets Cam Ranh Bay, Vietnam 5 August, 1970

August 22, 1970

List Of 91 Rescued from Christena

(Figure 0-2 Rescued Persons)

	Last Name	First Name	Residence
1.	Allen	Rueben	Montserrat
2.	Arisbeth	Carlton	Montserrat
3	Bartlette	Joseph	Nevis
4.	Blake	Robert	Jessup's
5.	Benjamin	Vincent	Coram Alley

	Last Name	First Name	Residence
6.	Browne	Arrington	Liburd Hill
7.	Browne	Clifford	Brick Kiln
8.	Browne	Dulcita	Keys Village
9.	Browne	Edna	Jessup's Village
10.	Browne	Franklyn	Camps Village
11.	Browne	Leonard	Prince William Street
12.	Browne	Roger	Camps Village
13.	Budgeon	Joseph	Jessups Village
14.	Budgeon	Luelia	Jessups Village
15.	Carlton	Tom	Brown Hill
16.	Chapman	Levinstone*	
17.	Charles	Meridith	Low Street
18.	Condell	Wyclide	Hermitage
19.	Clark	Edward	Hermitage
20.	Depusoir	William	Brick Kiln
21.	Demming	William*	
22.	Davis	Everson	Cotton Ground
23	Elliott	Ivan	Gingerland
24.	Edwards	Lionel	Round Hill House
25	Francis	Rudolph	Powell's Village
26.	Freeman	Samuel	Rawlins Village
27.	France	James	Clifton Village
28.	Herbert	Alice*	
29.	Harris	Vincent	St. Johnston's Village
30.	Hendrickson	Ronald	Gingerland
31.	Hanley	Eustace	Gingerland
32.	Hinds	Robert	Round Hill House
33.	Huggins	Fitzroy	Cotton Ground
34.	Jeffers	Belinda	Bath Village
35.	Johnston	Charles	Cayon

	Last Name	First Name	Residence
36.	Johnston	Charles	Jessup's Village
37.	James	Jonathan*	
38.	Johnston	Llewellyn	Jessup's Village
39.	Kelly	Edmund	Gingerland
40.	Lewis	Wilson	Jessup's Village
41.	Martin	Julie	Bath Village
42.	Martin	Joe	Craddock Road
43.	Matthews	Tyson Frank	Cayon
44.	Morton	Frank	Gingerland
45.	Morton	Vincent	Cayon
46.	Moore	Charles	Cayon
47.	Mason	Samuel	Conaree
48.	Mulraine	Shermelle	Sugar Factory
49.	Merchant	Edward*	
50.	Nisbett	Carlton	Brown Hill
51.	Richardson	Alice	Bath Village
52	Richards	Euste	Gingerland
53.	Roberts	Copeland	Low Street, Charleston
54.	Robertson	Joseph	Cayon
55.	Richards	Wendell	Ponds Pasture
56.	Sage	Leroy	Ponds Pasture
57.	Stapleton	Vincent	Happy Hill Alley
58.		Clive	Craddock Road
59.	Swanston	Victor	River Path, Gingerland
60	Sargeant	Laughton	Cotton Ground
61.	Sargeant	Livinstone	Cotton Ground
62.	Trotman	Livinstone	Rices Village
63.	Tyson	Oswald	Cotton Ground
64.	Wilkinson	Wendell	Church Ground
65.	Williams	Diana	Main Street, Charlestown

	Last Name	First Name	Residence
66.	Williams	Leroy	Cotton Ground
67.	Ward	Job*	
68.	Wilson	Aubrey*	
69.	Kelsiek	Ian	Cayon Street
70.	Uddenburg	Herman*	
71.	Brisbane	Michael*	
72.	Lake	Samuel	Brighton Estate
73.	Simmonds	Malcolm	Low Street, Charlestown
74.	Prentice	Gerard	Police Headquarters
75.	St. Clair*		Craddock Road
76.	Duncan	Terrance	Brick Kiln
77.	Brookes	Ivor	Brown Hill
78.	Simmonds	Victor	Crook's Ground
79.	Storrod	Earl	Hickman's
80.	Tross	Grenville*	
81.	Huggins	Phillip	Fothergill
82.	Weekes	James*	
83.	Warner	Cecil*	
84.	Rawlins	Cliva*	
85.	Liburd	Devon	Cole Hill
86.	Procope	Conrad	Dorsell Village
87.	Wenham	James*	
88.	James	Leroy	Bath Village
89.	Martin	Joseph*	

* = Missing Data; Author's Note: Two persons in the original list were
listed twice. Only 89 survivors were actually listed then. The
latest count does suggest 99 persons, not 91 survived the sinking.

Saturday, August 29, 1970

Government Moves Too Late

THE SINKING OF THE *M. V. Christena* with the loss of so many lives has indeed taught our government a bitter lesson. There is no evidence that on the spot checks were made to ascertain that there was no overloading of this boat. This week we find that all of a sudden there has been a late move to enforce the law whereby boats plying between St. Kitts and Nevis can only carry a specific number of passengers.

The *M. V. Lavina* and the lighter *Princess Royal* are privately owned. It is understood that the latter has been stopped from transporting passengers until it is equipped with lifebelts. The fact that the government's ferry boat, *Christena,* was plying between the two islands without the enforcement—of restrictions as to the number of passengers, has left us with a feeling of deep apprehension. It is vexatious that such a painful tragedy should have occurred for the government to show some concern for the people's safety.

AS A RESULT OF THIS BELATED ACTION a number of Nevisian market vendors trading in St. Kitts are experiencing difficulty returning to their homes. They go to the Treasury Pier after trying for several hours to earn a few pennies from the sale of ground-provisions here in Basseterre and are left behind some not knowing where to spend the night. What is now urgently needed to prevent this embarrassing situation is the establishment of a proper ferry service.

THE *M. V. BARFISH,* TEMPORARILY CHARTERED for $9,600 per month, arrived here three weeks ago and has reportedly undergone structural modification at the Factory Pier before beginning its run yesterday morning. From what

Bradshaw said in the House of Assembly on August 6th, it was believed that this boat was in perfect passenger form and would serve for one month. The alterations to the vessel now seem to indicate that it may remain indefinitely. The charter is an expensive one and people are looking forward to see that some speedy action is taken by the government to purchase a decent boat large enough to safely carry many passengers. Such a vessel could have been obtained long ago by sensible appropriation of public funds.

August 22, 1970

VHF Radio Was Out Of Order

Is it true that the radio telephone link between the St. Kitts and Nevis police stations was out of order some two months before the *Christena* disaster? Just before the start of the Inquiry on Monday morning, Attorney General Eugene Walwyn drew Commissioner Justice Renwick's attention to the newspaper and the foregoing question it contained. And he requested that the editor or reporter should be made to appear before the Commissioner in order to give necessary information if they had it, since the Commission was seeking certain information to establish certain facts relative to the *Christena* disaster.

On the following Tuesday, the Chief of Police, Mr. John Lynch Wade, confirmed in his evidence that the VHF radio set in Nevis used for inter-island communication was out of order some time before the *Christena* tragedy. But in reply to the question from Justice Renwick, Mr. Wade said he did not know when the radio went out of operation.

Whitman T. Browne, Ph.D.

August 29, 1970

Nicholls Writes

During the past two weeks since the fatal disaster of the *Christena,* several persons have been energetically trying to do something to help to bring relief to the distressed people of the State, who are living both at home and abroad. The government has launched "The *Christena* Disaster Fund" and I am pleased to learn that a sum of $24,000 has already been given by the British Government along with other contributions. The question is "How is the money collected going to be distributed and who is going to manage the distribution?" When we examine the facts relative to the handling of money by our government, right away we have to say point blank that we do not want the government to handle such money matters at all. In the first place, the government owes a lot of money here and there, and they might be willing to use any money they can muster towards their national debt. Have they paid off the $130,000 debt they incurred just to embarrass PAM by purchasing an old building? Would it not have been better if they had sold the *Christena* for what they could have gotten for her and make the money up with the $130,000 and buy a good boat, or take the money and extend/improve the Nevis airport, which did not even have lights on it for a plane to land on it that crucial moment?

It is my opinion that a *"CHRISTENA* DISASTER FUND COMMITTEE" should be formed consisting of Dr. Herbert, Dr. Simmonds, the Minister of Social Services, Mr. Almond Nisbett, Mr. Fred Parris and a representative from the Red Cross, to account for all monies received for the disaster and the subsequent planning for its distribution. It is also my opinion that Mr. Almond Nisbett be made Chairman of the Committee and that all contributions be made payable to the "*CHRISTENA* DISASTER FUND COMMITTEE," c/o Mr. Almond Nisbett. By so doing, all money received would be properly channeled to serve the purpose for which it is intended and will not get into the hands of the vultures whose lack of management is only bringing disaster and sadness on our State. I can assure you, Madam Editor, if this suggestion is taken, many, many people will send hundreds of dollars home for this effort and soon there would be much consolation at home. Thank you for the space in your valuable paper.

Wilmoth Nicholls, St. Thomas

August 29, 1970

High Time

The sight of the neglected mass graves of those victims of the *Christena* disaster whose bodies were recovered and buried at Springfield Cemetery is to say the least shocking. Almost one month has passed since the sad occurrence and yet the ugly sight of unfinished graves remains just as they were left by the bulldozers that opened and closed the earth upon the last mortal remains of those whose lives were suddenly snatched from them. We often hear telegrams as well as letters of sympathy addressed to the Premier read over Z.I.Z. These should at least remind him that his task in so far as those unfortunate souls were concerned is not complete. Surely, Mr. Premier, it is high time that the resting place of the mortal remains of the *Christena* victims be made to look like graves of human beings and not like those of beasts. This is no favor that is being asked; it is but a simple act of decency: High Time. (A *Survivor*).

Whitman T. Browne, Ph.D.

Saturday, September 5, 1970

(Figure 0-3 Fate of the *Christena*,

By H. Ritz, August 20, 1970)

When I think about the many sea disasters,
And the ships that lie beneath the sea so cold;
Then it brings to mind "the fate of the *Christena*,"
And it has to be the saddest story told.
If you care to stop and listen to my story,
But no doubt, you've heard it many times before;
About the sinking of a Caribbean ferry,
On a sunny afternoon, just about four.
They had boarded the ferry-boat *"Christena"*
To sail out across the dark blue sea:
Not knowing that the fete-day they had planned for,
A day of sad mourning would be.
With gay hearts they set sail for Nevis,
An island, not many miles away;
Ne'er dreamt, as they left St. Kitts island,
What fate would befall them that day.
She sailed on her course with her burden,
But she seemed to be laboring with her load;
All at once, as though demons possessed her,
She pitched, and then over she rolled.
It seemed that all hell broke loose that moment,
It happened "so fast," so they say;
With a shudder, she sank to the bottom,
Taking many to a watery grave that day.
Some swam to shore, and some were rescued,
And a little girl clung unto some debris,
As she floated in that shark infested water,
A boat came by, and plucked her from the sea.
Friends searched for days for their loved ones,

And could not understand that it could be;
With tear-strained eyes, and hearts that are so heavy,
They still stand there, staring, at the vengeful sea.
'Twas not the amount nor the damage,
Nor the value of all that it cost;
But the sad tale that comes from those waters,
Where the lives of so many loved were lost.
(Repeat) But the sad tale that comes from those waters,
Where the lives of so many loved were lost.

(Written and dedicated to the memory of those that lost their lives, those that survived, and those who lost loved ones on that fateful last ride of the Christena)

CHAPTER SIX

Photographic Reflections

(Photographs By Author, Except Where Noted)

Launching Christena
(*Labor Spokesman*)

The Christena
(S. Joseph)

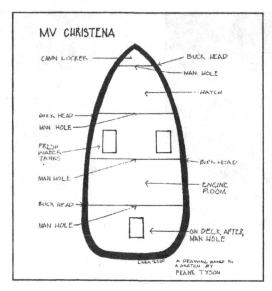

MV Christena Lower deck: Showing Bulkheads
(*Frank Tyson*)

Captain Skeete   Captain Tyson

Devon Liburd   Rupert Wade

Gathering the Dead-1
(*Barbados Advocate*)

Gathering the Dead-2
(*Barbados Advocate*)

Constructing Mass Grave

Placing the Coffins

Final Rites
(*Barbados Advocate*).

Christena Ceremony (Br. Guyana : *Labor Spokesman*).

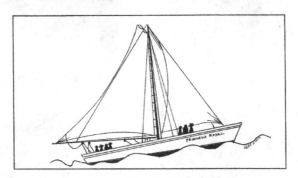

Memory of the Sail-boat Days

Whitman T. Browne, Ph.D.

Joshua Halliday

Wyclide Condell

Earle Parris

Luella Budgeon

Victor Swanston

Diana Richards

Malcolm Simmonds

King Barkey

Dulcita David

Joe Martin

Livinstone Sargeant

Oswald Tyson

167

Whitman T. Browne, Ph.D.

Roger Browne

Arrington Browne

Ian Kelsick

Clifford Browne

Franklyn Browne

Edna Browne

168

Michael King

Captain Anslyn

James Weekes

Charles Chapman

Charlestown Harbor (1980s)

The retired *Sakara*

Marking *Christena's* Spot—1

Marking *Christena's* Spot—2

Whitman T. Browne, Ph.D.

Diving the *Christena*—1

Diving the *Christena*—2
(*Ellis Chatterton*)

Diving the *Christena*—3

Diving the *Christena*—4
(*Ellis Chatterton*)

Memorial Plaque:
To Members of Gingerland Methodist Church
(*Jeffrey Nisbett*)

Christena Memorial—1 (Nevis).
(*Jeffrey Nisbett*)

Christena Memorial—2 (Nevis)
(*Deli Caines*)

CHAPTER SEVEN

Innocence, Ignorance, and Reality

It is strange, but true. As far back as present-day Nevisians and Kittitians can remember, their islands have boasted a special interdependence, although various forms of rivalries have stretched and strained that special relationship—one forged from historical, genetic, economic, and political ties. Through the years, however, this interdependence has existed in changed and changing forms. The St. Kitts-Nevis Labor government, under Robert Bradshaw, had the ferry *Christena* built by Sproston's Limited, of Guyana, in 1959, because the islands' interdependence required a more efficient form of travel. That was also a time when many social and economic changes were occurring in St. Kitts-Nevis. Emigration to England and the U.S. Virgin Islands was booming. Significant negative shifts away from local agriculture were also occurring.

Generally, agricultural production on the islands was in decline. Hundreds of Nevisians and Kittitians were leaving the cotton industry on Nevis and the sugar industry on St. Kitts behind, to migrate elsewhere. Time had also caught up with the proud lighters (sailboats) that for many years had been the predominant means of maintaining that essential communication, trade link, and people exchange, between St. Kitts and Nevis. However, in time, age, emigration and improved technology, made names such as *Gotham, Lady Nisbett, Oceana, D. L. V, Victoria, Vagabond, Crown, Sakara* etc., obsolete. Yet, those were once household names throughout Nevis: famous lighters that plied the waters between Nevis and St. Kitts before there was a *Christena.* And the people who witnessed them still cannot forget those races. That was a time when nature was harnessed and coupled with human skill to win sea races, and create hero-captains. During the time of *Christena, Princess Royal, Sakara, and Valiant* were fading residuals from that era, and most of the hero sea-captains had become mere memories. Also, by the 1970s, emigration, growing decline in sugar production, and increased democratization of education were having negative effects on the type and quantity of goods shipped weekly, from Nevis to St. Kitts. Historically, sugar plantations had come to dominate the economy of St. Kitts. That kept Kittitians dependent on the Nevis "turnhands" coming to St. Kitts to sell their agricultural products. And, that remained the order of things between the islands for a long time. Likewise, those hucksters from Nevis depended on the trips to St. Kitts. The trips encouraged entrepreneurship and provided physical survival for many Nevisians and their families.

Because they were at the mercy of the winds, one day the trip to St. Kitts could be one hour, another day it could be ten hours or more. However, the traders became at ease and comfortable with the lighters. But changing times, new boating technology, the unpredictability of the winds, on which the boats depended, and the problem of finding competent sailors forced the government to do the inevitable. Since the ferry service between the two islands was a necessity for both people, government moved to maintain it, and to enhance its efficiency. To help achieve those goals, the *Christena* was custom made for the people of St. Kitts-Nevis. It was to replace the sailboats, and in the process make ferry service more dependable and efficient.

When *Christena* arrived in St. Kitts, June, 1959, there were groups of people, who had doubts about its ability to carry out the travel and trade between the islands successfully. For example, one sea captain and businessman, Joseph Astaphan, was openly critical of the ferry's structural design and safety features. The claim that it was custom made for travel between St. Kitts and Nevis did not prevent people from concluding the *Christena was* generally not very seaworthy. Some specifically said that the ferry was unfit for service, plying the sea between St. Kitts and Nevis. Right from the start, however, the government readily accepted the selection and structure of the ferry, *Christena*. Its specifications were seen as meeting the special requirements for travel and trade between the islands. The authorities virtually saw the ship as an innovation in sea transportation, in the Caribbean generally, and specifically between St. Kitts and Nevis.

According to Arthur Anslyn, his father worked in the St. Kitts Nevis ferry service for some 24 years. From his observations and long experience, Captain, Edward Anslyn, made specific suggestions about the structure of the ideal ferry for St. Kitts-Nevis. Meanwhile, because of its shallow draught and high structure, many Nevisians and Kittitians saw *Christena* as more suited for use as a riverboat. It had 3.3 meters draught and a 12-meter high top structure. No part of the ferry reflected the carefully thought out suggestions of Captain Edward Anslyn. Actually, the physical structure of *Christena*, as it came to St. Kitts-Nevis in 1959, evoked in a large sector of the society, pictures of the death trap that it eventually became. Yet, *Christena* was accepted by the government of St. Kitts-Nevis, backed by claims of it being unsinkable. In its lower structure were five bulkheads which, when closed, created a vacuum effect. They were designed to keep the ferry afloat. It did not matter the sea condition or the load aboard. During a prior incident in 1960, when *Christena* sprung a leak, and on the scores of occasions when it was overloaded, it was probably the proper functioning of those bulkheads that prevented disaster.

However, the structure of the ferry was only one factor that continuously endangered the success and safety of its service between St. Kitts and Nevis. That *Christena* survived as a major means of transportation between the two islands for some eleven years, without a prior tragedy, was remarkable. For all those years, the government carelessly ignored impending doom. Meanwhile, thousands of citizens, in their innocence and trust, ignored danger and the certainty of approaching death. They showed awareness to neither situation. Although the signs of impending danger were there, and at times could be clearly seen, generally, most travelers ignored them. Despite a number of mishaps, there were those who actually concluded that the *Christena* was unsinkable. However, evidence of its vulnerability was everywhere.

James Ponteen, captain of the *Christena,* was in some ways a caring man. He got to know his regular passengers and developed strong bonds with them. Many of the hucksters who travelled regularly were his friends. That was the reason why, even though he was already at sea that fateful afternoon, the captain returned to the pier for one of his regulars, Pappie Liburd. However, his charm and friendliness to passengers aside, as a sea captain, Ponteen was poorly trained and not very competent. He had a number of mishaps that repeatedly brought his competence into question, but nobody in government bothered about the danger. Yet, those types of mishaps signaled grave danger to everyone, who cared to see what was going on with the *Christena.* For example, once, on a routine service trip to Barbados from St. Kitts, Captain Ponteen missed his route to Barbados and was sailing way off course unaware that he was sailing north, more toward England. It was reported that a passing ship warned him, so he rerouted to Barbados. Later, on two different trips from Barbados to St. Kitts, Captain Ponteen lost his way. One time, he found himself off St. Croix, U.S. Virgin Islands. The other time, he ran aground off St. Lucia, in the Windward Islands, and had to return to Barbados for additional repairs. Even during trips between St. Kitts and Nevis, there were times when Ponteen had navigational problems. On one occasion, during a squall, the *Christena* almost grounded, off Pinney's Beach on Nevis.

Those incidents were not well-kept secrets on St. Kitts-Nevis. Many people in the government and in the broader community knew about such incidents and talked about them. However, there was no evidence that Ponteen was challenged or reprimanded about his performance as a sea-captain. He continued in his post as captain without reprimand, or training, provided by government. Evidence that the government had some concerns was noted only on the few occasions when Captain Joseph Astaphan was approached about taking the ferry to Barbados for routine repairs. On his refusal, because of doubts, Captain Astaphan held about the ferry's seaworthiness, the task was always left for Captain Ponteen. Seemingly, the emotional stress Ponteen, his family, and the crew must have experienced, on those occasions, did not matter to the government. Neither was the physical threat to the captain and his crew given serious consideration. However, for a variety of reasons, it continues to appear as if the reality of danger always surrounded the *Christena*. Notwithstanding, the government and the people dealt with the matter in innocence and ignorance. Few people bothered to speak openly and consistently, about what they saw as threats to passengers' safety. Rather, the notion evolved, became popular, and was accepted: the *Christena* was unsinkable.

Captain Ponteen was not the only person who worked on the ferry, but lacked the proper training. According to the first mate, at the time when the ferry sank, except for the engineer, none of the other crew, including the first mate, had formal training for the tasks they performed. Although there was a technological leap in travel between the islands, with the once popular lighters becoming stand-by transportation or obsolete to some travelers, progressive thinking about safety on the part of government and the people, virtually stood still. During the time of the lighters, crews learned their tasks on the job by trial and error. Many persons who can recall those times, would remember that becoming an efficient worker on the lighters, was a long, harsh, and painful experience. Many of the student sailors became apprentices after leaving grade school and had to put in many years of observing and learning before they became good at their jobs. Sometimes, the student sailors gave up and tried something else.

Learning to become a competent seaman on the lighters was a difficult task for a number of reasons. Like any other profession, sailing has its secrets. Since sailors often had friendly, but intense rivalries, they held carefully guarded sailing secrets, and did not pass them readily to some of the apprentices. There was always the matter of loyalty. Further, some of the seasoned sailors were selfish, harsh, and not good teachers. They often swore at the trainees and hardly ever complimented them for anything done well. Other factors relative to training, included the hardships related to working on boats that depended on wind, for propulsion. Then, there was the small pay. At times it was not even forthcoming. There were apprentices who took to sailing, because it was attractive. Then, there was that thrill, a haunting and exhilarating danger, from being on the sea for very long hours. When government moved to improve the efficiency, safety, and the technology of the ferry system, it should have looked beyond just the basics, and included other tools needed to accomplish the task. The careful selection and training of personnel should have been considered. That should have received critical attention, since it would ultimately determine the success of the venture.

The lighters were essentially cargo boats that carried passengers, because there was no alternate manner to travel between the islands. The ferry that replaced them was expected to focus on transporting passengers. It moved more than one hundred passengers each time it traveled between the islands. The situation, where one ferry boat moved over a hundred passengers, was a new phenomenon. Usually, two or more lighters traveled at one time. Since mass travel between the islands was not as popular then as now, it was abnormal in that era to find one lighter traveling with more than one hundred passengers, on any one trip between the islands. Consequently, the danger of losing so many lives, as occurred in the case of the *Christena,* was not often present, at other times. The requirement for safe travel between the islands via the then, new and improved ferry service, demanded more from sailors. They were required to function in a much more complex system than the one their predecessors operated. Hundreds of adults and children were traveling for business, pleasure, and other reasons. It was the government's responsibility to ensure that the captain and crew were prepared for those changes. However, it was not done. Just as in the days of the cargo-lighters, the crew learned the skills needed through trial and error. This was an important factor in the whole *Christena* episode. Probably, proper training about how to keep the ferry safe for passengers could have averted the *Christena* tragedy. In an interview with Frank Tyson, he said a loud "Yes," to that.

Despite all the government's efforts to avoid blame for the incident, clear evidence existed that government officers erred greatly in how they handled the *Christena* affair. The ferry's design should have been examined by local experts, or by experts from Britain, since St. Kitts-Nevis was a British colony at that time, and they turned to Britain for expert advise on everything. The government could also have consulted the expertise of boat builders in Anguilla, or the Grenadines. Further, the questions about the boat's structure and safety led to many other issues.

People in the Caribbean find themselves constantly responding to challenges from the sea. In some instances, the sea has been a life-giving friend, providing food and other resources. At other times, the same sea destroyed all hope for some people. Numerous Caribbean stories, tell of the romance between the people and the sea. Some of those stories are captivating; others are happy, while many are sad. For example, there is one story about a tidal wave that covered Jamestown, the first capital of Nevis during the 1680s. Another story is about the slaves who supported the French and helped to defeat the British on St. Kitts. When they did not receive the freedom promised, many of those slaves built rafts and fled from an area in St. Kitts, now called Hilden's. They migrated to the next island, St. Eustatius. None of these stories, however, is as dramatic, or painful, as those in which hundreds of islanders die by drowning from boating mishaps.

Sea travel among the islands of the Caribbean has a long history and tradition. It goes back to the Siboneys, Arawaks, Tainos, and Caribs. Today, sea travel is still important to the islands because of economics, politics, and leisure tourism. There is also now travel associated with drugs and other criminal activity, becoming increasingly destructive to the Caribbean. Unfortunately, hundreds of young and old Caribbean people continue to die at sea because of overcrowded boats, bad weather conditions, poor seamanship, and an inability to swim. Wherever such challenges present themselves in the Caribbean, it is crucial that the people learn from their historical experiences and work toward their long-term survival, whether at sea or on land.

With this in mind, the people who travel from island to island frequently should ensure that their travel is under safe boating conditions. They should not simply be satisfied with comfort, where there is no real safety. For example, by the 1980s, it could be noted that many Nevisians made the crossing to and from St. Kitts without fear. After the *Christena* and some level of instability in the inter-island travel, lighters such as, *Valiant, Princess Royal and Sakara,* were there to fill the gap. But, from the ease with which the passengers made the journey, it hardly seemed that just over 10 years ago, people from the two islands shuddered in anger, fear, and pain, as they buried relatives and friends—dead from the sea.

On the issue of government's responsibility, it must have been known that *Christena* traveled under overloaded conditions, almost daily. That was not reflected in ticket sales. Mr. Julian Cox, Permanent Secretary, and the government executive directly responsible for the ferry service, pointed out that there was never a time when the money collected showed excess sales from the money collected. The system used on *Christena* for issuing tickets and collecting the money was unreliable. On most occasions when the ferry traveled, few passengers purchased tickets. The person collecting the money could have turned over to the government treasury whatever amount he saw fit. For example, according to Mr. Cox's testimony, there was never any more money turned over to the treasury than would account for 155 passengers traveling. If that was the case, one would have to suspect that someone on the ferry had devised a system to conceal the extra money collected. That afternoon, for example, the ferry was carrying more than two times the number of passengers it was registered to carry. A recent updating of the *Christena's* passenger load that afternoon suggests there were about 236 persons who died, while 99 survived.

Those warnings, verbally, and editorially, by concerned citizens, about overloading the ferry, and its possible threat to passengers' safety, were all ignored. It is not documented that the Ministry of Communications, responsible for the ferry service, did anything to hold a serious investigation, or to correct the problem, in a responsible manner. During the Commission of Inquiry hearings, Mr. Julian Cox admitted receiving two letters that came to his Ministry, protesting overloading of the ferry. He also acknowledged that his Ministry did little to correct the problem. One interviewee arrived at a very interesting theory as he reflected on the ferry *Christena*, and the results of its sinking. The person suggested that changes occur in St. Kitts-Nevis society only as a result of death. He pointed out that even Lee Moore, a former Premier of St. Kitts-Nevis, and former leader of the Labor Party's opposition, in the House of Assembly, recognized this. Moore once made similar comments at a public meeting in Basseterre. According to the theory proposed, people who could have affected changes to prevent the *Christena* disaster, did not care to do so. They recognized that if the ferry sank with a great loss of life, as actually happened, there would be political pressure against the government, and that could lead to its downfall. That did not happen instantly, but it was one of the changes that did come to St. Kitts-Nevis, and seemed to be related to *Christena*, in some way. Seemingly, the mishap did, in ten years, what pro-planter class politics and politicians, on St. Kitts-Nevis, could not do in over twenty years of trying—change the Labor government. On the surface, that theory seems just an interesting perception, however, once the events leading to the tragedy and those that followed are examined, the theory does not appear to be all wrong. One aspect of that theory that remains very frightening, however, is the human coldness it suggests about politicians, in their craving for power. If members of a society sat, planned and waited for the death of others from the same society, so that they could achieve personal and political goals, then, questions must be asked about whether anyone can prosper and be happy, from the fruits of such wicked machinations.

However, after this theory is put aside, even when other suggestions about causation are put aside, including the overcrowding, there were still many arrows of culpability and guilt due to negligence that could be directed at the Labor Party government. Its responsibility for citizens' safety was ignored. Later, it also avoided its contractual responsibility to compensate them. The government used as defense, an escape-clause written in small print at the back of the tickets. But, how could a government absolve itself from the guilt of such a tragedy, when the ferry's sinking was largely a tragedy of errors, on the part of its managers? The sinking was an unfortunate fact of St. Kitts-Nevis history, at a time when the colonial experience still openly cocooned Caribbean people, and cradled them in innocence and dependency. That unwitting ignorance also blinded political leaders to their responsibility. In too many instances, groups of people struggle for change from their condition of existence, but remain unconscious of their true reality. During the 1970s, despite the growth and evolution of local politics in the Caribbean, the culture of colonialism was an ever-present reality in all the islands. Despite the challenge by the citizens, to reach for change and revolutionary development, there is always that confounding legacy of colonialism, haunting minds, ideas, and values. Thus, too many Caribbean citizens become dwarfed in time, because they refuse to, or are barred by false consciousness, from analyzing the impact of colonial experiences on their future achievements and prospects.

The *Christena* incident, is one unfortunate mishap in recent Caribbean history, that still demonstrates the human cost, when innocence, ignorance, and blind dependency, come together and breed false consciousness in the lives of a people. When the ferry sank, everyone cried for a time, some longer than others. There were citizens who even vowed that such an incident would never happen in St. Kitts-Nevis again. But, in reality, politicians and other leaders of the islands appeared to have sat back and allowed the tragedy. The problem was, that British colonialism bred innocence, ignorance, and dependency, leading to an existence with a false consciousness, and to an endemic syndrome of general passivity and acceptance in the islands. Meanwhile, material-driven politicians appear to keep saying to themselves, and believing it, "Oh Caesar, live forever." So they manipulate the islands' politics to get elected, then ignore the rights of the people to freedoms, rights, and democratic participation in the islands' politics, social development, and history.

In Caribbean societies and their politics, one often sees a hold-over of the colonial syndrome. At times, this reaches down to every level of life on the islands. Sometimes there is ignorance of the need for a more dynamic view of management's role, among Caribbean leaders. When this is the case, it impacts every life on the islands, fostering fear, uncertainty, and instability among the citizenry. There is an inability to accept challenge, and to lead change, derived from critical thought, even when it promises better for the people. At that other time, ignorance of the islands' politics and its prospects, was a direct result of alienation from any participation by working class citizens in the decisions and processes that guided their islands. Unfortunately, in the twenty-first century there is still a concerted manipulation and alienation of the Caribbean masses, and Caribbean politicians are culpable. Too many leaders are in politics, not to promote wellness and success for the citizenry, but for themselves. The idea of Caribbean political leadership today, is that land deals and other money-making schemes can be arranged with the highest foreign bidders. Caribbean islands are quietly being resold. The poor people are losing access to beaches, cultural traditions, and the peace the islands once boasted.

However, the history of Caribbean people demands that the leaders take a stand on the side of enlightenment, true independence and change. When governments fail to represent the people well, and provide for them only new requirements of false consciousness, then the people must act to secure their right to thrive; not to flounder and drown into nothingness. Whatever successes have been attained in the Caribbean, the societies paid for, again and again, often with sweat, tears, and blood! The gains in the people's access to involvement and power, after the *Christena* tragedy, should never be lost. Both the political and democratic processes must serve the people's interest. Further, after the horrid costs of slavery, through our forefathers to us, Caribbean people cannot watch their lands being sold again so that they can be relegated for a second time, to the roles of gardeners, field-hands, and housekeepers. If the present trend of increasing poverty, massive land sales, and little food production continues, then the entire Caribbean area, through poor leadership, lack of critical thought, and personal greed, can see George Beckford's fear of persistent poverty in the Caribbean come true. Further, with the growing reality of global warming, there hardly appears to be any ready relief from the present Caribbean dilemma. The area has not truly learned from its traumatic history, including that of the *Christena* tragedy. There have been few lasting rewards from the people's many painful sacrifices.

Presently, there is growing concern and fear among contemporary Caribbeanists, about the direction the Caribbean area is taking. Some people are suggesting that the Caribbean islands are doomed to the alienating influences of pious missionaries, seemingly benevolent entrepreneurs, and a persistent client-state relationship with the technologically advanced world. We are forty plus years beyond the *Christena*, but neo-colonialism continues and prospers, in the Caribbean. Colonizers, colonial structures, and the relations they foster were as much alive in the 1970s, as they were in the 1880s. Now that we are into the twenty-first century, the strategies have changed, but colonialism with its control intent continues. Drugs have replaced sugar-cane, youths drop out of school, and jails are full of people who once said there are no rules in society. And, Black "plantation-minds" have replaced White "plantation-minds," among the elites and leadership throughout the area. The masses are kept poor, but the elite leaders and their families, get richer.

The senseless death of the masses continues, as in the *Christena* incident. And, the phenomenon is taken lightly. In the U. S. Virgin Islands, for example, one political leader suggested recently, that there should be little concern for groups of young Caribbean people, "who kill one another." There is no empathy or symbolic show of feeling, for those "lesser" others. Rather, they are passed over as limited to the history of the damned—a people who are, in time, forgotten. Consequently, there is no real guilt about corruption and lawlessness in society, except that which the bereaved masses bear and share with one another.

However, contrary to such an accepted view, neither ignorance nor innocence should signal bliss in Caribbean societies. They are both residuals from an era of colonial domination and subservience to foreign cultures. In time, they foster only a false consciousness about the true Caribbean reality. Yet, the two phenomena continue to find acceptance in the day-to-day being of many Caribbean people, stifling critical thought and dwarfing objective consciousness. Thus, the region remains an easy target for exploitation and domination. Many Caribbean leaders, with a false understanding of their roles in Caribbean history have become slaves to materialism, instead of serving as agents for freedom and change on the islands. Even at this point in their history, however, Caribbean people can examine their past to recreate their future. They must heed the wisdom of their own prophets and heroes. They must become an aware people about all that is around them. Then, they must study and learn from events that come to shape their lives, rather than simply wait to be shaped by these events. Marcus Garvey still shouts to Caribbean leaders and people, "Hold on to your land!" a matter he emphasized, when he visited St. Kitts back in 1937.

One day after the disaster, at a mass service on Nevis, an Anglican preacher from England suggested that one should not attribute the disaster to, "God's will," Fr. Eke encouraged the societies to examine the disaster in detail. They were to search for the causes, then avoid such mistakes in the future. The misery in Caribbean lives is often human-made. As Fr. Eke the English preacher hinted, place blame where it belongs. Demand answers! Demand change! While the population might have failed to grasp Eke's hint to them, the political leadership did not. The people were beginning to understand and appreciate such calls to consciousness raising. Both Kittitians and Nevisians were being called from that comfort of dependency, so often harbored in colonial societies. Unfortunately, Eke was later deported from Nevis. The government allegedly reasoned, he was riling up the people, when he noted the *Christena* tragedy was a failure in human leadership. It was not the will of God.

CHAPTER EIGHT

Politics and the Disaster

The 1960s and 1970s, were times of flux and change, in Caribbean history and politics. Colonialism was still alive and well in the area, but political and social developments were bringing new challenges, including the promise of greater Caribbean based autonomy. The Caribbean colonies were no longer of prime economic importance to Europe. Some of the British colonies had progressed to independent nations. Britain also granted Associated Statehood status to islands such as Antigua, St. Kitts-Nevis and Anguilla, Dominica, and some others, on their way toward independence, too. Meanwhile, the socialism initiated in the area by labor unionism, St. Croix, from 1915; St. Kitts-Nevis, and some other islands, from 1940; helped to shape the emerging politics of many former British colonies. In the case of Cuba, the new politics bred and unprecedented level of Cuban nationalism and independence. Cuba also experienced unprecedented levels of political discontent amidst new levels of academic development, and new political directions. Meanwhile, other Caribbean governments, including St. Kitts-Nevis started honest efforts to democratize their higher education programs, and to remake the social world their people had come to know. Over time, frequent discussions about critical issues in Caribbean history and politics, and about the future of the islands became the order of the day. Many thought the era of blind acceptance, and imposed alienating politics was ending. A new brand of politics was seen to be emerging in St. Kitts-Nevis. Admittedly, that growing dream of change in the islands, was deeply indebted to the labor movement in Caribbean societies and politics. However, many benefactors from that new and emerging politics, have refused to acknowledge an indebtedness, or to appreciate that labor union legacy—the classic case of Caribbean false consciousness.

The new Caribbean politicians argued that times had changed and their education, along with new types of exposure, had prepared them to be better leaders in the area. On the other hand, those tried, tested and seasoned heroes of the labor movement, such as Nathan, Challenger, Bradshaw, Southwell and others, used their stories of sacrifice, shared experience, and political expertise to keep themselves at the forefront of the leadership arena. However, the time came when such Labor Party stalwarts found themselves facing new and internal challenges. They were being forced to be on the receiving side of the political firing line. Some fell during the intense verbal fire. It became a disruptive political civil war in the islands. Other seasoned politicians stood their ground. They were skillful enough to survive, make indelible contributions, and create legacies from their time, which are still honored.

Always at issue in the islands has been which group should control political power and patronage. Who should make the critical decisions about shaping the islands' future? Accordingly, deep and intense rivalries developed between political parties and among the citizenry. Ordinary citizens from all levels of society found themselves embroiled in the selfish politics that continued on the islands, and a time came when the vote began to lose its meaning. Democracy too, started to lose its intended application in the islands. Meanwhile, political party battles became more divisive. Under such circumstances, it was inevitable that the politics and the politicians would weave the *Christena* incident into the web of an intense, evolving, and shifting politics.

Political Parties

Despite ongoing political skirmishes, during the 1970s, the Labor Party dominated the politics of St. Kitts-Nevis, under the leadership of Robert L. Bradshaw. Up to that time, none of the rival political organizations managed to withstand the attacks of labor unionism with much success. However, Caribbean society and Bradshaw's government were entering a new era. Throughout the area another wave of political instability was emerging, as some of the veteran labor leaders were being challenged by a younger political set, in some ways driven by intellectualism and a desire for participation in the political process. It was probably part of a global philosophical uprising, over forms of governance, and also about strategies for economic and social success, that brought positive shifts to the area, during the early 1900s.

By the mid 1970s, the Labor Government in St. Kitts-Nevis was facing growing and credible opposition for the first time. The Labor Party was learning that its costly trial and error, colonial-driven politics, was being subjected to scorching criticism. Any mistakes or political blunders became fodder for the opposition's political machine. The growing political opposition and its leadership, were certain their men could do things better. The People's Action Movement party (PAM) had been founded in St. Kitts by 1965. Among its founders were business men, Michael Powell and Richard Caines, medical doctor, Kennedy A. Simmonds, and lawyer, Dr. William Herbert. Over the years, these men played leading roles in the party. Meanwhile, co-founders such as Colin Perierra and other elites from the former Democratic Party opted to work from behind the scenes. Bradshaw was very skillful at making opposition against his Labor Party, the party of the masses who worked on sugar cane on St. Kitts, a class war.

Over in Nevis, there had always been opposition to the government on St. Kitts in general, and to Bradshaw's government in particular. The *Christena* disaster simply served to further unite the opposition against the government on St. Kitts. It came together as the Nevis Reformation Party (NRP) in October 1970. Lawyer Simeon Daniel, with businessmen Levi Morton, Zephaniah and Horace Liburd, Ivor Stevens and Uhral Swanston, spearheaded the venture. The drive for Nevisians to unite in an anti-St. Kitts political party got its biggest push from the *Christena* tragedy. However, when the sinking of the ferry occurred there was already much political ferment in St. Kitts, Nevis, and Anguilla—the entire colony. It did not matter who formed the government, or what role they played in the *Christena* incident. Further, as the government's organization responded to what had become an unprecedented disaster in the islands, with some 250 persons dead, its management and ordering of the society was quite inept. For that reason, and for others, including the fact that almost 400 persons were packed on a ferry registered to take 155 passengers, the political opposition to Bradshaw and his Labor government was harsh and bruising. Many citizens, including members of the opposition parties, leveled the inevitable criticism, as leaders of the government responded, trading political blow for political blow. At that time, however, attack as the best defense did not help Premier Bradshaw, Deputy Premier Southwell, Attorney General Moore, or Minister of Education Bryant. The people were burdened by their losses, angry, becoming increasingly politicized, and were in no mood to allow the government's attack strategy to work.

Generally, the two societies (St. Kitts and Nevis) thought government deserved blame for the disaster. The crew was untrained, the ferry was repeatedly overcrowded, but the government did nothing about the complaints. Also, on such an afternoon with so many people travelling to Nevis, a second trip should have been arranged. A further, even more fundamental argument for Nevisians, was that so many persons from Nevis died because the government kept Nevisians dependent on St. Kitts. Nevisians travelled to St. Kitts to trade, to receive government services such as passports and tax clearances, for medical attention, for higher education, for promotions in government, and to get to the outside world by plane. Such truths were well known in Nevis. The experiences were limiting, and humiliated Nevisians. But the government on St. Kitts defied any blame.

However, two prior incidents referred to in Commissioner Renwick's inquiry, showed that government officers had, for several years, received warnings about overcrowding on the ferry. There were two others situations mentioned in the local newspapers, as far back as 1959 and 1960. The government failed to learn from those cases. They clearly warned that the ferry *Christena* often travelled with a passenger count beyond its 155 limit. However, there is no record that anything was ever done to correct the situation. Julian Cox, then Permanent Secretary in the Ministry of Communications and Works, admitted at the inquiry that letters had come to his Ministry complaining about overcrowding on *Christena*. Two of those letters were particularly noteworthy because of their origin. On July I, 1959, Mr. Maguire, a warden of Nevis, wrote to the Harbor Master complaining about the overcrowded condition of the ferry as it traveled to Nevis. Hugh King of Delisle Walwyn and Co., the insurer of the ferry, also wrote a complaint about its overcrowding. He wrote the letter on January 26, 1960, in response to an article published by the *Labor Spokesman*, a pro-government newspaper, written earlier in the same month. The article referred to an incident when the ferry was crossing to Nevis from St. Kitts and had sprung a leak. The captain was able to make a quick decision and took *Christena* into the safety of Ballast Bay instead of continuing toward Nevis. On that occasion, 192 passengers were aboard. The ferry was carrying 37 passengers above its registered capacity of 155. *The Democrat* of January 20, 1970, made reference to that *Labor Spokesman* article. It was written just six months before the horrible tragedy occurred.

Government officers responsible for the day-to-day operations of the ferry service were often irresponsible and careless. Such carelessness could hardly have gone on as long as it did, without members of government becoming aware. Many of them, all on St. Kitts, travelled frequently to Nevis. Further, the society is small and the politicians usually institute networks of informers on both islands. Usually, they inform about anything that is said, for or against the government. When stories are critical of the government, they are normally reported, and serve as a prelude to political vindictiveness. The government encouraged such stories. While those about their handling of *Christena* would have been welcomed, they were simply not addressed to foster the needed change to the ferry's operation. Few people except die-hard supporters of the Labor government rejected that it had a role in causing the disaster. As far as the opposition political parties were concerned, the Labor government's perceived negligence, following such a devastating event, was a God-send. It boosted attention to their politics and they rode the event for every inch of political mileage it offered.

Unfortunately, such party politicking became a weapon against the best interest of the citizenry. The interest of the politicians in getting and keeping political power, superseded real concern about the welfare of a suffering and disillusioned people. Only token financial or other commitments were made to victims of the disaster. No comprehensive policy was devised to improve the immediate condition of Nevisians, so that they could avoid the frequent travel to St. Kitts. Part of the government's concern became getting another ferry so that the travel from Nevis to St. Kitts could be facilitated. At that time, there was no structural or policy change in the way government treated Nevis. Some persons even interpreted the sinking of *Christena* as an event allowed by the insensitivity of government to the concerns of Nevisians. There had also been a longstanding idea among Nevisians that, as their population decreased through migration or deaths, they would become more open to control from St.

Kitts. Irrational as that view might have appeared then, some Nevisians argued that the neglect of the ferry and its eventual sinking could well have been part of the government's hidden political agenda. Further, Premier Bradshaw had also promised Nevisians "blood in the streets" if they attempted to follow the Anguillan, 1967 example, to secede from St. Kitts. It was almost inevitable, after the *Christena* sank, rumbles of secession started to get louder on Nevis. Nevisians consistently reexamined their heavy dependence on St. Kitts, and resulted in a determined effort to change the political structure and the relationship that existed between the two islands, with St. Kitts being at the center, while Nevis struggled at the periphery.

In 1970, there was evidence everywhere that the population on Nevis was diminishing, showing a decline of more than 2,000 people by 1980. And the decrease was continuing. Emigration, the aging of the population, and the loss of young people in the *Christena* incident, contributed to the trend. Historically Nevisians have emigrated to better themselves economically and for other personal reasons. The politics meted out from St. Kitts did not help the situation. During the same period, population growth on St. Kitts was much more vibrant from natural birth. It also benefitted from migrating Nevisians and Anguillans. Today, however, although migration from Nevis has continued, immigration from Guyana, Jamaica, and the Dominican Republic, is reversing that 1970-1980s population decline trend on Nevis. Undoubtedly, the political relations between the islands, contributed to that wish to migrate from Nevis during the 1970s. Meanwhile, the present shifts in demography will impact the islands, in terms of future society, culture, and politics.

In 1961, a group of Nevisians led by Wilmoth Nicholls and Eugene Walwyn, then the two elected representatives for Nevis in the House of Assembly, went to St. Kitts and demonstrated against the political link between the two islands. At that time, Walwyn was the leader of a Nevis party, the United National Movement (UNM). However, by the time of the *Christena* incident, Walwyn and Nicholls found themselves on different sides of the political discontent between the islands. Walwyn had shifted his politics and supported the Labor Party. Nicholls, on the other hand, remained a staunch supporter of the growing argument for Nevis' independence from St. Kitts. Admittedly, personal experience had shaped each man's response to that matter. Although both men made an earlier commitment to the people of Nevis, Walwyn had served as Attorney General for the Labor government, and, over time, became committed to stand with the government's position on the *Christena* issue.

Nicholls, meanwhile, was making a new life in the U.S. Virgin Islands. Fred Parris, was another Nevisian elected to the House of Assembly, but he was on the PAM ticket, in opposition to the government. When the Labor government summoned a House of Assembly meeting on August 6, 1970 to pass a "Sympathy Resolution" on behalf of the families who lost loved ones in the accident, Parris took time to express his displeasure at the government's handling of the whole affair. He also suggested that government compensate all the people, particularly the direct survivors of the disaster. Shortly after the accident, the *San Juan Star* newspaper of Puerto Rico ran an article based on an interview with Mr. Parris. He took a strong anti-government stance arguing that the *Christena* incident gave another reason why Nevisians should sue for secession. Parris maintained that the loss of so many citizens from Nevis served to reopen serious historical wounds between the two islands. He also noted that many public statements made by government about the disaster were false and could not be verified.

Further, Nicholls, reacting to the tragedy from the US Virgin Islands, expressed annoyance that the House of Assembly met only to offer condolences to the people. He thought the politicians should have had some kind of in-depth discussion of the matter. For Nicholls, a broader debate about such an important event, and its possible consequences to the State was necessary. However, on August 6, 1970, the government argued against such a debate.

It could have aggravated the government's position with the citizens. A general election was just months away. Also, since the Commission of Inquiry still had to function and report its findings, those proceedings could have been influenced by the politics and by such a discussion at the time. No doubt, the first matter served as the more important factor for avoiding a debate in the House.

A very pressured and angry Bradshaw, responded to Parris' position and statements on the disaster with anger and his usual disdain for the opposition. He also suggested that Parris might have to answer certain statements made about the Christena incident in a court of law. However, such harsh, high-handed and uncompromising response to criticism was typical of Bradshaw, while he led St. Kitts, Nevis, and Anguilla, during the 1950s to the 1970s. There was also that certain arrogance about his political style.

Election, May 10, 1971

General election in St. Kitts and Nevis was constitutionally due in 1971. The new politics was disruptive, but, the election had to be scheduled. It would come less than a year after the disaster. Even so, it would no doubt be a test of strength for the government, but the government had the authority and controlled the timing for the election. It was quite a challenge, but those in power thought the people ought to have enough time and focus on alternative events that would make them forget *Christena*. However, for opposition parties, the *Christena* disaster and the sudden loss of some 250 lives in St. Kitts-Nevis, remained a critical election issue. Kittitians were rallying to the PAM on St. Kitts, and some Nevisians on Nevis, too. But the party had credibility problems in its leadership. Dr. Herbert, the party's president, was a brilliant, charismatic lawyer, but his father's link to the plantocracy and its elite Democratic Party left his son, Dr. Herbert, disconnected from the masses he sought to represent, as a leader of PAM. Over on Nevis, few Nevisians remained loyal supporters of the Labor government by 1970-1971. However, prominent Nevisians such as Stanley Henville, a businessman at Charlestown, Edread, and Eugene Walwyn, and a few others, kept rallying to the Labor Party. Notwithstanding, that political banner had become tattered and hated on Nevis. While the general population on the island wanted change, a few die-hard supporters of the Labor Party could not see any change in their lifetime. One night, shortly before the 1971 election, some Labor politicians came to Nevis to hold a meeting. As usual, their equipment was connected to Stanley Henville's place for electricity. However, when Bryant and Moore attempted to address the people, the meeting was disrupted permanently. Police Inspector Delsol and other police officers protecting the politicians could not hold back the crowd. Nevisians were in no mood to hear anything from visiting Labor politicians. Eventually the meeting was abandoned. During an interview with the author on May 2, 1999, Moore spoke of the rancor and hate he sensed at that meeting.

In the ensuing election, Daniel of the NRP opposed Parris of the PAM for the St. George-St. James seat on Nevis. Daniel's party was new, but he used the *Christena* disaster and its aftermath to argue love for Nevis and a Nevis nationalism stance. It was not a new message, but with people still mourning the loss of loved ones from the *Christena* mishap, that type of argument evoked strong emotions among Nevisians. However, Parris (still on the PAM ticket) defeated Daniel that year. He too, had capitalized on the *Christena* disaster and was ridiculing the government. He also had the distinction of being the only person to challenge the Labor government in the House of Assembly about the disaster. Two other positive things Parris had going for him were experience in the House of Assembly, and growing sympathy on Nevis for the PAM. He won handily, but by the next election he too, like Walwyn before him, had made peace with the Labor camp, and crossed over.

Eugene Walwyn and Ivor Stevens opposed each other for the seat in the St. Thomas, St. Paul, and St. John constituency. Because Walwyn had openly shifted to the side of Labor, he could not win an election again on Nevis. He had burned his political bridges on the island. To this day, Nevisians have not forgiven him for the betrayal. Many Nevisians felt slighted when Mr. Walwyn took a pro-Labor position in a Nevis matter as vital as the *Christena* disaster. In the meantime, Ivor Stevens too, who probably more than anyone else had made the disaster issue his political motto and talking point, simply could not let up. Seemingly, at the time, he wanted "blood" from the Labor government. He also intended to work for the collapse of the Labor government. For Mr. Stevens, its fall would be sweet revenge for *Christena*, and for other personal matters. Many years after the incident, talk about how the sinking impacted Nevis, remained one of Mr. Stevens' most frequently used points for criticism of the Labor Party government.

On St. Kitts, as well as on Nevis, the *Christena* disaster was an issue in the 1971 elections. But there were two other important issues. Both signaled new thinking, and new trends in Caribbean society and politics. The two issues were mechanization of sugar cane harvesting and a miniaturization of St. Kitts, Nevis and Anguilla, as a political unit. The British had moved to cut Anguilla from St. Kitts-Nevis after the Anguillan revolt, and Anguilla came into its own around 1967. There was even an attempt by Anguillans to invade St. Kitts and kidnap Bradshaw. Although the case by the government was unsuccessful, there was plausible evidence to support aspects of the government's argument and to show collusion from St. Kitts by certain members of the PAM party. Thus, for the election of 1971, the Labor government found itself in a very difficult position. It had to defend charges of complicity in the *Christena* disaster. Also, it could not justify to Kittitians and Nevisians, then, why it imported a number of untested harvesting machines to work in the sugar industry. The machines had to be abandoned because of their inefficiency. The terrain of the land appeared to have been a factor not accounted for before the purchase.

Meanwhile, whether there was an attempt to overthrow the Bradshaw government clandestinely, was still a hotly debated matter on the islands. To prevent Nevisians from moving in the same direction as the Anguillans, in time, soldiers were stationed on the ferry and on the island. The government became leery of all opposition to its policies in both St. Kitts and Nevis. It also accused the opposition of actively planning acts of violence against the government. However, most Nevisians and Kittitians felt the government's stability was never threatened. They considered the heightened militarization of St. Kitts-Nevis that came about after the Anguilla invasion incident as unnecessary.

Today, one very interesting question is, "Was Robert Bradshaw a liar or a prophet?" By the 1980s, Kennedy Simmonds, one of PAM's leaders during 1971, was one of the loudest preachers for militarization of the Caribbean. In 1983, for example, he supported the US invasion of Grenada. As Prime Minister, he too became concerned and wanted to promote political stability in the area. Probably he could rationalize and defend such a position at that time. For him and his fellow leaders of the PAM, that was understandable. Their party held power then, in an increasingly turbulent Caribbean.

Seemingly, from every angle, the 1967 instability on St. Kitts-Nevis, followed by the *Christena* tragedy of 1970, was an opportunity for Simmonds' PAM party, not a threat. Those events worked in favor of the movement against the Labor Party, so that the opposition became stronger through the 1970s. By 1980 there was a major shift in political leadership on St. Kitts. The weapons in the arsenal of the new St. Kitts-Nevis government, became such that it made the weapons of Bradshaw's time appear insignificant. It was like Enfield 303s, versus M-16s. The shift toward heightened militarism showed that a government in power will go to every length to defend its authority and privileges. Prime Minister Simmonds did just that. If Bradshaw was alive, he too would have identified with that. There is a natural desire to defend what is considered one's political turf, even to the point of making elective politics predictable.

The list of issues on St. Kitts-Nevis made for a keen, dirty election contest in 1971. PAM politicians labeled the Labor politicians murderers who hated the people, and who had killed scores on the *Christena* . . . They also referred to the Labor government's militarization as a stocking up of guns to kill even more citizens. At a very large meeting in Pall Mall Square, St. Kitts (now Independence Square), PAM's candidates called on the Labor government to resign in the interest of the people. The government was also accused of ineptness, confused policies and insensitivity to the needs of the people. In response, government politicians accused the leaders of PAM of being alienated from the true ideals of the masses, and traitors to the movement for a just society. Labor politicians also leveled accusations at PAM party politicians. They were accused of collusion with Anguillans in an attempt to overthrow the legally elected government, on June 10, 1967.

Despite the intensity of the contest, the Labor government won the seven seats on the island. However, there were rumors of ballot box substitution and other unfair election practices. None was publicly substantiated. After the election, some known supporters of the opposition lost their jobs without any explanation. Others left the island to live elsewhere. Certain foreigners who supported the opposition were also deported from the islands. At the same time, a number of Labor government supporters were exalted to loftier positions in the civil service. The promotions occurred despite questions regarding their qualifications and competency to do the jobs. On Nevis, one of the two seats went to PAM and the other went to the newly formed Nevis party, the NRP. However, while the 1971 election battle was lost in St. Kitts by the opposition, that was not true about the war. The opposition continued to use the *Christena* matter effectively, intending to shift political loyalty away from the Labor government.

After 1971, politics in St. Kitts-Nevis would never be the same. Finally a spirited and hungry opposition to the Labor government had been firmly established in both St. Kitts and Nevis, and, the *Christena* matter was playing a significant role in that development. Soon, little doubt remained that the Labor government was vulnerable and losing the poise and security it had during the 1960s and 1970s. Meanwhile, the PAM and the NRP parties were unrelenting in their criticism of the Labor Party, and were gaining popularity with the people. Although the Labor government survived the 1970s, even winning two elections after the *Christena* mishap, it would not make it through the 1980s.

Election 1975

Between the elections of 1971 and 1975, the issue of the *Christena* tragedy and its aftermath did not go away. The government instituted a special welfare program to serve the needs of the people with problems related to the disaster. As much as was possible, orphaned children were placed with families or in friendly homes in St. Kitts-Nevis or abroad. Thousands of dollars were also collected locally and from abroad to assist those in need. Everyone did not, but a number of persons received some form of assistance. However, there were numerous complaints about the management of the funds overseen by government. In a number of cases some families in need got no assistance. It was a good thing that the Anglican Church, along with some other private organizations stepped in and helped. By the time the government announced that it would accept no more claims from victims of the tragedy, two things were evident: the government had not pledged one cent of its own funds to help the victims, and no proper public auditing had been done, with respect to the large sums collected by the government from donors. Even into the 21st century, the donated *Christena* money and how it was spent can still be an emotional issue on St. Kitts-Nevis. Thus, the *Christena* matter remained a political problem beyond the next election, held in 1975. During the campaign of 1975, both secession for Nevis, and independence for St. Kitts-Nevis were campaign issues. The Labor government won the seven seats in St. Kitts again. The NRP easily won those in Nevis. Thus the two islands remained divided politically and ideologically: One was for separation through secession; the other for unity through independence from Britain.

Election 1980

In the next election, 1980, the Labor Party lost its position as the dominant political force in St. Kitts-Nevis, and that lasted for the next fifteen years. However the PAM did not win majority support immediately, neither did the PAM, ever reach that level of political dominance on St. Kitts, which the Labor Party had attained. Meanwhile, on Nevis, the NRP was still on a roll. It won the election again and remained the peoples' party. The NRP in Nevis was now an important political force, and looked as steady as a rock—at least for that time. Things had become more and more strange for the Labor Party, and that situation began to emerge just before the islands surged into the 1980s. Destabilization and uncertainty for them began when the party experienced some leadership set-backs in the late 1970s. First Bradshaw, then Southwell, two of its legendary champions, died in 1978, and in 1979, respectively. Supposedly, this resulted in a brief internal war of succession, since there were some questions about the best labor leader to succeed Bradshaw. On January 25, 1979, Dr. Simmonds won a seat for the PAM, in a by-election against the Labor Party. That was an unprecedented event in St. Kitts history and politics. For both the Labor Party and the PAM, it was a foreboding of events to come.

Just over one year later, on February 18, 1980, the Labor Party was humbled at the polls, losing three of its seven seats.

Those three seats were lost to the PAM. The Labor Party held on to the other four seats. Suddenly, Nevis became kingmaker. The NRP Leaders, Daniel and Stevens, joined forces with Simmonds, Powell, and Morris of St. Kitts, to form the first coalition government in the history of the islands. However, in every way, it was a coalition of convenience—not one made in heaven. The existing circumstances brought the PAM and the NRP together, as the politicians responded to an unprecedented situation. It was one that pushed them beyond themselves. It also presented an opportunity to make and to rewrite the islands' history.

There were three major developments in St. Kitts-Nevis' social and political history that contributed to that reshaping of the islands' destiny. From its inception in 1970, the NRP preached secession from St. Kitts. By the mid-1970s, Robert Bradshaw was talking about becoming an independent nation with Nevis as part of that nation. Again, and again, the NRP highlighted the destruction and pain to Nevisians caused by the *Christena's* sinking, which, in time, became woven into the wave of anger and protest on Nevis. In unison, Nevisians repeatedly made the demand for secession from St. Kitts. These were often platform themes for the NRP. Both issues garnered strong support for the NRP and evoked anger toward St. Kitts. Even in the area of sports, one island was always poised to crush the other without mercy. The intense rivalry continued into the 1980s. Back in 1971 and 1975, Fred Parris of the PAM and Simeon Daniel of the NRP had fought bitterly over the St. George-St. James seat. As usual, the infighting was dirty. Ill-feelings were left among the NRP and PAM candidates, Stevens, Daniel, and Parris. However, the PAM politicians on St. Kitts skillfully avoided confrontations with Nevisians. Later, when Daniel defeated him in 1975, Parris defected to Labor.

The PAM and NRP held common positions on the *Christena* disaster. They supported the Anguilla break with St. Kitts-Nevis and agreed on "no independence for St. Kitts-Nevis." They also continued to criticize the policy mistakes by the Labor government. Those two factors, plus the fact that each party now operated only on its own turf, kept the PAM and NRP on fairly good terms, but still suspicious of each other—a fact that Mr. Daniel never allowed the Kittitians to forget. Thus, PAM and NRP politicians had a history of agreeing on issues related to the *Christena* disaster and some other issues in St. Kitts-Nevis.

Another uniting factor for the two parties was the reality that PAM and NRP were constantly standing in the cold of opposition, instead of being in the warm, active seat of government. Finally, because of their blood connections to Nevis, PAM politicians Simmonds and Powell, could readily extend hands of peace and friendship to the NRP. Another factor often overlooked was that Ivor Stevens was a born Kittitian. Deep down, he wanted the islands to work together. Those subtle forces played a role in uniting the opposition politicians on both islands. At the same time, the opportunity for power, presented on February 18, 1980, was one in a lifetime. It was a chance that they could not agree to refuse. Before the terms of the coalition agreement were finalized, however, there were some disagreements over who should get what positions in the new government. PAM's politicians came to Nevis with, as they said, "no plan." The Nevisians requested and got the Finance and Communication Ministries. Suddenly, a PAM-NRP coalition had come into being. The two groups of politicians accepted the challenge to make policy decisions for St. Kitts-Nevis, during the brave new 1980s.

New Directions

Even as the 1980s sped by, *Christena* was a frequent theme in St. Kitts-Nevis politics, but the politics of the *Christena* disaster did not end there. It continues to haunt society to this day. Many who suffered in the disaster still lament that the government forgot them. Others such as Captains Skeete and Anslyn argue that the societies have forgotten those who died. At that point in time, there was no memorial to their honor. But that situation started to change during the leadership of Premier Vance Amory. The memorial change thrust, continued under Premier Walcott Parry. For a number of reasons, it was easy for the opposition political parties to criticize the government. They capitalized on the events surrounding the *Christena* tragedy and used their arguments to enhance their popularity with the people.

However, it must be understood that the times in which people live, and the conditions under which people exist, affect every aspect of their lives. Their politics, social relations, and responses to events, are all controlled by day-to-day understanding and responses to events in the society—their cultural meaning and ethos. The whole society was still emerging from the colonial cocoon and struggling for enlightenment. Dependency was a way of life. There was fear of responsibility, innovation, and independence. A PAM-NRP government, in 1970, would probably have made mistakes, similar to those made by the Labor government. However, to opposition politicians, those management shortcomings of the Labor Party seemed opportunities. They promised to innovate, recreate, and do everything right if the people gave them the chance. Eventually, they got it. Unfortunately, they too, seemed to have forgotten the cause, and the people for whom they became champions.

Like the politicians from the Labor Party era, the PAM-NRP politicians discovered that innovative management in colonies is a challenging task to pursue. They also learned that political management style can often be a function of the era in which a people live. Accordingly, there was enough circumstantial evidence surrounding the *Christena* tragedy to destroy the Labor government's credibility. Hardly anyone in the society accepted its plea of innocence. But, in retrospect, enough evidence is available to support the argument that the opposition parties over-politicized the disaster. In both St. Kitts and Nevis, politicians played on the emotions of a sad, broken people, blinded by grief. The moment was ripe for guile, political opportunism, and promises of heaven.

Reaction to the disaster eventually lost sanity and normality. A time came when the tears and concern for victims of the tragedy were replaced by divisive political ideas, and a certain amnesia seen often in the actions by calculating creatures of politics. The PAM-NRP politicians expressed much anger over the way the Labor government handled the ferry, the disaster, and the survivors. But there were other things that the PAM-NRP government could have done at that time to show tangible evidence of concern for the victims and their survivors. They did little more than to politicize the event, so that they could win the support of the pained and disillusioned masses.

A survey could have been carried out to find out who the survivors of the disaster were. Interest could have also been shown in how they have adjusted to such a traumatic experience over time. Some people on the islands are still in need of help because their parent or parents died in the disaster. Other people associated with the event failed to get a proper education because no one provided the means to that education. The PAM-NRP government came to power almost ten years after *Christena* sank. If its politicians were really concerned about those who suffered from the disaster, they could have done more to alleviate the victims' condition. In 1998, there were still many sad stories of school drop-outs, hunger, and neglect of the victims. The Labor government made a lame attempt to mark the mass gravesites in St. Kitts. But the PAM-NRP government, abandoned that effort. Today, it is difficult to locate those graves.

There is now more than one memorial sight on Nevis. Thanks to an effort led largely by Sonny Skeete, Nevisians are no longer limited to the old memorial that had become cracked and faded. What Skeete started as a one-man effort to get Kittitians and Nevisians to remember the *Christena* has now taken on a vibrancy on Nevis. Memorials are now in place so that all can look back to August 1, 1970. Seemingly they are now well kept, too. But while Nevis leads the way, in this matter, St. Kitts lags far behind. Both islands lost citizens, and both islands were haunted by the aftermath of the disaster. However, it is beginning to appear that few people on St. Kitts have seen wisdom in pausing to draw attention, and to memorialize victims of the tragedy. Nevisians and Kittitians must still reflect on, and remember, what the two people endured together, as a result of that tragic event. But, it is still strange that there is no memorial to the *Christena* on St. Kitts, to this day. Not even the mass graves there are marked anymore!

One is tempted to suggest that there may be thoughts that it will also bring back the horror of an earlier downfall by the Labor Party. But, what about all those other St. Kitts politicians who once championed the rights of the *Christena* victims? Has the event been conveniently forgotten? Have the politicians who used the event, like others in the society, who looked at the scene in pain and horror, come to a point in time when they have no place in their lives for the memories? Or, has it been that like voters in an election, the *Christena* event served its political purpose then, and now has lost its value? In reality, a people are a product of all their experiences. There is something to be learned from each one. Further, this is still true. When a people fail to value and pass on their historical and cultural experiences, as legacies to the ages, their heritage and its true meaning becomes easily reshaped and dwarfed by others, over time.

For Nevisians and Kittitians, the full *Christena* story is one of both failure and new beginnings. Despite the sacrifice and the pain the event brought to the islands on one hand, because of the same tragedy, the politics and people in Nevis were given new meaning and impetus to go forward and rewrite their story. Today, PAM-NRP politicians can only blame themselves for their unfulfilled promises. They built up the aspirations of citizens throughout those years when the disaster was needed as a battle axe. It worked well for them, but not for the people.

During the 1980s the unity of mind and spirit encouraged by the *Christena* tragedy vanished from the islands. There were opportunities to reach for new directions in the societies, but the people stood, still divided by politics. People were encouraged in their new materialistic lifestyles to say, "ump, ump, ump" when they could only say, "wee, wee, wee." Materialism has overwhelmed the islands and changed the ethos of the societies.

Erich Fromm, in his book, *The Sane Society*, suggested that when greed for material things becomes the driving force in society, such a society is on a path to insanity and destruction. It cannot go on indefinitely without the eventual resolution of an inherent, and destructive dilemma. The life and politics in St. Kitts-Nevis since *Christena*, in many ways, failed to heal the painful and historic wounds some citizens experienced. At that time, when the dramatic events brought all the people together, their unity was manipulated by politicians in cunning ways, for selfish gain. Even at this time, there are still chasms, deep and wide, between the people. Social relations and status in society are determined by the material things one owns, politics, and other subtle human-made status symbols. There is little time spent in grasping the meaning of the politics, or in the finding of human common ground, through the acceptance of our shared humanity. Today, as in the time of *Christena*, politicians and other leaders of human societies fail to communicate with the citizenry in complete honesty. Yet, in St. Kitts-Nevis, other Caribbean nations, and around the world, few people appear to grasp and understand the insanity politicians can inflict on the lives of those others. There are still lessons to be learned from the *Christena* story. But the story must be known. Then, those who know the story must ask the who? where? what? and when? questions. It is now over forty-two years after the event. Maybe people can now ask the hard questions, accept the real answers, and also develop a broad appreciation as to how the *Christena* tragedy impacted society, and changed lives in St. Kitts-Nevis.

CHAPTER NINE

Commission of Inquiry

REPORT ON THE
CIRCUMSTANCES SURROUNDING
THE SINKING OF THE
M. V. *CHRISTENA*
OCTOBER 1, 1970
COMMISSION OF INQUIRY
J.D.B. Renwick, Commissioner
Basseterre, St. Kitts, B.W. I.

Report

I was appointed pursuant to the provisions of the Commissions of Inquiry Act, Chapter 288 of the Laws of Saint Christopher, Nevis and Anguilla, by His Excellency, the Acting Governor, to hold an inquiry and investigate the circumstances surrounding the sinking of the *Motor Vessel Christena* on her scheduled voyage between the Islands of Saint Christopher and Nevis during the afternoon of Saturday, the first day of August, 1970 and to report to His Excellency in writing my findings and to make such recommendations as may seem to me meet in the special circumstances of the case. I was directed to hold the meetings of the Commission in public, to hold the first such meeting on or before the 31st day of August, 1970, and to present my report on or before the 15th day of September, 1970. Meetings whereat evidence was taken were held at the Courthouse, Charlestown, Nevis on Monday 17th, Tuesday 18th, and Wednesday 19th days of August, 1970, where 25 persons gave evidence, and at the Courthouse, Basseterre, St. Kitts on Monday 24th, Tuesday 25th days of August, 1970, Tuesday 1st and Saturday 5th days of September, 1970, where 20 persons gave evidence.

Boat Design*

The Motor Vessel *Christena* was designed and built by Sprostons Limited, Georgetown, British Guiana at Georgetown aforesaid for the Government of Saint Christopher, Nevis and Anguilla and completed in May, 1959. In the builders certificate she is described as follows: "The frame, keel and deck of the vessel are of steel. She has one mast, two decks, oblique stern, elliptical stern, hard chine built.

Dimensions

The general dimensions are as follows:

Figure 1 Dimensions of *Christena*

Length.. 66' 0"
Main Breadth 16' 0"
Depth in Hold 4' 5"
Depth from top of deck at side amidship to bottom of keel 5' 6"

* Subtitles are the editors' and not in the original report.

Round of Beam Nil
Tonnage measurement is estimated at 22.66"

The Certificate of Survey as is required by the Merchant Shipping Acts, 1894 to 1952, gives her length at 62' 10", and her registered tonnage as 33.74. In addition, the vessel had 5 water-tight bulkheads. She was powered by 2 Caterpillar Diesel—D326-F F. Marine engines made in 1958 by the Caterpillar Tractor Company, Peoria, Illinois, U.S.A.

Capacity

The vessel was designed to carry a maximum of 5 tons in the forward hold, 100 second class passengers on the main or lower deck, 30 first class passengers on the upper deck and a crew of 5. The makers however increased the number of passengers to be carried on the lower deck to 120. From the drawings which were produced in evidence I found the following:

Figure 2 Capacity of *Christena*

Length of upper deck	44.0
Uncovered portion of upper deck	13.9"
Height of cabin on upper deck	6'10"
From ceiling of upper deck to lower deck	13'9"
Draught	3'5"
Freeboard	2'1"

The M. V. *Christena* provided a scheduled passenger and cargo service between the islands of St. Kitts and Nevis. From Monday 26th August 1968 (except when away for docking) she made two return trips to Nevis daily except on Thursdays and Sundays. She was also available for charter. Passengers on the upper deck paid $1 each way, while those on the lower deck paid 50 cents each way.

The charges for freight were as follows:

Small packages, baskets of goods and sacks of flour 10 cents each
Bags of sugar (large) 50 cents each
Small stock 35 cents per head
Passengers were allowed one hand package free.

Operation

The Ministry of Communication, Works and Transport was responsible for the administration, operation and maintenance of the *M. V Christena*. She was manned by a Captain, James Ponteen, a mate Frank Matthew, an engineer, Charles Moore, an assistant engineer, Conrad Phipps, and 5 crew members. I have been unable to ascertain whether any member of her crew received any formal training in navigation. The probability is that their experience was purely practical. Tickets for each trip were sold during the voyage by Captain Ponteen, or, during his absence, by a clerk in the Ministry who was especially assigned to dealing with matters concerning the *Christena*. Each morning after the *Christena* had returned from Nevis, the clerk would check the number of passenger and cargo tickets sold against the actual cash receipts. Having verified that, he would make out a deposit slip to the bank and hand over the cash and deposit slip to the Captain, and the latter would make the deposit in the bank. The Captain would then lodge the deposit slips half monthly at the Treasury.

Docking

The *Christena* docked as follows

Table 1: Docking of *Christena*

Date in	Date out	Country	Cost
28/3/60	27/4/60	Barbados	$9,529.65
12/12/60	4/1/61	Barbados	$3,419.12
23/11/61	14/2/62	Barbados	$14,800.00
27/2/63	30/3/63	Barbados	$7,416.30
24/4/64	12/5/64	Barbados	$6485.75
20/10/64	28/11/64	Barbados	$4,007.93
14.8/65	16/12/65	Barbados	$31.388.39
9/5/67	14/8/67	Tortola	$14,543.00
16/2/68	12/5/68	Barbados	$22,344.88
9/2/70	7/5/70	Barbados	$42,282.79

The Central Foundry Limited of Barbados, a firm of Dock and Foundry Owners, Ship-builders, Marine and General Engineers, repaired the *M.V. Christena* whenever she was docked in Barbados. During her last docking repairs were effected to the engines, propeller shaft assembly, toilets and wash basins, life rafts, bilge pumps, windlass, main and auxiliary exhaust pipes, top deck, lower deck, hatch, hand rails, pipe rubber, bilge and suction pipes. In addition electrical and carpentry work were carried out. From all this it can be seen that the *Christena* was docked annually when all necessary repairs were effected. *The Christena* returned to St. Kitts on Tuesday 17th May 1970 and resumed her normal schedule beginning with the afternoon trip on 19th May The passenger carrying capacity of ships plying between St. Kitts and Nevis is fixed by the Passenger Regulations, Chapter 155 of the Laws of Saint Christopher/Nevis and Anguilla, Revised edition 1961.

Regulations

The Regulations state as follows:

"2. Number of Passengers (1) The number of passengers to be carried by ships of over 20 feet of keel between the islands of St. Kitts and Nevis, or going coastwise in either island shall not exceed two passengers for each one foot of keel, or not to exceed six passengers for each registered ton. The Passengers (Motor Boats) Regulations which were made some 15 years later modified regulation 2(1) of the Passenger Regulations above quoted and provided as follows:

"3. Number of Passengers Restricted. Notwithstanding anything to the contrary contained in the Passenger Regulations, the number of passengers which may be carried at anyone time in any motor boat shall not exceed the number determined by the Comptroller of Customs on the written application of the owner of such motor boat, and the number of passengers so determined shall be legibly painted in a conspicuous place on such motor boat to the satisfaction of the Comptroller of Customs." In these Regulations, the expression "motor boat" means any motor boat carrying passengers between the islands of St. Christopher and Nevis.

Passengers

In the Passenger Ordinance, Chapter 155, the word "passenger" is defined as follows: ". . ." Passenger' means any person carried in a ship, except

(a) a person on board the ship on the business of the ship, (b) a person on board the ship either in pursuance of the obligation laid upon the master to carry shipwrecked, distressed or other persons, or by reason of any circumstances that neither the master nor the owner nor the charterer (if any) could have prevented or forestalled, and (c) a child of one year of age." In spite of the foregoing provisions, at no time was an application in writing or at all made to the Comptroller of Customs to have the number of passengers which may be carried by the M.V. Christena determined. From that it naturally follows that the requirement that "the number of passengers so determined shall be legibly painted in a conspicuous place on such motor boat to the satisfaction of the Comptroller of Customs" was not observed.

Letters

Julian Byron Cox, the Permanent Secretary, Ministry of Communications, Works and Transport, deposed that he had personally never received any information or complaints about the *Christena* being overloaded. He went on however, to produce from the records two letters dealing with this matter. The first was dated 1st July 1959, from W.L. Maguire, Warden of Nevis and the other was dated 26th January 1960 and was from Delisle Walwyn & Co., Ltd. Suffice it to say that no reply was sent to Mr. Maguire while the reply sent to Messrs. Delisle Walwyn & Co., Ltd. was not as polite as it should have been and the action therein promised was not taken. I have however come across another letter which in part deals with this matter. This letter was addressed to the Honorable Minister of Communications & Works and a copy placed on the personal file of the Captain of the *M. V. Christena*. The letter is dated 20th May 1961 and was written by Cecil O. Byron, then Acting Warden of Nevis. The first paragraph of the letter reads as follows:

"I travelled yesterday to St. Kitts, by the *M. V. Christena,* for business with His Honor the Administrator. Captain Ponteen was aware of my presence on the launch as I had reason to suggest to him, soon after we embarked, that he should consider whether it was advisable to take the Motor Vessel back to the Charlestown Pier in view of the large number of passengers on board and the somewhat disconcerting experience we had suffered in regard to the balance of the vessel as soon as it had set out its course. The Captain however decided to proceed and we arrived at Basseterre without further incident."

It will be noted in this paragraph the Acting Warden dealt with two matters viz., the large number of passengers on board, and the balance of the vessel. I shall deal with the second of these matters later. In his letter the Acting Warden dealt with other facets of the operation of the *Christena*. I was unable, however, to find on the file any reply to any of the points made by the Acting Warden or of any action taken as a result of that letter. These three letters were written to the Ministry responsible for the running of the vessel and each letter contained an allegation of an expressed concern over the overcrowding of the vessel. These warnings apparently evoked no action from the Ministry.

I am of the opinion that as time went by people having become more accustomed to and confident in the vessel, were not as alarmed by the vessel being continuously overcrowded as they had been soon after she went into service.

Overcrowding

On Tuesday, 12th July, the Captain of the *Christena* at his own request was permitted to make two trips to Nevis at the end of that day's play in the final match of the Leeward Islands Cricket Tournament played between St. Kitts and Nevis. Mr. Cox saw the *Christena* leaving for Nevis on the first of her said trips. He was of the opinion then that she was overloaded. Next day he called in the Captain and told him that the boat was overloaded. This the Captain denied. A check of the cash receipts by him showed that the boat was not overloaded. Mr. Cox then went on to state that he told the Captain that he was not satisfied with the amount of people he had seen on the boat and that he, the Captain, was risking people's lives and if he didn't care about his, he should have some thought for young children, women and old people on the boat. I would like to point out that checking the cash receipts would not reveal whether the boat was overloaded on anyone trip, since the receipts covered two round trips to Nevis and in the case of the check on 13th July related to five round trips, viz. one on Saturday, 3 on Sunday and 1 on Monday. The revenue returns clearly show that for every period covered thereby more passengers travelled first class than second class. I find this hard to accept and it should have alerted the Ministry and the Audit Department, which audited the accounts that a physical check of passengers using the *Christena* was necessary. Besides the exhortation to the Captain by the Permanent Secretary, nothing was done. It is my view beyond question that on many occasions by whatever yardstick is used the number of passengers carried by the *Christena* greatly exceeded the number that it should have carried.

As the mate said whenever the *Christena* was the only passenger boat on the St. Kitts-Nevis run she would be overloaded. Dulcita Browne, a witness who impressed me as being honest and truthful and was a regular commuter said *"Sometimes when the Christena put out the amount of people, you think is a steamer bring these amount of people."*

What Happened

On Saturday 1st August, 1970, at about 3:30 o'clock in the afternoon, the *M. V. Christena* cast off and began leaving the Treasury Pier, in Basseterre. There were three latecomers and the Captain brought the vessel back to the Pier and picked them up. The boat was crowded with passengers. This was August Bank Holiday weekend. In addition to the usual turn-hands, i.e., those who had come from Nevis to sell their vegetables and other produce in St. Kitts, there were holiday makers, relatives intent on spending a weekend with their loved ones and families in Nevis, Nevisians returning home after a week's work in St. Kitts, Nuns going on retreat and others. There were more than three hundred men, women and children on board. They realized that the boat was overcrowded but thought not so much of the danger they themselves helped to create but rather of getting to Nevis. Most passengers were crowded in the stern of the vessel, as that was where the passenger accommodation was situated. Passengers were sitting wherever they could find a place to do so, even on the handrails and places where they knew they were not allowed to sit. As the vessel swung towards Nevis it rolled to the starboard side, stayed there for a while, came back on even keel, and then rolled to the port side.

The sea was calm, the wind moderate to light, and visibility was good. The Captain was obviously concerned with the trim of the vessel. He ordered his crew to move some crates of sweet drinks amidship and the passengers away from the gunwale to the middle of the boat and not to move around. While some passengers obeyed him, a goodly number heaped abuse on him. The vessel continued to roll from one side to the other and on each occasion water washed over the stern. The Captain handed over, as was his custom, the wheel to the mate and began collecting the fares. A small fishing boat on its way to Nevis, was just ahead of the *Christena*. Wade and Parris, its occupants, signaled to the *Christena* to reduce speed as she was seen to be shipping water in the stern. This signal was either not seen or, if it was seen, was not understood. As the *Christena* was about to enter the Narrows, i.e., the channel between St. Kitts and Nevis, but while she was still sheltered by Nags' Head, she rolled over to the starboard side. Victor Swanston, who was standing in the bow of the vessel, jumped overboard and dived to avoid the propellers. As he came to the surface, he was churned up in the wake of the vessel. He started to swim and saw the vessel, with only 10 feet of the bow and its mast out of the water. People were screaming, crying and praying, trying to get out of the stricken vessel and holding on to its bow and mast. In a very few short minutes, at about 4:10 pm, she sank.

Why did the Boat Sink?

Why did the *Christena* sink after having sailed for over half an hour, having covered nearly half the voyage to Nevis and in almost ideal weather conditions? To answer this question, since inspection of the hull revealed that it is intact, I must refer briefly to the design of the vessel. She was a vessel which drew under four feet of water. **In** order to come alongside the Treasury Pier she had to be of shallow draught. On the other hand her superstructure was over 13 feet high and she was of normal beam. This type of construction would, to my mind, mean that she would roll a good deal. On this, her final voyage she carried relatively speaking, little cargo. With an overcrowded upper deck and little cargo to act as a counterbalancing force it is obvious that *Christena* capsized. Having capsized the stern filled and because she was buoyant in the bows this part of the vessel was the last to sink.

Malfunctioning

Inspection of the hull by divers showed that the steering mechanism was at that time malfunctioning. It is not possible on the available evidence to state the cause of the malfunction or when it arose. The divers found that the steering wheel and rudder are locked hard starboard and that turning the steering wheel does not affect the position of the rudder. If this malfunction had arisen before the *Christena* capsized, the helmsman would not have been able by steering to help right the vessel on her last roll to starboard and this malfunction could have been a contributory cause to her capsizing. **In** my view this malfunctioning could not by itself have caused the loss of the vessel. Why after capsizing she sank so quickly I am unable to say as inspection of the bulkheads has not been possible.

Life jackets

There were 25 life jackets for adults in the Captain's cabin and 58 on the rack on the upper deck. On the lower deck there were 95 and 40 life saving jackets for adults and children respectively. In addition, there were 5 buoyant seats, each with a capacity of 18 persons. In my view the *Christena* sank so quickly after she had rolled over that there was not sufficient time for people to get the life saving jackets. The fact that the buoyant seats had not floated lent weight to the evidence, which was denied by the mate, that they had recently been bolted down to the deck.

Seats

The true position, however, is that the seats were not bolted, but having floated jammed the companion ways and other exits. Two probable reasons for this are firstly, the vessel sank stern first, thereby trapping the seats; and secondly, a part of the upper deck which was originally uncovered had been covered with plywood to provide shade and shelter, this covering would naturally have the effect of boxing in the seats. So, tragically, what was designed as lifesaving equipment trapped persons in the vessel making escape there-from nigh impossible.

Position of the Christena

The exact position of the *Christena* was first ascertained by Captain Phillip Miller by using electric sonar equipment. This was confirmed by *H.M.S. Sims.* It was marked by a white foam buoy, a yellow anchor rope and a 121b. anchor. The *Christena* is lying in 11 fathoms of water, latitude 17 degrees 12.2 minutes North and longitude 62 degrees 39.8 minutes West; 9/10 of a mile from Nags' Head. This position has been confirmed by the divers.

The first boat on the scene was a small fishing boat which was manned by Wade and Parris. The latter had actually seen the *Christena* sink. They took a few people into their small boat and landed them on the rocks at Nags Head. From there they proceeded to Cockleshell Bay to get help. No one was there so they crossed the Narrows and went to Jones Bay, Nevis, where they met a fishing boat, *Sea Hunter 1*. She had just returned from a fishing trip and was being docked. Captain Miller had already gone ashore. Wade told the mate of the *Sea Hunter 1*, Winston Skeete, also known as Sonny Boy, that the *Christena* had sunk and without further ado,

Skeete, together with Wade, Parris, Robert Jeffers, Rupert Maynard and Foster Huggins, set off to the disaster area. In the meantime those who could swim were trying to reach Nags' Head. Others holding on to empty soft drink cases, some to benches and other floating objects. A number of men were holding on to an empty drum. One woman who had her youngest child swept out of her arms by the force of the water on the final roll of the vessel was saved for as she put it, "God was merciful to me He sent a bag with 3 breadfruit in it and is that I held on and take my own time swim till Cliff Dwellers' boat pick me up." Stronger swimmers encouraged the weaker ones. Upon this scene came a small boat with Michael King at the helm.

Michael King

Michael King's evidence is very important so I will deal with it in some detail. Let me begin by saying I accepted his evidence as the untarnished truth. He stated that he was on his way to Nevis, accompanied by his wife and four daughters, brother and his wife, and sister. As they were passing Nags' Head, one of the children drew his attention to some people waving at them from the rocks at Nags Head. His boat was between 50 and 100 yards off Nags' Head. He then turned around and saw several people swimming in the sea further out. He then realized that the *Christena* must have sunk. He dropped off the ladies, children and baggage on the nearby rocks and with his brother went to the disaster area. I will continue **in** King's own words "We saw the ship *Hawthorne Enterprise* about 4 miles off shore. Our first plan was to go out to it for help but seeing so many people around us drowning, we stopped to pick up one and a second and then next we knew we had a boat load. We realized that by the time we got the *Hawthorne Enterprise* on to the scene most of the people would have drowned. By this time we had about 10 people onboard the little speed boat, which was all it could carry and we headed for shore. At this point we saw the *Sea Hunter*–we saw it in the disaster area, and we went to her to off-load the survivors we had on board." There was one elderly lady who was actually drowning—she was going down and coming back up—and he jumped overboard and managed to save her and get her aboard with great difficulty. He took everyone he rescued to the *Sea Hunter.* He made about 4 such trips.

Sea Hunter

The *Sea Hunter* then took 63 survivors and 3 dead bodies back to Jones Bay. There they were met by George Bradley, Government Secretary. The survivors were taken to the hospital where they were treated, some discharged and others detained. The *Sea Hunter* put back out to sea, this time with Captain Miller in command, and continued rescue operations and the painful task of recovering dead bodies from the sea.

Hawthorne Enterprise

One important matter demands my attention at this juncture. I refer, of course, to the allegation that a ship, the *Hawthorne Enterprise, had* been contacted by radio by the *Sea Hunter* and not only had she refused to give assistance after having been told that the *Christena* had sunk but someone on that ship had used indecent language to Sonny Boy Skeete. This allegation is undoubtedly the only one on which there was a sharp conflict.

Charles Moore

Charles Moore, the engineer on the *Christena,* stated in evidence that soon after the *Christena* sank he saw "the ship, bows on to the *Christena* where it had gone down." As he was at that time heading towards Nags' Head, he turned back and swam towards the ship as it would be much better for him if he could be picked up early rather than have to swim all the way to Nag's Head. The boat was then about two miles off Green Point. Suddenly, he saw the boat turn away and go back to sea. He was later picked up by Michael King and put on the *Sea Hunter.*

Sonny-Boy Skeete

As he got onboard the *Sea Hunter,* Sonny Boy Skeete asked him to assist him with the radio and to try and call any station. Continuing Moore deposed that he called and was answered by the *Hawthorne Enterprise.* After the indecent language he heard Sonny Boy speaking to the Police Launch. Frank Matthew, who was rescued by the *Sea Hunter* after Moore had already been on board, on the other hand said he could actually read the name of the *Hawthorne Enterprise* painted on the bow of that ship, so close to him was she while he was swimming. He went on to say that he overheard parts of the conversation between the *Hawthorne Enterprise* and the *Sea Hunter* 1ncluding Charles Moore stating "this matter will have to be reported." Sonny Boy Skeete related how he asked Moore to call as he could get nothing. Moore, he said, got the *Hawthorne Enterprise,* and he spoke to that ship. He went on to state that he also contacted a yacht and the Police Launch.

It is not necessary in my view to go into the alleged conversation with *the Hawthorne Enterprise* in detail. It is agreed by all that Moore and Matthew were landed at Jones Bay when the *Sea Hunter* took its first lot of survivors to Nevis. This was done when Captain Miller was not on the boat. As the evidence of the Chief of Police and Mr. Cox clearly shows, the Police Launch had not left Basseterre yet so the evidence of Moore and Skeete that they had contacted the Police Launch is not true.

Unreliable Witnesses

Further, I do not believe Matthew when he said he was able to read the name of the *Hawthorne Enterprise* on the bow of the ship while he was swimming. The most reliable witnesses estimated the distance that the ship passed from the disaster area as being between 2 and 4 miles. I am firmly of the opinion that it is not possible to read 6 inch high by 1 inch wide letters at that distance. Skeete, Matthew and Moore all gave statements to the police describing in great detail their accounts of the events. In not one of these statements was any reference made to the *Hawthorne Enterprise made*. This omission is all the more serious when it is recalled that Moore is alleged to have said that this matter will have to be reported. When each was asked by me why he did not refer this important matter to the police, Skeete said he was doing so and was prevented from doing so by the policeman who took his statement and this the policeman denied, and neither Matthew nor Moore had any comprehensible reasons for the omission. It is not surprising therefore that I find no truth whatever in their accounts of their supposed contacting of the *Hawthorne Enterprise.*

Captain Stanley Wynter

But the matter does not end there. Captain Stanley Wynter, Master of the *Hawthorne Enterprise,* appeared and gave evidence before me. He impressed me as an honest and trustworthy witness. He categorically denied having known anything about the sinking of the *Christena or* having had any radio conversation with the *Sea Hunter* at all. The evidence of the boatswain added great weight to his Captain's testimony.

I am well aware that Captain Wynter had said that he was waiting for an important weather report from the radio station on Tortola which he got at 6:30 pm., whereas the boatswain had said that he did not know that the Captain was listening for a weather report and he did not hear any weather report. To my mind this shows even more clearly that their evidence was true since if they were fabricating they would surely have tied off this loose end.

Mr. Christian

Before finally leaving this aspect of my report I feel constrained to allude to another pertinent matter. Mr. Christian had informed me that he had cabled the United States Coast Guard in Puerto Rico, whom he said kept a 24 hour watch on 2182 kcs—the wavelength alleged to have been used throughout—and that he would like to produce this reply whatever it contained. I told him I would permit him to produce the reply he received. This was on Tuesday 1st September being the day on which Captain Wynter gave his evidence. On Saturday, 5th September, Mr. Christian produced the reply he had received on 1st September and which reads-

"RE SINKING CHRISTENA BETWEEN ST KITTS NEVIS AUGUST FIRST. REVIEW OF SEARCH AND RESCUE CASE FILE NR 4271-70 DOES NOT INDICATE A MAYDAY MESSAGE RECEIVED SAN JUAN STATION THAT DAY."

After this telegram had been produced, the Attorney General produced the following telegram from the United States Coast Guard, San Juan, Puerto Rico and which was received on 27th August,

"REUR TELEGRAM 37 26 11552 BG THIS STATION
HEARD NO DISTRESS CALL FROM FIV SEA HUNTER
AT TIMES IN QUESTION STOP THIS STATION
FIRST HEARD OF POSSIBLE DISTRESS AT 2313 GMT
WHEN OUR RADIO STATION OVERHEARD TWO
BOATS DISCUSSING BRINGING IN BODIES ON
2182 KH2."

This latter telegram, in my view, shows without doubt
that the reports made against the Hawthorne Enterprise
are entirely without foundation in fact. The conversations
overheard by the Coast Guard in San Juan fit precisely in
point of time with the conversations between the Sea Hunter
and the Police Launch evidence of which was given both by
Captain Miller of the Sea Hunter and the Chief of Police.
The telegram by inference shows that the Coast Guard would
have picked up messages transmitted by the Sea Hunter 1,
and messages sent by the Hawthorne Enterprise. The fact
that the only communication they overheard took place at 7:
13 pm speaks volumes.

It is a pity that the frankness which prompted the production
of the telegram arose only after Captain Wynter had been
warned that his alleged misconduct was an offence against
the laws of this State, after his cross-examination and that of
the boatswain of his ship and after his counsel had not only
undertaken to produce any reply he received from the U.S.
Coast Guard but had in fact produced the reply he received.

Dr. Simmonds and the nursing staff of the Alexandra
Hospital, Nevis, augmented later by medical and nursing
personnel from St. Kitts rendered yeoman service tending
the survivors.

Whitman T. Browne, Ph.D.

Bodies

The task of recovery, identification and burial of the dead proceeded with dignity and dispatch. From all the available information, 57 bodies were identified. A list of these is attached hereto as Appendix A. Whilst trusting that I do not cause further sorrow to the bereaved, I must point out that there have been doubts expressed as to the identification of Kirsten Olivia Liburd, and that although the body of Clarent Forbes was identified and his address given as Sandy Point, none of the residents of Sandy Point who have been contacted can confirm the identification.

Recovery of dead bodies was effected on Sunday, Monday and Tuesday the 2nd, 3rd and 4th days of August, respectively. With the passage of time identification of the bodies became virtually impossible and so had to be abandoned. All necessary health precautions to prevent the outbreak of disease were taken. In Nevis 6 unidentified bodies were buried while in St. Kitts the number of such bodies was 60.

I regard the ascertainment of the number of persons who sailed on the 1st August as of paramount importance. With this in mind, I personally prepared three lists, namely: a. a list of the persons whose bodies were identified; b. a list of the persons reported as having sailed on the *Christena and* missing; and c. a list of the survivors.

These lists were given wide publication and were checked by the Ministry of Health, the Government Secretary, Nevis, the Police and other interested persons.

The list of missing persons is attached hereto as Appendix B, and the list of survivors is Appendix C. There are a few persons who were reported as missing but subsequent investigations have been unable to reveal anything whatsoever about them. I have attached those names as Appendix D.

Recommendations

By the terms of my appointment I was enjoined to make such recommendations as may seem to me meet in the special circumstances of the case. No evidence was given on this aspect during the inquiry and unfortunately in the time and with the information available, I have not been able to produce as comprehensive recommendations as I would have liked. Here, however, are a few personal random thoughts.

I feel that an immediate study should be made to determine the present pattern and future aspects of coastal trade both in passengers and cargo between St. Kitts and Nevis. This study should reveal the economic viability of such trade and whether or not it should be subsidized. It should also lead to finding out the most suitable boat for such trade.

The present statutory provisions governing coastal trade between St. Kitts and Nevis are to be found in more than one Act, Ordinance and Statutory Rules and Orders. The legislation is quite old, and while it contains provisions which deal with the safety of the passengers, it is in the main geared to curb smuggling, e.g. the only vessels which trade coastwise that have to be registered are those under 30 tons.

The records show that in the past twelve years, 4 privately owned vessels which were engaged in operating a scheduled passenger service between St. Kitts and Nevis were lost—one during a hurricane, one by fire, one at the Charlestown Pier and one while riding at anchor in Basseterre. Fortunately no lives were lost but the inescapable inference must be drawn that these vessels were not sea worthy.

Whitman T. Browne, Ph.D.

I recommend that new and comprehensive legislation to govern and regulate coastal trade both passenger and cargo be enacted. I do not intend to go into detail as this will be trespassing on the draftsman's province but I will indicate the broad topics with which such legislation should deal. In making my proposals I am deeply conscious of the fact that coastal trade must not be made difficult or expensive and that getting from one island to the other must be achieved with the minimum of inconvenience and red tape. However the safety of the passengers must be the prime consideration.

In the first place the legislation should provide for the licensing of all vessels irrespective of ownership and size engaged in coastal trade. The license should be of not more than 12 months duration and should be issued by the Comptroller of Customs who should keep a register of such licenses.

A license should only be granted after the vessel has been inspected and certified as being safe for the carriage of passengers by some competent person or authority.

To qualify for such a certificate a vessel will have to: a) possess an adequate amount of watertight bulkheads; b) pass a stability test; c) possess sufficient life saving equipment, viz., life buoys, life saving jackets and rafts; d) be equipped with adequate fire protection device; e) be equipped with efficient radio receiver and transmitter; and f) where appropriate, have efficient mechanical and electrical installations, special emphasis being paid to any equipment which is a necessary part of any system vital to the safe navigation of the vessels, such as propulsion and steering systems.

A certificate as being safe for the carriage of passengers should be not more than 12 months duration.

As regards the number of passengers which a vessel will be licensed to carry the present provisions that this should be based on the length of the keel or registered tonnage of the vessel although already modified by the Passengers (Motor Boats) Regulations before cited needs closer examination and expert advice on this should be obtained.

The legislation should lay down the criterion to be followed when determining the maximum number of passengers a vessel will be allowed to carry. Breach of this provision should be severely punishable.

As far as I am aware no legislative provision here exists for issuing certificates of competency to Captains of ships engaged in carrying passengers coastwise. I recommend that this be introduced. In the beginning, the legislation should provide that

Captains of such ships should satisfy the examiner that: a) their eyesight is normal as regards form and color vision; b) they have a working knowledge of the Regulations for Preventing Collisions at sea; c) they have a thorough knowledge of the different lights carried at night by all types of craft; d) they understand how to go alongside piers and jetties; e) they know what action to take in case of fire, man overboard, taking a boat in tow, being taken in tow, losing a rudder, engine breaking down, etc.; and f) they can use ship to shore radio, etc.

More subjects should be added to the preceding list dependent on whether the ship will be operated at night and the number of passengers she will be permitted to carry. In my view, to be a Captain of a ship carrying over 100 passengers, such a person should hold at least a valid 3rd Mate's Certificate.

In order to easily control the number of passengers being carried by a ship, the practice of collecting fares during the voyage should be stopped immediately. All tickets should be numbered consecutively and sold to would be passengers before they board the ship. These tickets should be presented by the passengers when about to board the ship. Never should more tickets be sold than the number of passengers the ship is licensed to carry.

Regulation of cargo traffic coastwise, will in the main be a matter for Customs and there are ample provisions elsewhere in the Caribbean which can be adapted to suit the local needs. I would like to point out that cargo dangerous in itself should not be carried with passengers. In a community as small as ours, it is not surprising that many and varied rumors were circulated following news of the disaster of the 1st August. I am pleased to state that although I relaxed the rules of evidence, those giving evidence showed remarkable candor and appreciation of the task I was asked to perform. I wish to put on record my gratitude to all and especially the people of Nevis who never said or did anything to cause me embarrassment in this Inquiry. My profoundest sympathy goes out to all the bereaved.

Dated this 1st day of October, 1970.
J.D.B. Renwick
Commissioner
(For the various lists of names see Appendix V thru IX)

CHAPTER TEN

Questions That Were Not Answered

Forty-two years have passed since *Christena* sank in 1970. However, there are many questions about that tragedy, which remain unanswered. Neither the government of St. Kitts-Nevis nor the Commission of Inquiry delved deeply enough to find real answers to all the questions people still ask. In dealing with the tragedy, the government found itself in an unprecedented and bewildering position. There were certain questions it could not answer honestly and other questions it could not answer at all. Meanwhile, that seemingly rushed, one-man Commission, was a contrived, quick, limited review and discussion, of a profound sociopolitical event, that would impact the islands' society and history for a very long time. The questions asked and answered did not seem to be as comprehensive or as probing as they could have been. Thus, the findings were limited and to some measure superficial. Essentially, the authorities asked easy questions and got the answers they wanted. Further, the intense politics surrounding the *Christena* matter, did not allow the hard, honest questions, or encourage insightful, reflective answers.

For example, these questions can now be asked. Was there a networking of Caribbean Lodges in this St. Kitts-Nevis matter, as it related to Captain Wynter? Did the Lodge phenomenon play as critical a role in 1970, as it did in the court case about the Anguillan invasion of St. Kitts, back in 1967? Too many Nevisians and Kittitians accepted a minimal review of a situation that was tearing their societies apart. There was little new information, questionable honesty in the politics, limited compensation forthcoming, and a rushed inquiry. Further, since a general election was due within months of the painful tragedy, any sharp focus on the government would have been a limiting factor for the government. The leaders understood the failures of the government in the tragedy. There could have been an impact on the election if they were really forced to answer the hard questions. That would have also increased the rancor and political discontent already present in a pained and increasingly divided society.

Seven of the hard, and most frequently asked questions, still being asked about the *Christena* tragedy, are discussed in this chapter. Only careful study and analysis of the circumstances, then, a thorough gathering of all possible facts, could have led to realistic, reasoned answers. However that did not happen. Many questions were never asked or answered. Those seven questions are noted and discussed here.

1. Why did *Christena* sink?
2. Was Captain Wynter of the *Hawthorne Enterprise* totally oblivious of the *Christena's* dilemma when he passed by?
3. Why did so few witnesses to the actual sinking testify at the Inquiry? (A total of 45 persons gave evidence to the Commission of Inquiry. Many of them were government and other people, not among the 99 who survived the tragedy).
4. What happened to the aid programs and the money donated to assist victims of the disaster?
5. Why did some individuals involved in the disaster behave in such an inhumane manner to those helpless others in distress?

6. Why didn't the government resurface *Christena?*
7. How did the sinking of *Christena* intensify the animosity between Nevis and St. Kitts?

The Sinking

Four theories were presented to explain why *Christena* sank. One group or another in St. Kitts-Nevis generally accepted three of them. The fourth is probably still not well known. Actually, most people who asked questions about the sinking might not have heard the new facts that came to light long after the political and verbal storms over the disaster had abated.

Obeah

Immediately following the sinking, obeah, or the supernatural, was a popular explanation on Nevis as the cause of the ferry's sinking. Probably the obeah theory became that popular because, having traveled on *Christena*, safely, for some eleven years, there were citizens who had come to believe the boat was unsinkable. A number of the surviving passengers made statements about seeing a strange man, whom they concluded was an evil spirit aboard the ferry. Later a story also began to circulate about someone who wanted to kill one man on board the *Christena*—its captain, Mr. Ponteen. However, there have always been problems with that supernatural theory. It seems simplistic, but during that period, on Nevis in particular, many superstitious citizens were prone to accept such explanations for sudden and seemingly illogical events in society. Despite other evidence, obeah served to discredit rational explanations, and to undermine human responsibility. If someone really had a grudge against Captain Ponteen; Why would that vengeance seeker use a ferry filled with innocent passengers for his attack on the captain? It was obvious; too many innocent people could be hurt. Why would a crowded *Christena* be the best place to carry out such a dastardly act? The captain could have been eliminated elsewhere at much less cost to the society. But then, such a person might also have known that the captain could not swim.

In retrospect, maybe a more creative suggestion would have been that supernatural means were used to sink the ferry in order that political animosities and criticisms about St. Kitts and Nevis politics, could intensify. However, that premise given for using obeah as the weapon to cause such tragedy, is still irrational. But, there are Nevisians who still accept the suggestion as credible. Ironically, despite quite a mysterious disappearance of Dr. William V. Herbert, along with other members of his family, in a boat, during 1994, there has not been similar talk about obeah. Maybe the politics of *Christena's* time was the better place to look for the why's of the disaster and its aftermath.

Bradshaw's government survived the overthrow attempt of 1967. However, by 1970, there were many chinks in the leadership's armor. They included, growing opposition to the government on both St. Kitts and Nevis. However, at that time, Bradshaw's grasp and command of the government was so exclusive of those others, particularly on Nevis, that some people might have concluded, only the supernatural could have defeated Bradshaw at the game of politics. Actually, even when it was well known that Bradshaw was dying, he continued to control and dictate the politics of St. Kitts-Nevis, until he died on May 23, 1978. Further, a final criticism of the supernatural theory is the cold inhumanity it suggests in the relationship between Kittitians and Nevisians. Whether the quarrel was personal or political, it is hard to believe a citizen of St. Kitts-Nevis would have planned, then carried out such brutal murders. There has to be another explanation of how almost 250 people came to such a sudden, untimely death, that afternoon.

Overcrowding

Overcrowding was another of the explanations for *Christena's* sinking. However, many passengers who were aboard the ferry could recall other occasions when it was more heavily loaded than it was that afternoon. One such occasion was when the Australian cricket team visited St. Kitts in 1965. *Christena,* reportedly, made two trips back to Nevis in the evening, to take back the passengers, it brought to St. Kitts on one trip, during the morning. And, that became the situation only because the authorities decided to monitor the ferry on the return trip. On another occasion, when it sprung a leak in 1960, even though overcrowded, there was no immediate threat of sinking. The manner by which it finally sank, allude to the fact that the bulkheads in the fore section were designed, when properly closed, to keep the ferry afloat under varying sea conditions. This fact also contradicts the overcrowding argument as the most critical reason for the sinking. The sudden roll which threw passengers overboard should have resulted in a righting of an overcrowded *Christena,* or caused it to roll over sideways. Further, it has been suggested by experts that if overcrowding was the most critical problem with the ferry that afternoon, it would not have sunk stern first.

Seemingly, the large crowd aboard mattered more in terms of the number of lives lost. The *Christena* contained close to 350 passengers, although its registered capacity was 155. Knowing what we know now, suggests that even strictly enforced precautions against overloading would not have averted the sinking. The boat was often overcrowded. That was its usual travel style on many of the runs between the islands. Anyone who claimed differently could not have been familiar with the condition of travel between St. Kitts and Nevis at that time. Regular travelers had become so accustomed to traveling under overcrowded conditions that they hardly bothered about it. There was actually a growing belief among the regulars about the invincibility of *Christena.*

Fate

There was the other argument that God sank the ferry. However, that too is being escapist and again, too simplistic. It was another attempt at finding a scapegoat beyond the physical human reality, and at the same time moving to avoid an examination of the facts and circumstances surrounding the incident. Such an argument would also have to explain under what circumstances St. Kitts and Nevis, more than the other Caribbean islands (or the rest of the world), incurred God's wrath leading up to August 1970. Undoubtedly, there were heightened and new demonstrations of religiosity in St. Kitts and Nevis after the disaster. However, Nevisians and Kittitians have always exhibited high levels of religious commitment and fervor. The colonizers were careful to dictate and control the behaviors of the colonized. They used labor, the court system, schools, and religious systems, particularly after the abolition of slavery. The "God's will," explanation for the accident probably sounded good to the embattled Labor Party government. By attributing the incident to God, that shifted blame and responsibility for poor oversight and inept regulations by the government. Little wonder then, that the government became angry and eventually deported the Anglican priest Fr. Eke, after he stressed in one of the memorial services that, "There was no sudden to the disaster. It was not an act of God, or fate," suggesting that the government's poor oversight allowed the tragedy to take place.

Manholes

The final theory for the sinking is that three manholes to the bulkheads at the stern of the ferry were inadvertently left open by the crew. Repair work was done on the ferry, Thursday, July 30, 1970, two days before it sank. Because the manholes were left open, water filled the bulkheads as the ferry traveled between St. Kitts and Nevis, Friday, July 31, then again August 1, 1970.

Wyclide Condell recalled working in the stern area of the ferry and welding the ferry's exhaust system on the Thursday. Frank Tyson also recalled that the manholes were left open by accident, after the welding was done on the ferry. Two dangerous situations then developed. The bulkheads in the stern lost their ability to produce a vacuum effect keeping the ferry afloat. The presence of water in the three chambers disrupted the normal equilibrium of the *Christena*. As more and more water entered the chambers, that condition, with the water moving about in the open bulkheads, made *Christena* easily sinkable. Actually, as the water moved about in the ferry's lower section, it became impossible to maintain even normal steering control or the equilibrium of the ship. Thus, the attempts by the captain to move people and cargo about to achieve balance proved futile. Further, the sea was calm. When disaster finally struck, water had filled the bulkheads to that critical level at which they could no longer keep the stern afloat. No water entered the bulkheads toward the bow. The ferry began to sink stern first. Its bow went under later. Eventually, the water in the stern area, the passengers, and the sea pressure pulled the entire ferry under. On Thursday, July 30, 1970, when the group of welders from St. Kitts Sugar Factory did repair work on the exhaust system, three manholes toward the bulkheads in the stern had to be opened. The exhaust system was reached inside those bulkheads. After the job was completed, the workmen did not close the manholes; neither did the crew.

Such an oversight on the part of the crew was a classic case of poor seamanship. Keeping the vacuums closed and functioning effectively was critical to keeping the ferry afloat. Because of their poor training, the crew did not understand how important to the ferry's safety such an oversight could be. The ferry traveled to Nevis, then back to St. Kitts, twice on Friday, July 31st. On August 1st, it went to Nevis in the morning and returned to St. Kitts. With each trip, water went into the lower section and entered the bulkheads through the open manholes. That was why passengers noticed the strange movement of the ferry as early as Friday afternoon. Mrs. Helen Bradley chose to return to Nevis the Saturday morning because she noticed the unusual sailing pattern, when she travelled on the boat to St. Kitts, "to get her hair done," the Friday afternoon. The situation got worse on Saturday morning. It became impossible for the *Christena* to stay afloat Saturday afternoon. That was why it sank. Even if there were just 100 passengers aboard, and not close to 350, the ferry would have met the same fate.

The Hawthorne Enterprise Affair

In retrospect, it appears that the conclusions reached, by the Commission of Inquiry, were agreed on, after listening to a number of second-hand, and in some cases, biased testimony. In areas where there were discrepancies, those pertaining to the men on *Sea Hunter 1*, were highlighted. The same strategy was not adopted regarding conflicting testimony from the men on the *Hawthorne Enterprise*. Seemingly, the one-man Commission of Inquiry heard reports from too few of the passengers who saw the ship in the area. Also, while the Inquiry chose to discard the discrepancies in the testimony of the Captain and boatswain of the *Hawthorne Enterprise*, it was harshly critical of explainable discrepancies in testimonies by men aboard *Sea Hunter 1*. On that matter, Mr. Renwick appeared biased and to favor the statements made by Mr. King and Mr. Wynter. They too were fallible human beings. But they understood the politics of the case.

The Inquiry failed to consider that the radio equipment on *Sea Hunter 1*, had a range of only 113 km, while the U.S. Coast Guard station monitoring for such calls in Puerto Rico was almost 333 km from the disaster site. Further, Justice Renwick's report made no reference to the fact that harbor pilot Joshua Guishard took a female passenger aboard *Hawthorne Enterprise* with Captain Wynter that Saturday afternoon. Neither did it deal with Joshua's conversation with *Hawthorne's* crew as *Christena* passed by on that final trip to Nevis. In a second interview, 1998,

Joshua continued to maintain his earlier (1980s) position on the issues. Despite their assertions, neither Commissioner Renwick nor Michael King was in a position to make a fully informed conclusion as to whether the captain of *Hawthorne Enterprise* knew *Christena* sank. Both men had too little, and seemingly, too biased information from which to make a fair judgment. Michael King came upon the disaster scene after *Hawthorne Enterprise* had veered away from the swimming passengers, and had left the scene. Sonny Skeete, unlike Captain Wynter, had no reason to lie. Further, it may still be revealing, in this matter, if it can be determined whether the Lodge system, or the Class system, was at work here in Captain Wynter's favor. It has also been reported that the PAM party, to which Mr. King was affiliated, wined and dined Mr. Wynter and supported the argument of his innocence in the case. It did not matter that Mr. Wynter was being accused of knowingly refusing to help citizens of St. Kitts-Nevis, as they died in the water. At the same time, Bradshaw was desperate for a scapegoat. The PAM party, under the leadership of Dr. William V. Herbert, Jr. was doing everything possible to prevent Bradshaw and his Labor Party Government from escaping blame for the tragedy that had overwhelmed the islands.

A careful examination of the evidence now available brings to mind many questions about the conclusions of the Inquiry. While the Commission cleared the captain and crew of the *Hawthorne Enterprise,* the available facts now seem to suggest a different view. Sonny Skeete must have known how to operate the radio on *Sea Hunter 1.* Also, in reference to what Frank Matthew-Tyson testified about the *Hawthorne Enterprise*, only a fool in the water would have started swimming toward a ship four miles away, while land was in full sight and less than one mile nearby. One or more of the crew of *Hawthorne Enterprise* must have told Skeete and Guishard, independently, that the ship was bound for Guadeloupe, on leaving St. Kitts. Someone from the ship gave them that information.

Shortly before *Hawthorne Enterprise* left St. Kitts for Guadeloupe, it took on a female passenger. Mr. Guishard, the harbor pilot, who took Mr. Wynter and the lady to the ship, confirmed that. In a public meeting during the height of *the Christena* controversy (November, 1970), government politician Lee Moore reportedly indicated that the lady gave the *Hawthorne Enterprise* as her St. Kitts address to immigration officials when she landed at Golden Rock Airport. When Moore was interviewed in May 1999, he said he could not recall the details of that matter. According to other reports the lady came to St. Kitts from Guadeloupe, via Antigua. It appeared that some prearrangement had been made for the lady to meet Captain Wynter and the *Hawthorne Enterprise* at St. Kitts. Thus, on the afternoon of August 1, 1970, the harbor pilot, Joshua Guishard, took Captain Wynter and a female passenger to the *Hawthorne Enterprise*.

Mr. Guishard was still aboard *Hawthorne Enterprise* when *Christena* passed by on its way to Nevis. At that time, the boat's crew was also preparing to sail. When *Christena* passed by, the large crowd aboard was noted by the crew of the *Hawthorne Enterprise*. Consequently, Joshua recalled that the crew's conversation shifted to the heavily loaded ferry. The men told Joshua that they were certain *Christena* could not make the trip across to Nevis safely. Joshua, however, expressed confidence that the two-engined ferry would make the trip to Nevis. Joshua then left the *Hawthorne Enterprise* and went back to his assignment. Shortly after, *Hawthorne Enterprise,* sailed out of Basseterre harbor behind the *Christena*. The ship's departure was delayed because Captain Wynter had gone to pick up a girl-friend from the airport. Also, if members of the crew suggested to Joshua that the ferry could not make the trip safely to Nevis, one would expect that when they left St. Kitts, behind *Christena*, there was no sudden forgetting of its apparent danger.

Since they sailed a short time later, the sinking could have become evident to them right after it happened. Initially, the distance between the routes taken by the ferry and the ship, as they left Basseterre that afternoon, was not very great. It was not surprising then, that the ferry's passengers claimed, *Hawthorne Enterprise* sailed toward them and then veered away as they struggled in the water. Unfortunately, the Inquiry also ignored that factor in the evidence. According to Sonny Skeete, Frank Matthew-Tyson, and others, who were aboard *Sea Hunter 1*, they saw *Hawthorne Enterprise*, and held a conversation with its crew, before it diverted and left the area. Some passengers who saw *Hawthorne Enterprise* turn away from the disaster, stated that the ship also laid-to, briefly, outside the area. Accordingly, it was still in the area, when *Sea Hunter 1*, arrived on the scene. Mr. King also noted that he intended to go toward *Hawthorne Enterprise*, and alert the ship about the sinking. Eventually, however, King chose to stay with the rescue operation. Time was a very important factor in saving as many passengers as possible, that were still alive and struggling in the water.

Meanwhile, if the *Hawthorne Enterprise* was indeed 4 miles away, as King later testified at the Inquiry, it is doubtful whether he would have seriously considered, even for a moment, help from the *Hawthorne Enterprise* as an option at that time. The ship was also moving away from the scene of the accident. Skeete did testify that the conversation between the crews of *Sea Hunter 1* and *Hawthorne Enterprise*, became unpleasant. When the men aboard *Sea Hunter 1*, explained what happened to *Christena*, the crew on the larger ship asked questions about the water's depth. That was a fair question. Skeete, at that time in command of *Sea Hunter 1*, stated: "I explained that I knew the area and offered to pilot *Hawthorne Enterprise* in, so that it could assist with the rescue." However, according to Skeete, the men on *Hawthorne Enterprise*, rejected his offer.

Skeete testified that someone on the ship emphasized that it was on a tight schedule to Guadeloupe. Seemingly, Skeete became angry and was involved in a heated exchange that involved the use of foul language between the crews, when the *Hawthorne Enterprise's* response to the disaster continued to be nonchalant and negative. After all was done, and no assistance was forthcoming from *Hawthorne Enterprise, Sea Hunter 1,* stayed with the rescue mission. *Hawthorne Enterprise,* left the area. Thus, a small boat was saddled with a very large challenge to rescue desperate, dying people, from a calm, but forever hungry sea.

Maybe the gravity of the matter escaped Mr. Renwick in 1970. But looking back at the situation today, the case does seem to beg the question, why would a sea captain make a decision to keep a schedule, when almost 350 human beings were struggling and dying in the water nearby? Further, there is a seamen's code of honor that one should rescue others at sea, and save lives in danger! The question remains, What made Mr. Renwick conclude, so readily, that Mr. Wynter was telling truth, but not Mr. Skeete? Another question that should have been asked was, Who had more at stake in the charge that *Hawthorne Enterprise* ignored a call for help from the *Sea Hunter 1*? Was it the men aboard *Hawthorne Enterprise* or was it the men aboard *Sea Hunter 1, who were doing everything to save lives?* If somebody lied, there should be a motive, and a good one, too.

Frank Matthew-Tyson was at the helm of *Christena* when it sank. But Frank did not cause the sinking. Further, after he was rescued, Tyson probably did more than any of the others who were aboard *Christena,* to assist passengers in distress. Frank did not need a scapegoat for *Christena.* Further, he did not know *Hawthorne Enterprise,* was about to leave St. Kitts behind *Christena.* Why would Frank create a story about seeing *Hawthorne Enterprise,* while he and others in the sea were trying desperately to save their lives? Sonny Skeete's only involvement with the disaster was to rescue people from the sea. He did not know Captain Wynter or anyone aboard *Hawthorne Enterprise.* Why would Skeete lie about the conversations shared between the two boats? He is a Nevisian, but his interest was in saving people from the sea, not in slandering Captain Wynter.

Obviously, the attitude of those aboard *Hawthorne Enterprise,* toward the disaster, disappointed Skeete. Men who live by the sea do not respond in that way to a disaster at sea. Were the men on that ship not showing disregard for all Nevisian and Kittitians? Obviously, Bradshaw, Lee Moore, and many others thought so. The leaders of the PAM party did not. They saw a political opportunity and openly befriended Captain Wynter, supporting him against the government and all those St. Kitts-Nevis citizens who claimed he left them in the water. The Inquiry attempted to settle the matter, but it was left embroiled in conflicting testimonies, and some obvious biases that favored Captain Wynter. The inquiry should not have been conducted by one person—it left more questions than answers.

Charles Moore and the crew of *Sea Hunter 1,* stated they had requested assistance with the rescue operation from the *Hawthorne Enterprise.* Captain Wynter, of the *Hawthorne Enterprise* denied this contact was ever made. From Commissioner Renwick's point of view, it was unthinkable that a man of the sea would turn his back on a vessel in trouble. According to Skeete, Tyson, Moore, and others caught in the tragedy, it was the inaction and nonchalance of the captain and crew, in view of the horrific circumstances, that angered them. However, from the evidence available at the time, the Commissioner could not accept that a seasoned seaman would have refused to give assistance to the *Christena* in its situation. But, the Inquiry never delved into a number of the related issues which were revealed later to the public. Mr. Renwick showed clearly that he was more accepting to the testimony of Wynter, over that of Skeete and all the other Kittitians and Nevisians who claimed they saw *Hawthorne Enterprise,* in the vicinity of the *Christena* accident.

Personal Issues

The Inquiry never asked a number of critical questions that were relevant to the *Hawthorne Enterprise* matter. If the Commissioner did additional probing, probably more light could have been thrown on the situation. Who was the woman Joshua took aboard with Captain Wynter just before the *Hawthorne Enterprise* sailed? What was the relationship between Captain Wynter and that female passenger? Was the captain involved in the discussion at the height of the crisis? Finally, another question to be asked would be, how did having that woman aboard affect the behaviors of the men on the *Hawthorne Enterprise?*

One critical factor ignored was the fact that if the *Hawthorne Enterprise went* to assist with the rescue, its schedule to Martinique would have been disrupted by days. After the rescue action, Wynter and his crew would probably have been required to give the government an official report of their role in the disaster. It was suggested later that the possibility of delay in the ship's arrival in Martinique amplified the possibility of the mystery lady on board the *Hawthorne Enterprise,* arriving home a day or two later than her husband, who had travelled abroad. Actually, the operation to rescue passengers and recover dead bodies from the sea took until the Tuesday, after the accident. Reportedly the woman had to be home by Sunday. Her husband was expected home on Monday.

Another factor that should have been accounted for, was that if Wynter was found guilty, his captain's license would have been in trouble. Meanwhile, Bradshaw needed a scapegoat. And, unlike Renwick, he was committed to believing the reports given by the citizens of St. Kitts-Nevis. Bradshaw did move to ban both Captain Wynter and the *Hawthorne Enterprise* from St. Kitts. He also threatened to report Wynter's action to shipping authorities in England, the Cayman Islands, and elsewhere. There is little doubt that Bradshaw kept his promise. He was a man who did what he said. Wynter, meanwhile, was committed to protecting himself and his career as a sea captain. If the evidence was conclusive and showed *Hawthorne Enterprise's,* captain and crew refused to help in rescuing survivors from the *Christena*, no one would have held much respect for them in the future. The ship's agent, Wynter, the Commissioner, and all those who took the captain's side in the matter knew this. Again, the hidden question

that can now be asked, in retrospect, is, What was the role of the
Caribbean's lodges, in the manner that matter ended?

Testimony of the Passengers

The latest count suggests that about ninety-nine people
survived *Christena,* yet fewer than one third of them gave
evidence to the Commission of Inquiry. Most of the evidence
came from secondary sources, Why did so few survivors testify at
the hearings? There were more than one possible reason. In the
short time between the accident and the hearings, many survivors
could not bear to relive that experience they barely survived. A
number of survivors had already moved to live away from St.
Kitts-Nevis. And, because of the rancor in the islands' politics,
there were people who were afraid and did not want to be involved,
particularly in appearing to be critical of the government. Some
of the people were also intimidated by the official and legal
settings. Then, there were passengers who merely saw the sinking
as the "Will of God"; there was therefore nothing to talk about.
Meanwhile, others concluded that government's negligence had
brought on the disaster. In that case, the Commission of Inquiry
could have been designed to be a show. Nothing significant was
expected to come from it. Eventually, many of the conclusive
statements were based on second-hand information. Some
people also reasoned the hearing was a waste of time. Those were
some of the factors that prevented eyewitnesses to the disaster
from testifying. Ultimately, the fact that only a limited number
of people who saw the sinking testified at the Inquiry must have
affected the findings. Accordingly, on certain crucial issues related
to the sinking, conclusions were drawn, based only on unreliable
second-hand information.

Disaster Funds

Various rumors circulated in St. Kitts-Nevis and many questions were asked about the money received to aid victims of the disaster. Money was distributed and a number of people received some measure of assistance. But, the general population disagreed with the manner in which the government agency handled the funds. It is still felt that a large portion of the money received did not reach people who had the greatest need. Three groups on St. Kitts-Nevis supervised distribution of the funds. Two were set up on Nevis and one on St. Kitts. Two groups were locked into the government, one each on St. Kitts and Nevis. The third group was privately organized on Nevis. The Government's organization was called the *Christena* Disaster Fund. The private one on Nevis was the Nevis Churches *Christena* Disaster Fund Committee. The two committees collected well over two hundred thousand dollars between them. However, even that amount was small, when compared to the extent of the need in society for financial assistance. Many people who needed aid got nothing.

The private funds on Nevis were managed by Mr. Spencer Byron, Fr. Edgar Blant, of the Anglican Church, John Esdaille, From the Wesleyan Holiness Church, Rev. Robert Cutberth, of the Methodist Church, and Rev. Simmonds from Emaus Chapel. Lawyer, Maurice Davis, on St. Kitts, and banker D. R. Walwyn on Nevis, were the chief managers of the government's funds. Each of these men had other persons working with him as assistants. The private group on Nevis kept accurate records of the funds received and distributed. In 1982, there was a balance of $535.78 on their records, and they still functioned. On the other hand, the main group set up by government handled its responsibility poorly. It did not keep the people informed about its activities. No running account was kept of the monies collected or distributed. The final disbursement from the government-managed account was made in 1981. Some time before that disbursement was made, a financial statement was tabled in the House of Assembly. However, the members of government did not discuss the matter.

There were rumors of mismanagement in handling the government-controlled funds, but nothing was ever made clear to the general public. The people were left groping in the dark for answers to their questions. Very little information was provided for them to go on. Today, it is hardly a wonder that the passage of time has not removed certain questions about mismanagement and misuse of those funds. There are Kittitians and Nevisians who remain skeptical about how that money collected by the government was spent. They continue to doubt whether the government-controlled funds, especially on St. Kitts, were handled with forthrightness and used to benefit the families who needed the most help. However, suggestions that Mr. Bradshaw kept portions of the *Christena* Disaster Fund, for himself, did not fit what the man stood for. Particularly under the circumstances of death from such a tragic event in St. Kitts-Nevis, Robert L. Bradshaw would not have stooped that low to steal from the money being collected. He was too proud, honest, and dignified a Caribbean leader to steal money from the dead and their families. While Bradshaw was ruthless as a politician, he was noble, as a human being. He actually cried with Nevisians over their losses. Notwithstanding, in view of the situation at hand, a shadow was cast on the forthrightness of the government. It failed in the manner by which the *Christena* money was managed. And, the society was not kept informed. Too many questions were left unanswered—probably an issue at the time, related to colonialism and false consciousness. Another factor at play in the matter was the politics. The opposition parties in both St. Kitts and Nevis, PAM and NRP, respectively, used every tactic available to criticize and destabilize Bradshaw's government. Even when it was baseless, an attack on Bradshaw's dignity, as a leader, was considered good politics for them. The truth in a matter, or its negative impact on the society, were often not considered by the politicians. All was fair in the war to control the hearts, minds, and votes of the masses.

Behavior of the Victims

The afternoon of the tragedy saw some cooperation among the terrified and distressed passengers, but seemingly selfishness dominated in a number of situations where cooperation was needed. Many of the former passengers found themselves abandoned in the water, and face to face with death. Scores of such people died in their hopeless struggle to live. Why did so many desperate passengers, struggling in the sea, experience such low levels of cooperation? Why did some passengers who could have helped others act with such cruelty to persons they knew, in some cases, even friends and family who were in distress?

The initial reaction of all the passengers to *Christena's* sinking was shock and fear. High levels of desperation and stress prevailed everywhere. It was a very frightening and uncomfortable situation, being thrown into the sea so suddenly. One can imagine the terror of those who could not swim. Most of the people there had very little experience in how to react under such stressful circumstances. They found it difficult to think clearly or to act constructively. It was a terror-laden situation riddled with chaos. Cooperation was scarce, except in a few cases. There were the three nuns who were seen holding hands, and supposedly died together. A herculean effort was made by a number of people to help Livinstone Sargeant and Ian Kelsick toward Nags Head. Franklyn Browne found his son, then swam along with his son and another boy until they were rescued. Then, there was that heroic effort by Dulcita David who shared her floating crocus-bag containing five breadfruit, with Edna Browne, and helped her survive, until they were both picked up. Meanwhile, the selfish and at times irrational acts included the actions of people who never swam a long distance before. On finding themselves in the water they started to swim for land, just about a mile away, as fast as they could go. Unfortunately, many of them could not keep the pace and faded in less than 15 minutes. Even for a seasoned swimmer, such a swim under the existing conditions could take more than an hour.

Many people who became distressed and desperate at the sinking, showed the worse side of themselves. They did anything necessary to survive. One survivor reported that she was advised to let others die while she concerned herself only with her own safety. One young man noted later that in the height of the confusion he struck a girl on the head, so that he could get the crate on which she floated. Then, there was the man who indicated he intended to be selfish by sticking a knife in the log on which he rode. The protruding knife signaled he was in no mood to share his sanctuary with anyone else. Thus, there were people who acted both foolishly and selfishly. They thought that more passengers could be saved if each person took care of himself or herself, only. Such persons refused to give any assistance even when they could have done so with no threat to their safety. At the same time, some people were afraid of being held, and drowned by others who could not swim, and were struggling desperately in the water.

Since many of the people in the water lacked the knowledge of proper water rescue skills, double drowning became a realistic possibility. To reduce that danger, some survivors simply avoided any contact whatsoever with others struggling in the water. They did not intend to be cruel. It was simply a strategy for self preservation. Today, we can look back and criticize or commend the actions of that group of desperate passengers struggling in the water, face to face with imminent death. While some of the actions were rational, other actions seemed far from that. Ironically, were we in the same situation of desperation, in retrospect today, no one is really certain about which group of those actors, he or she, would have been found.

Whitman T. Browne, Ph.D.

Resurfacing The Christena

And now, the question, Why didn't the government refloat *Christena*? Only 20 meters of water cover the infamous ferry, and many divers have found the area an easy dive. However, there are many reasons why the *Christena* was not refloated. The government would have to import labor and equipment at a cost to refloat *Christena*. It would not have been worth the effort, in an attempt to use the ferry again for transportation between St. Kitts and Nevis. After the sinking, with so many persons having lost their lives, because they were trapped onboard, few Nevisians or Kittitians would have relished traveling on *Christena* again. They would see it as, "The boat of the dead." Further, the societies are much too superstitious to sail comfortably in a boat where so many persons died. Then, a recovery of such large number of dead bodies that were trapped aboard could also have caused the crisis in society to be prolonged. Tears would flow again and anger reignited too, if *Christena* were refloated. At the same time, the government would be providing an added cause for confrontations and arguments about compensation—matters the Government wanted to avoid at all costs.

Maybe someone would have bought *Christena* for scrap iron, or for other sentimental reasons. However, the money made from the sale could not have paid for the physical or emotional cost of *Christena's* loss to the people in St. Kitts and Nevis. There were also those who might have called such money, "blood money." No matter the reason, the refloating of *Christena*, in the 1970s or 1980s, would not have delighted or excited many people in the islands. Such a move would not have had positive meaning for the society. It would not appeal to the people of St. Kitts-Nevis today either.

Despite the time distance, even now, more than forty years since it occurred, the memories of the incident are still painful and devastating to a number of families in St. Kitts-Nevis. It is still the case that very little prodding is needed to bring back memories of that 1970 horror in St. Kitts-Nevis. Even younger Nevisians and Kittitians who did not experience that drama, can learn to envision and appreciate its impact on the islands.

Undoubtedly, there are other perspectives on the questions and answers presented here. The concern is with the fact that the government and the Commission of Inquiry, authorized by the government, left many of these questions unanswered. Meanwhile, a still dazed and very gullible society sat back, and seemed quite satisfied with inadequate answers. In some instances, the questions asked received no answers at all. Maybe, if demands were made of the authorities with persistence, more meaningful answers could have been found. Blame for the disaster would have also been laid somewhere. And the power of the people would have been demonstrated to the government, and to politicians aspiring to lead. Meanwhile, such failures of justice in colonial societies do speak to the pervasiveness of the citizens' entrapment in false consciousness.

They failed to use all the opportunities afforded by the disaster, to assert themselves as one people. At that time, Nevisians and Kittitians failed to capitalize on the power of their united influence, and demanded from the government that their voices be heard. The people also allowed certain vested interests in St. Kitts and Nevis to use their organizational affiliations to manipulate the right of a people to find the truth, and to know all about the incident. Today, Kittitians and Nevisians still suffer because of that mistake. If everyone, government and people, grasped the opportunities to sue for real system changes, after the *Christena* tragedy, the relationship and trust between the government on St. Kitts and the people of Nevis, could have developed more rapidly.

St. Kitts-Nevis Rivalry

It was not a surprise to many: *Christena's* sinking intensified the animosity on Nevis for St. Kitts politicians. As early as the

---

1960s, Nevisians and Anguillans, had been very angry and dissatisfied with their subservient relationship and a consistent domination from St. Kitts. The evolution of the labor union and the Labor Party on St. Kitts, was a response to the earlier plantations' control, and planters' dictatorship on the island. Meanwhile, that plantation system had withered and died in Anguilla and Nevis. Accordingly, the idea of labor unionism dictating the way forward on Nevis and Anguilla met with much resentment. But, St. Kitts politicians, under the leadership of Comrade Robert Bradshaw, did not accept the obvious cultural and ideological differences, that had evolved among the three people. Neither did they consider how such differences can impact political aspirations.

There were repeated protests on Nevis over the ideological and political dictatorship from St. Kitts politicians. Eventually, the Anguillans went beyond protests. They rebelled against St. Kitts-Nevis and moved to disrupt the government, by allegedly attempting to kidnap Robert Bradshaw, on June 10, 1967. Nevisians did not go as far as the Anguillans, but they too were angry, felt alienated, and wanted to follow the path of rebellion ignited by the Anguillans. For a number of years, the government on St. Kitts was very concerned about the break-away of Nevis, or any action similar to what had taken place on Anguilla.

At that time, another important matter being contemplated on Nevis was the creation of Nevis' own political party. There was growing refusal to accept the Labor Party as a political party for Nevis. After *Christena's* sinking killed so many Nevisians, the people on the island became more disgusted with the idea of being subjected to leadership from St. Kitts. They wanted separation and their own political party, with Nevis-based leadership and more. Actually, they went back to that old call for secession, initiated back in 1882—a matter that always brings Nevisians together, against St. Kitts. Further, immediately after the ferry sank, the discontent on the island made it easy to organize Nevisians. Just about three months following the ferry's sinking, Nevisians rallied, organized, and created the Nevis Reformation Party (NRP).

Right from its inception, the NRP made secession from St. Kitts its rallying cry. The leaders held that Nevis politics is for Nevisians to manage, and took issue with both the Labor Party and the new party on St. Kitts, the People's Action Movement (PAM). Both St. Kitts-based political parties had some following in Nevis. Back then, the leadership of both parties on St. Kitts saw Nevis and Anguilla as colonies, and St. Kitts as the dominant partner. With the coming of the NRP, however, Nevisians moved to end that perceived relationship with St. Kitts. The animosity over the loss of lives from *Christena* and the antagonism that evolved with the coming of a new breed of Nevis politicians, all came together in the NRP. Suddenly, Nevisians were energized politically, ideologically, and in their determination to be independent from St. Kitts. Throughout the 1970s, most Nevisians supported the NRP, its anti-St. Kitts actions and pronouncements. In a referendum held in 1977, almost 100% of the Nevisians who voted, did cast a vote in favor of their island's secession from St. Kitts. During the entire 1970s there were times when the two islands barely avoided bloody physical battles. And, throughout that period, the *Christena* incident and secession for Nevis were always factors woven into the fray. Lee Moore, a politician from St. Kitts, spoke repeatedly about the rancor he sensed in Nevis when he visited. Unfortunately, the report by Mr. Renwick left many people dissatisfied. No one was blamed. There was no compulsory compensation. And, the subtle politics in the matter seemed obvious. Some of the concluding statements also appeared designed to placate the wounded and hurting people. Accordingly, that report about the sinking offered Nevisians little comfort. There was little in it to assuage the pain from the great loss, or to relieve the bewilderment that overwhelmed the people on the islands.

CHAPTER ELEVEN

Riding Out the Storm

One haunting dilemma for human societies is the continuous presence of death. It is always in the shadows or somewhere—waiting. Sometimes the visits of death are expected. Strange as it may seem, there are people who wait to die. At other times, as in the case with the *Christena*, death's visits occur unexpectedly. Many people on the two islands were caught up in the *Christena* drama. Some became emotionally disoriented due to the sudden loss of one, two, or more members of the same family. In a number of cases, the dead person was the chief provider for a family. At a time when they were not prepared for such drastic changes, Nevisians and Kittitians, people accustomed to sunshine, little rain, and not much to worry about in their lives, found themselves facing a sudden devastating tumult—more in the order of a thunderstorm.

There were six important factors that came together and aided in the survival of society in St. Kitts-Nevis. These things kept Kittitians and Nevisians sane and hopeful beyond *Christena*. They were (a) the islands' historic emigration linkages; (b) the eventual acceptance of the physical reality of the tragedy; (c) one's inherent capacity to respond psychologically to experiences;

(d) the concern of philanthropists; (e) the human will to survive dramatic events in their lives; and (f) the islanders' belief in God.

Emigration Linkages

For many years after the abolition of slavery in 1838, Kittitians and Nevisians have migrated within the Caribbean and to other parts of the world. They can be found in Europe, North America and countries such as Panama in Central America. Because of how they were socialized, and the knowledge about what it took to survive on the islands, there were also long-term family commitments. Many people who migrated maintained social, physical, and economic links with their birthplaces. These they did through monetary gifts, occasional visits, and at times providing political voice for the islands. That was the case during the time of the Harlem Renaissance, at the vibrancy of Pan Africanism, and in the early years of labor unionism. For some, the connection happened intermittently, but particularly during times of special events—accidents such as the *Christena,* at carnival, at Culturama, during ceremonies such as Carifesta, and more.

When the *Christena* sank, many Kittitian and Nevisian families were left in social and economic disarray. To such people, families, and friends who migrated, became a source of emotional and financial support. Also, some of the family links that were broken or had become rusted were mended. In time, many old linkages between the islands and their migrants became revitalized, as a result of the disaster. There were also struggling people in great need, who found friends and family they never knew before. By the time news of the accident spread throughout the world, many people with family and friends on Nevis or St. Kitts reacted with fear, shock, and great concern. They knew the *Christena.* They knew the general area where the tragedy occurred. And, some knew a number of the people who died there.

In a very short time, interested people and the government, created information networks to span time and space across the

Whitman T. Browne, Ph.D.

world. Telephone calls and telegrams reached across the Atlantic, linking Europe, Africa, and the Americas with St. Kitts-Nevis. Whether the news was just sad or totally unbearable, people wanted to know more—even though there was very little good news. There was desperation for details. Even as the sad stories kept coming, the expatriates mobilized for action. Committees were formed to collect money, clothing, and food. Some people wanted to go home to their families and help, or simply to be there, to see things for themselves. Eventually, thousands of pounds from England, dollars from the U.S., Canada and throughout the Caribbean, were sent to St. Kitts-Nevis, from families, friends, and well-wishers. Some people went further. They made arrangements and helped some of the people left in despair emigrate, so that they could start again elsewhere. It was almost a psychological imperative that some of the survivors begin a new living experience, some place away from the disaster area. Its impact had crippled the societies in both St. Kitts and Nevis, at least temporarily. In a way, it was that global solidarity with friends and families that proved a useful buffer to counter some of the physical and emotional disruption on the islands, after the disaster. Caribbean family networks around the world became a powerful and useful vehicle to provide emotional and physical support.

The majority of Caribbean families during the 1960s and 1970s were still, in some measure, extended families. Emigration from this family setting, tended toward stronger family bonds and an unusual commitment to sharing and caring. It did not matter the physical distance between the members. Even today, this peculiar bonding continues to have an important impact on the area's economic survival and demographic shifts.

In 1970, it was virtually unthinkable for Nevisians and Kittitians abroad not to come to the aid of their families, back on the islands, particularly at a time when they were in distress. For many of the expatriates, coming to the aid of their distressed families back home was considered a critical commitment and an important responsibility. Further, for many Caribbean people, family does matter greatly. It is a blood contract. The findings of the late social anthropologist, Richard Frucht, support this argument. The anthropologist noted that throughout the 1960s, Nevisians abroad made a critical financial contribution to the economic and physical survival of their island. There were also times during the 1960s and 1970s when the financial contribution to the island from family abroad surpassed the island's GNP. That connection with their migrants remained an important factor for the islands, as they moved beyond the accident and its aftermath.

The Psychological Impact

Generally, the reality of the *Christena* disaster had two different impacts on Nevisians and Kittitians. Some people were so emotionally paralyzed by the tragedy that they used avoidance as a strategy. At the same time, other persons sharing that common situation sought to maintain their grip on the reality. They developed an existential approach to the disaster, and it aided their will to survive. For example, as Charles Freeman came face to face with his reality, he depicted behaviors that were both existentialistic and altruistic.

During the early weeks and months following the tragedy, Kittitians and Nevisians were dazed and wounded by the experience. But, one's ability to rationalize such a situation, so that the stress was lessened, did come into play. Some of them had great difficulty coping with the shock, the loss, or their prospects for the future. Consequently, a variety of approaches in the move ahead had to be found. There were irrational thoughts, including illusions about reality, as many persons wrapped themselves in protective cocoons to shield themselves from the horror of their existence. In some situations, the desire for avoidance was so great that not even time has changed that painful reality for many such individuals. For some, their *Christena* experience is still too traumatic to relive and talk about. They simply refuse to discuss their *Christena* experience with anyone.

Three such cases were those of Francis Griffin, Dulcina Wallace, and Annette Lewis. One of the saddest cases of avoidance is that of Annette Lewis, a very beautiful Nevisian woman. She lives at Mount Lily. Her husband Calvin Lewis was returning to Nevis on *Christena*. Neither Annette nor anyone else has seen him since. Suddenly, this woman's normal life ended. At one time Annette had a severe struggle dealing with the reality of her situation. She was seen frequently in different areas of Nevis, acting and doing things others labeled abnormal. Today Annette Lewis is still a strikingly beautiful woman, but her mind now seems to focus on a different world with a different reality, from the one in which she once lived, loved, and shared with her family.

If fairy tales or wishes became reality, maybe her husband would have appeared, kissed Annette, then she would wake from her world of different images and a different music. During an interview in 1998, Annette appeared to be coping better with her reality. However, not everyone chose to avoid the *Christena* fall-out. In a "free" society, such a situation would be unthinkable. Ironically, those who chose avoidance might have come through the experience emotionally damaged, but relatively sound physically. For such persons it was a no-win situation. Everyone who was close to the *Christena* disaster and survived the experience lost something, particularly the younger victims. Unfortunately, the total dimension of that loss may still be a mystery. No one has really bothered to find out all about it. St. Kitts-Nevis societies still do a poor job at nurturing and healing, when it comes to the matter of mental health.

Assistance

St. Kitts and Nevis are small societies with limited resources. They could not have rebounded from the devastation caused by *Christena's* sinking, at the rate they did, without assistance from people throughout the world. As Nevisians and Kittitians groped uncertainly in their time of deep despair, other people empathized with them. The willingness to give aid did not depend only on blood relationship. It also came because of that shared human connectedness, and in response to the fact that the citizenry was in need of both emotional and material support.

When the call went forth, philanthropists in Canada, the U.S.A., England, the Caribbean, and other areas of the world, many persons without any connection to anyone in the Caribbean, did what they could to ease the pain left by the disaster. Thousands of dollars were sent to the government or to private groups on St. Kitts and Nevis. Many of the people who donated money had never visited the Caribbean; neither did they know anyone in St. Kitts-Nevis. What such persons knew was that people were in need. That was what mattered.

The citizens in the islands can hardly look back, since August 1970, without recognizing the role of philanthropy in the societies' revival. Many children left without parents needed food and clothing. Others were unable to attend school or to manage normal daily living without some form of assistance. There were cases where close families took in relatives who needed homes and someone to care for them. In cases where comfortable living depended on an increase in available physical space, some of the donated money was used to ensure that it was attained. More often than not, there was need for money to meet new demands suddenly forced on the limited resources of the societies. The government did not have access to such resources, and even the help from families abroad was not enough to meet all the demands, without added assistance. All the donations by philanthropists were welcomed. They went a long way in ensuring civility, sanity, and survival on the islands. They contributed greatly to a lessening of the disaster's impact on the lives of Nevisians and Kittitians.

Yet, as with numerous situations surrounding the *Christena* incident, the exact role of the philanthropists still has to be determined. Almost everyone heard about the large sums received in St. Kitts-Nevis to aid victims of the disaster. However, very few people understood how that aid was distributed or how it contributed to a lessening of survival stress in their societies. An inefficient bureaucracy, particularly on St. Kitts, did affect the flow of aid to needy persons. Twenty-eight years after the tragedy, there was Edna Browne of Jessup Village, for example; she was still in need of aid, but got none. Meanwhile, sad to say, there were other people who lied about their losses to get extra aid, and in some cases they got it. In retrospect, without gifts from people who agonized with, and about those others in distress, most people of St. Kitts-Nevis would have struggled much longer to achieve order in their lives, after the *Christena* experience. Ultimately, despite the thousands of dollars sent to the islands, there were additional needs. Other home-grown strategies had to be devised, woven in, and used as part of the long-term healing process.

God's Will

Most Nevisians and Kittitians acknowledge some measure of belief or degree of association with the Christian religion. Historically Christianity has been used and manipulated in many dimensions of life on St. Kitts-Nevis. Consequently, in 1970, God, like witchcraft and politics, had to be woven into the tragedy. To some Nevisians and Kittitians, the disaster became acceptable because it was "a warning from God." He was using it to reprimand the people of St. Kitts-Nevis and to warn them about their sinfulness. A time close to August Monday could not be better for such a warning. It is a time when citizens of St. Kitts-Nevis and other Caribbean islands celebrate with abandon. Usually, as they do so, they push God away from their lives and activities. Besides this passive fatalistic notion accepted by certain people on both islands, there was another view about God's role in the matter. An Anglican priest suggested to a mass gathering on Nevis, Sunday, August 2, that the *Christena's* sinking was not God's will. Fr. Eke could not see a loving God deliberately participating in such an act of sudden mass death. To him, the best explanation for the tragedy was human error. Eventually, Fr. Eke's "not God's will" statement took on ugly political dimensions. According to reports, he was banned by the government from working in St. Kitts-Nevis. While the government was seeking absolution from the matter, Fr. Eke's statement was a subtle attempt to direct blame at mismanagement by the government.

However, perceptions of God and Christianity also served distressed Kittitians and Nevisians in another way. The teachings of Christianity promise the thousands of Nevisians and Kittitians that God will deliver them in their distress. Such people were convinced that through prayers, confessions, and contriteness, God will succor them. According to their Bible, God delivered Shadrach, Meshach, and Abednego. He also comforted the relatives of Lazarus. Over and over, the victims and their relatives were admonished to put their whole trust in God, expecting deliverance. Brother, Charles Freeman, who lost his wife, spoke of the comfort and hope he found when he read Psalm 46. Many persons were seeking any help. Everyone struggled with a disruptive present, and a fearful, uncertain future. Initially, throughout the two islands, many prayers and memorial services were held. For some people, August 1, became a special day for prayers and fasting, because of the pain from the *Christena*. However, some healing did come with time. The pain decreased, then the special sessions of prayer and fasting stopped. Notwithstanding, over the years, hundreds of Kittitians and Nevisians agreed that they moved closer to religion and God after the *Christena* disaster.

There was a yearning for supernatural deliverance from such a traumatic experience in the islands. Both history and culture, as Nevisians and Kittitians know them, have suggested that deliverance from such trauma is beyond human control. They were taught that God alone, through His son Jesus, could bring peace and tranquility back to their lives; and the people believed. To many victims, help and recovery came in miraculous ways. God honored their trust and prayers. If a survey were done to ascertain what gave Nevisians and Kittitians most help through the *Christena* experience, the conclusion would be God and religion.

Any suggestion that religion and the associated rituals only serve as placebos would be sacrilegious in St. Kitts-Nevis. Their God is known to provide the deliverance He promised—and He did. To think or to suggest otherwise would be unnatural. After all, God gave guidance and protection beyond the disaster. He also brought healing to their lives.

Human Will

Another factor on which survival beyond the *Christena* disaster depended, is the human being's innate will to innovate, change, and survive the stresses of life. Once the "will" factor was accepted as a strategy, there was hardly a recognition of buffers to stress and pain. Deliberately planned moves were made to counter the disaster and its effects. Clifford Browne, Arrington Browne, and Frayco Weekes, went back to the sea despite their ordeal with *Christena*. Daring and innovation counted. Eventually, the two societies felt the need to change and the challenge to innovate for survival. However, no change comes easily. Those who died in the disaster were the islands' sacrifice for political, economic, and social changes. They are their "lost generation." Other individuals also sacrificed and served as agents of change during that difficult time. They did not lose their lives, but the disaster took a physical and emotional toll on them. Only in time were such persons appreciated as catalysts for change and renewal in St. Kitts-Nevis. After all, it was emotionally difficult for Kittitians and Nevisians to move on, live "normally" and forget their losses after *Christena*. Existence under such a stressful condition was always a challenge. At times, hunger struck adults and children alike. Because of the disaster, some the old patterns of living, on the islands, eventually died too.

The *Christena* disaster was more than a dramatic and painful event in St. Kitts-Nevis history. It was also a precursor to a number of profound economic, social and political changes on both islands. In time, some of the changes did place new demands on the societies. Thus, in themselves, the changes became new challenges beyond the disaster. However, strategies for innovation and reconstruction did evolve in both St. Kitts and Nevis after *Christena*. How effectively those strategies were harnessed for good, may be a matter for time and historians to determine. At first the survival strategies came slowly, probably because of the nature of dependency promoted by colonialism. However, since the situation at hand was unprecedented in the islands' recent history, neither Nevisians nor Kittitians had a model to keep before them, while they attempted to bounce back from the horror and the loss, which came to the islands, because of the *Christena* tragedy.

All through the experience, a colonial Government, inexperienced in disaster management, groped along, using trial and error to inform its decisions. Ultimately, though, some survival strategies were found. The people did move on. Despite the disillusionment that came and permeated the societies. And, despite the long, lingering, aftermath of the event. However, the disaster and its aftermath bred such mistrust that the islands' unity was further threatened. To many people, the government's neglect of its oversight responsibilities led to the disaster.

The Labor Party was concerned that opposition politicians on both islands were seizing every opportunity to lead citizens away from supporting the positions of the government. However, despite all the perceived uncertainty and the confusion in 1970, the government's machine and organization held together. Amidst all the uncertainty, some citizens did find the fortitude that helped to buoy them and provide hope to their lives, beyond that tragedy. Eventually, change and gradual stability came to the society. Over time, too, both change and the growing stability were legitimized by the two sides—the people and the government. Some of the economic and financial assistance that came to St. Kitts-Nevis was from one government to the other. But a great deal was from ordinary people whose hearts were touched by the tragedy.

The government and the churches were the organizations with the structure and staffing to reach out and distribute the aid to Nevisians and Kittitians who needed help. In a number of instances, when the aid programs did not reach some villagers, neighbors and friends had compassion and gave help. In cases where children were left without responsible adults as guardians, the oldest sibling, or other adults in the community, took on the roles of overseers, role models, and providers. A once vibrant Afro-Caribbean tradition in the area, the idea of common ground and community togetherness found meaning again. Nevisians and Kittitians were caught up and united in struggle. This was coupled with a determination to survive, despite overwhelming odds. Unfortunately, such a community spirit on the islands has not survived the disruptive influence of cultural exchanges, migration, and the powerful influence of foreign mass media in the area. Notwithstanding, that desire and commitment to family and community bonding was once a useful residual of African culture that some Caribbean societies sought to emulate and preserve. Two distressed Caribbean societies, St. Kitts and Nevis, were severely burdened by their losses. However, while they were pained by its reality, many remained sane enough to grapple with the ideas of change and survival. Some also became hopeful and reflective enough to find renewal and change, to reach beyond what at one time for them seemed to be destiny.

It is now a common experience in the Caribbean, as elsewhere in the world. The Christian sects on St. Kitts-Nevis talk more Christianity than they demonstrate. Yet, the emotionalism, the terror of the present, and the power of hope in the future, keep the promises of Christianity attractive to a people grounded in spirituality, but victimized by their historical experiences. After the disaster, Christian churches on the islands had every opportunity to be good Samaritans, and some did act the part. Church leaders in the Anglican, Methodist, Wesleyan Holiness, Seventh Day Adventists, Roman Catholic and other Christian sects, took up the challenge and cared for many of the people in distress. It was a challenge that provided new and rewarding experiences. Through a variety of programs and strategies, they used the trust of the people to demonstrate how caring can be done, at times, by the churches. Many people in distress were visited and comforted by church leaders and church members alike. Food baskets were shared with those who were hungry. And, for a number of years after the disaster, special services in memory of the "dearly departed," were held annually at the churches. At the Gingerland Methodist Church, for example, plaques were erected, bearing the names of church members who died. They can still be seen on the wall.

However, as the churches moved to do their Christian duty, succoring the needy, and more, they also benefited from an increase in membership. Nevisians and Kittitians who interpreted the disaster as an omen went back to church in large numbers. For many citizens, that time in St. Kitts-Nevis became a period for deep soul searching and catharsis. Numerous broken covenants with God were renewed or mended. Thus, during the total crisis, as happened again and again, with Africans in various areas of their Diaspora, the church played an important role in survival and renewal. Many citizens of St. Kitts-Nevis found in their church organization the type of emotional and other support they needed to buoy them, as they moved through troubled times. It was not abnormal that the political leaders also bought into that religious fervor. Bradshaw, Southwell, Bryant and even the acting Governor Milton P. Allen made speeches filled with solemn, religious pronouncements. They too read the times and resorted to a politics of prayer and praise. This was not unusual since religion is such a commonly shared Caribbean experience. Thus, leaders in the political sphere, use religion frequently, in their search for common ground, on which to meet people in distress. And, also as stratagem, when on the campaign trail.

Notwithstanding, the praying, the conversions, and the religious renewal did not appeal to everyone. To some Kittitians and Nevisians, the disaster was evidence of a curse on the State and the government, not so much on the individual. Those who thought that way saw the islands' politics as defying the natural laws of justice, freedom, and equality. Particularly on Nevis, where there was greater loss from the sinking, emigration became an avenue to survival, and a strategy by which to elude the perceived curse on St. Kitts-Nevis.

Shortly before he died in 1997, Ivor Stevens reflected on that time. He claimed that the situation on St. Kitts was, "Maneuvered to create further hardship in Nevis." Consequently, the thrust toward emigration continued as the order of the day for Nevisians. In some cases, Nevisians desperate to get off the island almost gave away the little property they possessed, in order that they could raise the money to pay their passages to England. Both those speedy land sales and the massive migrations back in the 1950s, 1960s, and 1970s, continue to impact society and politics on St. Kitts-Nevis today. Meanwhile, some lawyers and politicians have also become embroiled in land grabbing for profit schemes.

Population Movement

By the time the 1970s came along, both Nevis and St. Kitts were experiencing waves of population movement. Some of it was an immediate response to *Christena's* sinking, however, much of the population shift that came later was related to politics, economics, and the growing consciousness raising that came about as a response to the effects of the *Christena* disaster on the State. Meanwhile, during the 1970s, England no longer practiced a liberal policy on Caribbean immigration. There was a growing tendency toward limiting immigrants from the colonies to England. At the same time, the fact that St. Kitts-Nevis was still a colony of England became a negative factor impacting U.S. immigration policy to the islands. Consequently, St. Maarten, Canada, Tortola, Puerto Rico, and the U.S. Virgin Islands became popular destinations for migrants from St. Kitts, Nevis. At times, even smaller islands, such as Saba and St. Eustatius came to be viewed by some Nevisians and Kittitians as more attractive places to live than St. Kitts or Nevis. Often, the immigration policies of the islands did not matter. Young people on St. Kitts-Nevis who felt trapped and who saw survival only beyond their own islands, found the will to dare. They devised ways and means to make the move away from their homeland. Quite often, as was noted repeatedly in the U.S. Virgin Islands, during the 1960s, and 1970s, a large percentage of that movement was illegal. Today, few if any of the Nevisians and Kittitians who left home during that time appear to have regretted leaving. One major drawback, however, was that these people's concept of the islands' social and political evolution became fossilized. After those citizens left home in the 1970s, particularly if they never took the time to revisit, they did not imagine the islands as evolving beyond what they knew. On their return to the islands to visit, some Kittitians and Nevisians were often shocked at how the islands have changed, and what they have become.

National Consciousness

For many Nevisians who remained at home after the disaster, the experience evoked a new burst of national consciousness. While politicians were rallying citizens' and contending to achieve political goals on Nevis, a number of young citizens, including Calvin (Cabo) Howell, Victor Martin, Lyra Richardson, Irma Thompson, Clifford Griffin, Tyrone O'Flaherty, Joseph Parry and others, channeled their energies into directions that were more artistic and creative. Ironically, that period, marred by death and pain, also became a time of Renaissance and renewal on Nevis.

The impact of a colonizing attitude from St. Kitts toward Nevis left Nevisians an angry people searching for independence. They were also searching for a Nevis identity, different from that of St. Kitts. During the early 1970s, Nevisians were losing appreciation for their cultural and art forms; so many persons had migrated, and the population that remained on the island,

Whitman T. Browne, Ph.D.

was either very young, or aging. In Nevis the sports program was being manipulated and virtually disorganized. There was also the crippling effect of a perceived historic inferiority to the programs on St. Kitts. Thus, a time came when young Nevisians wanted change and renewal, in the island's sports and arts—something different from what they had come to know.

Instead of continuing to have a carnival at Christmastime, an appendage to the celebration on St. Kitts, Nevisians were determined to disassociate themselves from that festival, while they created one to call their own. It was from such reasoning that Culturama was created on Nevis, by 1974. At its inception, the emphasis was on the arts, cultural traditions, and other forms, endemic to Nevis. However, the government on St. Kitts saw Culturama as a challenge to its sovereignty in Nevis, and at one point interfered with its development. In the ensuing struggle for identity and relevance, the Culturama celebration became both a subtle political force, and a powerful vehicle for cultural renewal on Nevis. It also contributed to human survival, and the sanity of some people, in the aftermath of the *Christena* tragedy. At the same time, cricket and net ball, two favorite sports on Nevis were reorganized and reinvigorated. Joseph Walcott Parry was a leader with the cricket thrust, while, Jeanette Grell Hull, was an inspiration to the netball effort on the island. By the late 1970s, Nevis had reinvented its cricket program. The island started to demolish St. Kitts in the sport and emerged with Antigua as the champion islands, and the teams to beat in Leeward Islands cricket.

After many years of having been humiliated at cricket by St. Kitts and Antigua, Nevisians everywhere looked forward to the annual cricket encounters against St. Kitts and Antigua, especially when it was with St. Kitts, at Grove Park in Nevis, or Warner Park on St. Kitts. For Nevisians, it was sweet revenge. St. Kitts cricketers were humiliated repeatedly, by Nevis cricketers such as Elquemedo Willet, Livinstone Sargeant, Deryck Parry, the late Lipton (Big Bird) Griffin, and others. Eventually, Elquemedo Willet became the first Leeward Islander to play test cricket

272

for the West Indies. Deryck Parry, Keith Arthurton, and Stuart Williams were other Nevisians to join that elite club a few years later. In time, that new dynamism in Nevis sport was to affect the entire Leeward Islands and West Indies cricket. By 1983, Vivi Richards, of Antigua, was captain of the West Indies cricket team. Willet remains a hero on Nevis, but in time, Parry appeared to have forgotten his historical origin and his debt to the African Diaspora. He went to South Africa and played cricket there, despite the existence of a government with apartheid policies in the country. Vivi Richards of Antigua rejected a similar offer referring to the money offer as "Blood money." Today, Parry has been forgiven on Nevis. He came back to the island and made stellar contributions to sports on the island.

The rebirth of cultural awareness on Nevis sparked much unity and a new political consciousness. It also encouraged a renewal of spirit among Nevisians, following the *Christena* tragedy. That spirit of renewal also came to serve as a source for defiance, denial, and creativity, all at the same time. Culturama was the symptom of an emerging, complex force in Nevis. It served to challenge the government of the day, on St. Kitts. It brought a new unity among Nevisians. And, it also helped instigate denial in certain cases, while it assuaged the hurt and pain that permeated the society from the August, 1970 tragedy. Little wonder, the government on St. Kitts hesitated in legitimizing Culturama, as it evolved during the 1970s. However, Nevisians remained undaunted and committed to the changes they desired on their island. Throughout those primal years of Culturama, thousands of Nevisians traveled to Nevis from abroad to show political and cultural solidarity at the programs. In time, Culturama became and still remains a reason for Nevisians to come home and visit Nevis—and a very special time for Nevisians. Ultimately, Culturama inspired Nevisians to new levels of creativity, self-confidence, and independence. This is still reflected, somewhat, in the drama, music, crafts, traditions, and other art forms seen at Culturama time. Culturama became Nevis' equivalent to the Harlem Renaissance. It inspired a people and ignited a revolution. While the *Christena* tragedy brought pain, hurt, and a certain avoidance of reality to Nevis, the coming of Culturama brought healing, renewal, and inspiration toward dynamism and change on the island.

If the inspiration and creations at Culturama-time were carried on throughout the year, Nevis can become a hub of creativity. The associated inspiration can also drive a continuous revival and renewal of the human spirit. However, not every aspect of societal adjustment to the aftermath of *Christena* had positive effects on the people of St. Kitts-Nevis. In time, one impact of emigration was that it increased the people's sense and yearning for materialism. Today, greed for material goods, has fostered a tendency to false consciousness. In the process, attraction to materialism has become an endemic, destructive force on the islands. Just as the once rampant inter-island rivalry did, materialism along with its associated culture and ideology, is taking a toll on the people of St. Kitts-Nevis, and the broader Caribbean. Many of the values and traditions that were once sacred in the islands have now lost their sanctity. At one time the area suffered at the hands of economic imperialism. To that is now added cultural imperialism. Meanwhile, that growing greed for material goods is causing Caribbean people to lose the war for physical and cultural survival—globalization is overwhelming them, and often the political leadership is too inept to counteract the trend. Presently, crime, gang activity, drugs, school failure, the failure of politics, and a growing alienation within societies, are destroying Caribbean islands.

Technology

The technological innovations that emerged in the world by the 1970s, along with the mass migrations from St. Kitts-Nevis to more economically viable areas around the globe, made the arrival of increased technology to the islands inevitable. Meanwhile, small foreign industries such as Curtis

Mathes (television manufacturing) and growing automation in agriculture on both islands, especially in fishing, encouraged vast changes in both production and marketing on the islands. There was also a reemergence of globalization and some economic domination in the area, via outsourcing. Eventually, even those traditional and institutionalized trade relations between St. Kitts and Nevis began to change. There have also been other shifts in the island societies, as they face the challenge to survive growing materialism, globalization, and an even more astute and powerful capitalism bent on increased profits. No country that has depended on agriculture for over 300 years, can survive such drastic disruption of its system of production, as has occurred in St. Kitts-Nevis, without experiencing challenges, due to all the associated changes. But, that growing shift, in St. Kitts-Nevis, from agriculture to tourism, is a path to tread gingerly. It can be problematic for the islands' future.

Demographic Changes

Demographic changes during the 1970s, had an important role to play in the direction taken by St. Kitts-Nevis. In light of so many Nevisians dying on the *Christena,* population shifts on the islands seemed to have been a natural result. That sudden death of so many Nevisians was followed by movement of people away from the island to live elsewhere. There was also the ongoing migration from the island in search of a better life. No small island could have come through such a tragedy successfully, without experiencing pain, drama, and change. Nevis has also continued to pay great social costs for its lost population. The large number of young Nevisians who died on *Christena,* along with the hundreds who left the island, depleted the population and lowered its fertility rate. The population on Nevis has, for a long time, been tending toward aging. Over the years it has also exhibited a lower level of productivity, since it lost so much of the creative dynamism the islanders once knew.

Although the *Christena* did not kill a majority of Nevisians, the rate at which the island's population was declining and aging tends to make the island's population an endangered group of people. Nevis had over 11,000 inhabitants in 1970. However, the 1980 census showed that there were fewer than 10,000 people living on the island. Now, in the year 2012, immigrants from the Dominican Republic, Guyana, the USA, Jamaica, and some returning Nevisians who migrated earlier, are causing observable changes in the island's demography and culture. This trend will certainly be an important factor shaping the island's future society.

Before *Christena* sank, the ferry's existence and functioning were minor political issues in St. Kitts-Nevis. After the disaster, they became very much a part of the islands' day to day politics. By the time *Christena's* drama subsided, they were battered and bruised, but Nevisians and Kittitians emerged a more sober, ideologically aware, and politically aroused people. They were more determined to change their destiny too. Nevisians rose up and moved to force important changes in the politics of Nevis and St. Kitts. It was a severe struggle, but eventually, change came to the islands' politics.

Not long after *Christena* sank, the government imposed very strict safety rules for passenger boats between St. Kitts and Nevis. Despite the declared safety intent, many citizens on Nevis saw the strategy as having an anti-Nevis intent. The new rules placed sudden and unfair demands on the sailboats that had historically plied between the islands. Suddenly, owners of the few lighters (sailboats) that remained on Nevis found they could no longer transport passengers between St. Kitts and Nevis. They accepted the safety rules as necessary, but they were being applied too stringently, and many years too late. Further, the sailboats had an enviable record of safe service between St. Kitts and Nevis. The story of *The Crown*, which sank on its way to St. Kitts from Nevis, about 1948, was one of the few real boating tragedies before the *Christena*. Only the captain and two other men died.

It was reported that Captain Bullar Hicks could not swim. The other two deaths were George Didier and Tommy Shark. Despite the initial dissent about the new safety rules, after the *Christena's* mishap, those initial safety moves made by the Labor government, laid the groundwork for increased consciousness about safety on the sea. Over time, new and more specific rules and regulations were drawn up for the ferry service between the islands.

The operation of the present ferry services does reflect a high level of concern for human safety. Tickets are sold in advance of boarding, and the number of passengers is counted carefully. Whenever there are large groups waiting to travel, multiple trips are made to either island. And at times, according to how heavy the passenger load is, the captain himself may be seen supervising the loading. Today, there are more than one ferry-boat available between the islands, and they have regular schedules. The authorities have also allowed many other amenities that were not available during the time of *Christena*. Some of these contribute to keeping people comfortable and safe.

Despite situations such as an unstable economy, less dependence of Nevisians on St. Kitts, and other intervening factors such as the love/hate relationship between the islands, there is now more ferry travel between St. Kitts and Nevis than at any point before. Such a situation does seem to reflect a certain confidence in the islands' ferry services. But it also speaks to the failure of what had become an overpriced five-minute plane ride between the islands. Presently there are some three or four different ferry services competing against one another. The government is no longer the dominant partner in the inter-island service, as was the case in the time of *Christena*. Two of these services operate seven days a week, and up to eight o'clock in the evening. However, while this does not allow travel from one island to the other up to midnight, as is the case between St. Thomas and St. John, in the U. S. Virgin Islands. An 8:00 pm., ferry today is certainly a travel revolution in St. Kitts-Nevis, when compared with that 5:00 or 6:00 pm., cut off back in *Christena's* time.

Whitman T. Browne, Ph.D.

Besides the travel service, there are other changes that have come to the islands since the disaster in 1970. Much of the change has been social and political. A greater variety of family structures exists today than in 1970. And, a number of new social networks have been formed on both islands. In time, these can serve as important buffers to crises, should some disaster strike again. Meanwhile, the high level of emigration has resulted in the persistence of remittances from relatives overseas. This does contribute to development and progress in the islands: better education, more economic viability, growing social mobility, and higher standards of living through participation in the growing revolution in communications and technology. Meanwhile, although it is at a lower rate, emigration still contributes to its peculiar forms of social distress on the islands---absentee parents, low levels of discipline, school drop-out, and sexual promiscuity, all with a high correlation to decreased parental authority. During migration periods, children are often left in the care of grandparents, aunts, cousins, or friends. Then, in the complex hustle of life, the guardians who replace birth parents, tend to exercise lower levels of authority over their charges.

Throughout the last forty-two years, as Nevisians and Kittitians moved to ride out the storm, they faced the issues of dependency, self determination, and interdependence squarely, on numerous occasions, and under varied circumstances. At times the issues at hand were examined in terms of how they related to the individual. At other times, they were seen as they related to the group on each island. Today, the political response to some of these emerging questions is still not clear. As St. Kitts-Nevis citizens attempt to move beyond the *Christena* tragedy, at times, it appears that politicians do deal with such issues, but only as expediency dictates.

The NRP collaborated with the PAM in forming a new government in 1980, even though it had campaigned since 1970 for independence from St. Kitts. As problems emerged between the two parties by 1985, both PAM and the NRP, started to examine their capacity to exist independent of each other. In 1998, Nevis, under the CCM, moved to legitimize the island's secession from St. Kitts. The vote fell a few percentage points short of the legal requirement. Meanwhile, on the individual level, the aftermath of the disaster forced creative independence on many persons. Desmond Tyson, Joseph Budgeon, and other fishermen looked beyond Nevis-St. Kitts, when the people refused to eat seafood caught in any area close to Nags Head or near where *Christena* sank. Puerto Rico and St. Martin, at least for a time, became new and vibrant markets for selling fish. For Charles Freeman, and other men who lost wives or girlfriends on the *Christena,* they too restructured their lives, because the women who managed their homes died in the disaster.

However, not everyone who sought after it has found fulfillment in life beyond *Christena.* There were children and some adults who suffered such great loss that emotionally they could not continue a normal existence. Such persons became the ward of others. There is an emptiness, that continues to haunt their lives. Thelma Parris, who was barely nine months old when her mother died in the tragedy, said: "I often wonder what it would have been like growing up in a family with my mother being there." *St. Kitts-Nevis Observer* carried a special article on August 1, 1998, to mark the 28th Anniversary of *Christena's* sinking. One of the persons interviewed, Franklyn Browne, my fourth grade teacher, and a survivor of the sinking, sent this message to all those whom the incident touched: "Cheer up, we can overcome some of our losses and we can bear these things with fortitude and carry on with our lives." It is now just forty-two years on from that tragic afternoon in St. Kitts-Nevis, August 1, 1970. There must be retrospect as well as prospect. God is still on his throne. The earth continues to turn. And, time moves on! Yet, their past should always be instructive to a people. Notwithstanding, one painful event from an earlier time, should not be the only force that shapes the patterning of their future life!

APPENDIX I

The Launching of the *Christena*

The Labor Spokesman, Wednesday, 20th, May, 1959.

At 10:30 a.m. yesterday, the Honorable CAP Southwell, Minister of Communication and Works, left the island by air for Trinidad where he will spend one day, after which he will leave for British Guiana. The Minister's visit is for the purpose of launching the new inter-island boat to replace both the *MV Anslyn,* which was destroyed by the hurricane Greta in 1956 and the *MV Rehoboth,* which was destroyed by fire last year. The launching of the boat will take place on, or about Saturday the 23rd, instant. About a year ago construction of the new boat was started at the building works of Sprostons in British Guiana. The boat will make daily runs between St. Kitts and Nevis, and is equipped to carry at least 100 deck passengers, 30 first class passengers, and up to four cabin passengers. She will be fitted with a small winch to enable the easy lifting of dry goods cargo. Wireless equipment for easy communications and quarters for its crew are also attached. The cry for this replacement boat was long and hard and the community can do no less than to breathe a sigh of relief at this announcement. It is hoped that the boat will set sail from B. G. next week, and it is due to arrive in our territorial waters on, or about the end of this month. The engineer of the *MV Silver Arrow* left here last week for B. G. where he will receive instructions regarding the working of the boat. After the craft is launched and proved satisfactory the Minister will leave the engineer who will accompany the boat with a crew designated by the makers of the boat. The overall length of the boat is sixty feet and is of all steel construction, fitted with two high powered engines; she will cruise at about 12 miles per hour and will likely cross from St. Kitts to Nevis in one hour or less. During the year, frequent visits were paid to B. G. by the Minister and the Hon. R. L. Bradshaw, with a view to speeding up work on the boat and to press for early delivery. Nevisians in particular will do well to note that the difficulties of travelling to and from St. Kitts, will be greatly reduced and that progress in this direction is not due to their attitude toward the Labor Government, but rather in spite of it. Tribute must be paid to Captain Anslyn as the keel of the new boat was laid on specifications suggested by him. It is to be hoped that the coming of the boat will cause Nevisians who are hostile to the Labor Government to realize that they will be enjoying a benefit brought about by the same Government. The development of estates in Nevis, reconstruction of roads, etc., are burdens which fall frequently on the majority party, elected by the people of St. Kitts, whose good work benefits the entire territory. The coming of the new inter-island, passenger cargo motor vessel will furnish another such example.

APPENDIX II

The Labor Spokesman

Sunday, 31st, May, 1959.

Showpiece of W. I. For St. Kitts, Nevis-Anguilla Govt.

Within a fortnight, this territory will see the development
of its sea transport for inter-island communication and
commercial reassurance between St. Kitts and Nevis. The
arrival of the *Sum-fun* last Friday and the early coming of
the *M/V Christena* which left British Guiana on the same day
will undoubtedly answer the problem of sea transport which
for some time relied purely on the *M/V Silver Arrow* for this
type of service. The history of the new government boat,
which is no doubt well known to this territory is reprinted
from *The Daily Argosy*, British Guiana for the benefit of
those interested: The new $130,000 *M/V Christena* which
was built by Messrs. Sprostons Ltd was launched last week
Friday afternoon by Mrs. Ram Karan, wife of the Minister of
Communications and Works about 5 o'clock. His Excellency
the Governor, Sir Patrick Renison K. C. M. G., and a number
of Government Officials were at Sprostons Wharf to witness

the ceremony. Also present was Mr. C. A. P. Southwell, Minister of Communications in his Government, who came specially for the event.

Memorable Event

It was quite a memorable occasion as Mrs. Ram-Karan pressed a button and sent the *Christena* sliding into the Demarara River. After the boat was launched His Excellency inspected it, and afterwards the guests repaired to the Mariner's Club for a reception ceremony.

Obtained Order

The story surrounding the obtaining of the order to build the vessel for the St. Kitts-Nevis-Anguilla Government began in November, 1956, when Sprostons were called in to advise and assist in repairing the damage to marine facilities after the October hurricane. Several crafts had been lost, including barges and a wooden passenger vessel. Sprostons Works Engineers visited St. Kitts for consultation and as a result two sugar carrying barges were built in Georgetown and shipped within two months. Sprostons then designed and obtained the order to build a new steel passenger vessel, capable of trading between the islands.

Show Piece

The *M/V Christena* has been built to Lloyd's Register of Shipping Approved Plans, is an all-steel, all-welded vessel 66 feet long with a beam of 16 feet, powered by two 170 B. H. P. Caterpillar Marine Diesel, giving the vessel a service speed of 12 knots. The vessel is designed to carry 125 deck passengers and 30 first class passengers, with cargo hold capacity of five tons, also accommodation for a crew of five. The vessel will be a show-piece in the West Indies and it is hoped further orders will materialize.

Other Speeches

Mrs. B. Ram-Karan deputized for Mrs. C. A. P. Southwell, who was unable to attend, due to unforeseen circumstances. Other speeches were delivered by Mr. John Thompson, General Manager of Sprostons, Mr. H. G. Mc Grath, His Excellency and Mr. Southwell, who congratulated the firm for the very good work they have been doing, and wished them all success in the future. His Excellency stressed the colony's great industries and declared that we are looking for a brighter country through such bright prospects.

APPENDIX III

The Labour Spokesman

Thursday, 11th June 1959

Christena Inaugural Cruise Thursday

Arrival Stimulates Lively Interest

After much anxiety on the part of the people of St. Kitts and Nevis particularly for the coming of the M/V *Christena* to replace the *M*V Ansyln, sustained curiosity was climaxed last Sunday when the boat dropped its anchor in the Basseterre roadstead. Captained by Mr. D. Hogarth, the boat which is built to carry passengers and cargo left the shipyard of Sprostons in British Guiana for Basseterre. For two days *Christena* floated in the seaport of Chaguaramas, Trinidad, the proposed area for the Federal capital site. Last Friday at 3:30 p.m., she weighed anchor and sailed out for our territorial waters. At a cruising speed of approximately 9 m.p.h., forty nine hours sailing brought her safely to Basseterre at 4:30 p.m. last Sunday. Within a very short time of the alarm—"The New Boat!" onlookers thronged the Treasury pier and the bay front to have the fist look at the beautiful all-steel boat.

Precisely at 5 p.m. she dropped her anchor at the signal of the Harbor Master, after half an hour circular cruise in port. During the week captain D. Hogarth and engineers T. Miline the firm's workmen supervised trial runs between the islands. These are to provide the new captain Pontin and engineer Hicks the opportunity of familiarizing themselves with the boat and their new duties.

Inauguration Ceremony

Acting for the Hon. The Minister for Communications and Works, who is absent, the Minister for Trade and Production will conduct the inaugural ceremony which commences at 2 p.m., this afternoon. Upon invitation, members of the public will participate in the official ceremony to mark the inauguration of the service. The function will commence at Basseterre when invitees will board the boat for a cruise to Nevis where other persons will join the party for continuation of the day's activities. It is believed that the function will last until about 7 p.m. According to report from our information service the boat will be on its official and regular route on Monday next week: The information received includes the itinerary for the daily run as here under appended:

Figure 0-1 Daily Run

| | Leave St. Kitts | | Leave Nevis | |
	a.m.	p.m.	a.m.	p.m.
Mon	7:30	3:00	9:00 *	
Tues		3:00	9:00	5:00
Wed	7:30	3:00	9:00	5:00
Thurs	6:00	1:00	8:00	2:30
Fri	6:00	3:00	9:00*	

APPENDIX IV

The Labour Spokesman

Saturday 13 June 1959

Minister Formally Hands Over Christena

Stresses Importance of Inter-Island Communication

The following is the address of Hon. W. E. Glasford, Minister of Trade and Production, on the occasion of the inaugural cruise made by the motor vessel *Christena* on Thursday: Your Honor, Honorable Mr. Justice Alleyne, Honorable Members of the Executive and Legislative Councils, Ladies and Gentlemen—I take pleasure in welcoming you here to join in the inaugural ceremony of receiving the newly-acquired Government Motor Vessel *Christena,* and representing it to the public that it is intended to serve. I am very sorry that owing to the strict limitations of boat space, it was not possible to invite the large gathering that should have fittingly matched this big occasion. Some 60 invitations could not have been issued for reasons of restricted accommodation and I do hope that those who have not been invited will realize how sorry we are at their absence and will not feel a sense of being unwanted.

Deputizing The Honorable Minister of Communications and Works has asked me to deputize on his behalf at this important function, inasmuch as he is now on his way to the United Kingdom to attend a Conference on Constitutional Reform for this territory. I am very happy to perform this task—especially so, for the simple reason that although shipping falls directly under the portfolio of my colleague's Ministry, as Minister of Trade and Production, I have a special interest in the part that this vessel will play in stimulating the flow of trade between the islands of this territory.

Inter-Island Travel

Indeed I cannot too greatly stress the importance of interisland movement in the economic development of these islands. Despite the strides that air transport is making, it is still true to say that the expansion of our trade will largely depend, in the days ahead, on the efficiency of our shipping. We shall need more and better boats to give effect to plans for the increased movement of population and goods. We shall need too, expert navigators, coasters, helmsmen and ordinary sailors to run these ships if life is to be safe and worthwhile.

Sailing as A Career

And so at this stage, I should like to express Government's appreciation of the services of the crew who have brought this motor vessel so expertly to St. Kitts. I think that it would be fitting for some of our local young men to take note of what can be achieved through skill of this sort. I should like to see a few of them come forward and display a more intelligent interest in navigation and all nautical matters since it would appear that this profession might offer a useful field of service in the future.

First Journey

The Motor Vessel *Christena* arrived in the Basseterre roadstead at 4:30 p.m. on Sunday, the 7th June, and dropped her anchor at 5:05 pm., after cruising about the harbour. She appeared none the worse for her long journey from the mainland coast of British Guiana where she was built. This boat has been constructed at a cost of $132,500 (W.I.) and was ordered to replace the *M.V.* "Ansyln" that was damaged by hurricane "Greta" in 1956. Funds for this purpose were provided through a grant from the United Kingdom.

APPENDIX V

List of Persons Identified
(One of Original Lists From 1970)

	Last Name	First Name	Address
1	Arthurton	Rodney	Jessups Village
2	Bussue	Lillian	Webbes Ghaut
3	Belle	Franklyn	Upper Market Street
4	Bertie	Sherwin	Cayon
5	Bloyce	Adolphus	St. Paul's
6	Browne	Robert	Needsmust Estate
7	Condelle	Anthony	Rawlins Road
8	Condelle	Irene	Hermitage
9	Comeau	Sister Amelia	The Convent, St. Kitts
10	Dineen	Sister Patricia	The Convent, St. Kitts
11	Duporte	Amelia	Government Road
12	Elliot	James	Morning Star
13	Esdaille	Florence	Brown Hill
14	Forbes	Clarent	Sandy Point
15	Forbes	Emily	Brown Pasture

	Last Name	First Name	Address
16	Francis	Kluivert H	St. Pauls
17	Freeman	Tamar	Stoney Hill
18	Griffin	B Lorraine	Butlers
19	Hanley	Bertram	Buckley's Site
20	Hanley	Eglantine	Church Ground
21	Hanley	Zena	Beach Road
22	Henry	Rosalyn	St. Kitts
23	Hendrickson	Marilyn	Clay Ghaut
24	King	Herbert Maxwell	Clifton Village
25	Huggins	Alice	Jessups Village
26	Hutton,	Frances	Cotton Ground
27	Jones	Olga	Cotton Ground
28	Jeffers	Rosalie Agatha	Jessup's
29	Jones	Edith	Government Road
30	Jones	Oretha	Mount Lily
31	Joseph	Carmen	Newcastle
32	Joseph	Venetta	Godwin Ghaut
33	Le Blanc	Sister Marie	The Convent, St. Kitts
34	Liburd	Mrs. E.P	Greenlands
35	Liburd	Elvira	Cole Hill
36	Liburd	Kirsten	Olivia Greenlands
37	Liburd	Marion	Church Ground
38	Martineau	Maude Lucilla	The Factory
39	McQuilkin	Linda	Brick Kiln
40	Mills	Vivian	Jessups Village
41	Morris	Ursula	Carty Alley
42	Nisbett	Herbert	Gingerland
43	Nisbett	Lilian	Hermitage
44	Pemberton	Helen	Zion Village

	Last Name	First Name	Address
45	Phillips	Berdie	United Kingdom
46	Ponteen	James	Newtown
47	Powell	Marion	Beach Road
48	Richardson	Yvonne	Pinneys Road
49	Stanley	Vivian	Burden Pasture
50	Stapleton	Yvonne	Brick Kiln
51	Sutton	Stanley	Maynard Yard
52	Swanston	Hanschell	River Path
53	Sweeney	Samuel	College Street
54	Tross	Marilyn	Rices Village
55	Tyson	Theodosia	Cotton Ground
56	Weekes	Avonell	Tabernacle
57	Williams	George (Jinks)	Government Road

NB: Doubts have been expressed with regard to the identification of the following: Clarent Forbes, Sandy Point; Kirsten Olivia Liburd, Greenlands; and Herbert Nisbett, Gingerland.

APPENDIX VI

List of Missing Persons:
(One of the Original Lists from, 1970)

	Last Name	First Name	Address
1	Allen	Ezekiel	Cayon
2	Allen	Miriam	Rawlins Village
3	Allen	Shirley	Rawlins Village
4	Archibald	Floretta	Brick Kiln
5	Archibald	Samuel	Bath Village
6	Arthurton	Amy	Jessup's Village
7	Arthurton	Bertranne	Cotton Ground
8	Arthurton	Emily	Jessup's Village
9	Audain	Valentine	The Factory
10	Bartlette	Errol	Government Road
11	Bartlette	Froncille	Government Road
12	Barzey	Ellen	Bath Village
13	Barzey	Mavis	Bath Village
14	Belle	Austin	Market Street
15	Browne	Monroe	River Path

	Last Name	First Name	Address
16	Browne	Muriel	Government Road
17	Browne	Harold	Government Road
18	Browne	Josephine	Zion Village
19	Browne	Olga	Brick Kiln
20	Budgeon	Gwendolyn	Jessups Village
21	Byron	Millicent	Greenlands
22	Cable	Allan	Nevis Street
23	Carr	Orilda	Cayon
24	Chapman	Sharon	Cooks Ground
25	Charles	Clementina	Newcastle
26	Clarke	Anita	Fountain
27	Clarke	Brenda	Simmond's Village
28	Clarke	Euphina	Craddock Road
29	Clarke	Leslie	Government Road
30	Clarke	Sarah	Simmond's Village
31	Claxton	Dahlia	Cox Village
32	Claxton	James	Jessup's Village
33	Claxton	Vernon	Chicken Stone
34	Condelle	Christine	Hermitage Road
35	Cornelius	Loretta	Craddock Road
36	David	Carl	Keys Village
37	David	Christena	Keys Village
38	David	Joseph	Keys Village
39	David	Leon	Sandy Point
40	David	Mavis	Keys Village
41	David	Verna	Keys Village
42	Davis	Lanyel	Cotton Ground
43	Daniel	Leontine	Cayon
44	Dore	Claristene	Pond Hill

	Last Name	First Name	Address
45	Dore	Jessica	Pond Site
46	Dore	Myra	Rices Village
47	Duporte	Wendell	Government Road
48	Elliott	Kennedy	Morning Star
49	Esdaille	Albertha	Craddock Road
50	Farrel	Zenneth	Durrant Avenue
51	Ferguson	Albertine	Webbe Ground
52	Ferguson	Emile	Webbe Ground
53	French	Daniel	Saddlers
54	Frank	Moses	Cotton Ground
55	Freeman	Augusta	River Path
56	Glasford	James	Craddock Road
57	Gumbs	Melvina	Tabernacle
58	Halliday	Lilian	Jessup's Village
59	Hanley	Conrad	Taylor's Pasture
60	Hanley	Hugh	Clay Ghaut
61	Hanley	Melford	Brown Pasture
62	Hanley	Rose	Government Road
63	Hill	Bethia	Morning Star
64	Hobson	Marilyn Myrna	Bucks Hill
65	Holland	Emily	348 W 118 St., N.Y.C. 54
66	Huggins	Nelson	Leroy Church Ground
67	Irvine	James	Lodge Project
68	James	Esther	Bath Village
69	James	Vernon	Dorset Village
70	Jeffers	Clifford	Maynard Yard
71	Jeffers	Dwight	Jessup's Village
72	Jeffers	Maurina	Mount Lily
73	Jeffers	Ralph	Bath Village

	Last Name	First Name	Address
74	Johnson	Clotilda	Jessups Village
75	Johnson	Michael	Nevis
76	Jones	Emily	Government Road
77	Jones	Iris	Government Road
78	Jones	Vida	Cotton Ground
79	Joseph	Louisa	Godwin Ghaut
80	Joseph	Sheila	Godwin Ghaut
81	Kelly	Avril (Cynthia)	Zion Village
82	Kelly	Eugene	Zion Village
83	Lanns	Verna	Liverpool Row
84	Lewis	Calvin	Morning Star
85	Liburd	Beryl	Brown Pasture
86	Liburd	Castro	Brown Hill
87	Liburd	Edric Paul	Greenlands
88	Liburd	Emerson	Bucks Hill
89	Liburd	Evelyn P	Brown Pasture
90	Liburd	Iris	Brown Pasture
91	Liburd	Kirsten	Olivia Greenlands
92	Liburd	Kirtley	Brick Kiln
93	Liburd	Elvira	Cole Hill
94	Liburd	Lillian	Brown Pasture
95	Liburd	Louisa	Brown Pasture
96	Liburd	Marianne	Webbe Ground
97	Libund	Thomas	Government Road
98	Liburd	Samuel	Rawlins Village
99	Martineau	Sheryl	Kittstoddart
100	Marson	Eva	Basseterre
101	Masters	Leroy	Government Road
102	Maynard	Charles	Sandy Point

	Last Name	First Name	Address
103	Maynard	Sadie	Sheriffs Village
104	Michael	Idetha	Phillips Village
105	Mills	Hennetta	Low Street
106	Mills	Maude	Cox Village
107	Morton	Calvin	Sheriffs Village
108	Morton	Clarice	Sheriffs. Village
109	Morton	Inez	Government Road
110	Morton	Irma	Maynard Hill
111	Morton	Orville	Brown Hill
112	Morton	Pearl	Maynard Hill
113	Natta	Annie	Phillips Village
114	Nisbett	Govan	Simmonds Village
115	Nisbett	Tony	St. Kitts
116	Nolan	Doldria	Greenlands
117	Nolan	Eulita	Nurses Headquarters
118	Nolan	Tessa	West Pond Site
119	Parris	Florence	Craddock Road
120	Parris	Hannah	Craddock Road
121	Pemberton	Calvin	Bath Village
122	Pemberton	Rufus	Webbe Ground
123	Phipps	Conrad	Sandown Road
124	Powell	George	Jessup's Village
125	Powell	Miriam	Stoney Hill
126	Powell	Sheryl	Grove Park
127	Powell	Yvette	Brown Hill
128	Prentice	Evanston	Mount Lily Village
129	Prince	Anthony	Lodge Village
130	Reid	Austin	Craddock Road
131	Richards	Assinette	Colton Ground

	Last Name	First Name	Address
132	Ritchens	Joseph	Craddock Road
133	Rouse	Leroy	St. Johnston Village
134	Saddler	Vernarine	Maynard Hill
135	Scarborough	Alicia	Gingerland
136	Scarborough	Duane	Gingerland
137	Scarborough	Inez	Gingerland
138	Smith	Edward	Zion Village
139	Smithen	Ivan	Cayon
140	Smithen	Christena	Craddock Road
141	Springelte	Keith	River Path
142	Swanston	Daryl	Jessup's Village
143	Swanston	David	Craddock Road
144	Swanston	Theodosia	Craddock Rose
145	Thompson	Marilyn	Brick Kiln
146	Trotman	Alton	Cole Hill
147	Trotman	Iris	Cole Hill
148	Trotman	Irvine	Rawlins Village
149	Tross	Alston	Rices Village
150	Tyson	Dave	Cotton Ground
151	Tyson	Kirsten	Cotton Ground
152	Wade	Yvelte	Bath Village
153	Wallace	Candy	Pond Pasture
154	Wallace	Lorna	Pond Pasture
155	Walters	Judith	Bucks Hill
156	Walters	Virginia	St. Pauls
157	Walwyn	Wentworth (Parks)	Bath Village
158	Wattley	Violet	Fawcett Village
159	Walts	Velcine	Gingerland
160	Webbe	Adina	Rawlins Village

	Last Name	First Name	Address
161	Weekes	Benjamin	Low Street
162	Weekes	Elroy	Saddlers
163	Weekes	Elroy	Webbe Ground
164	Weekes	Louisa	Tabernacle
165	Weekes	Louisa	Craddock Road
166	Weekes	Nicholas	Camps
167	Weekes	Rita	Tabernacle
168	Wheeler	Amelia	Craddock Road
169	Williams	Kirtly	Brick Kiln
170	Williams	Vernon	Clay Ghaut

APPENDIX VII

List of Survivors
(One Early List From, 1970)

	Last Name	First Name	Address
1	Allen	Reuben	Montserrat
2	Arisbeth	Carlton	Brown Hill
3	Bartlette	Joseph	Craddock Road
4	Benjamin	Vincent	Coram Alley
5	Blake	Robert	Jessup's
6	Brisbane	Michael	North Square Street
7	Brookes	Ivor	Brick Kiln
8	Browne	Arrington	Lambert Inn
8a	Browne	Orrington	Liburd Hill
9	Browne	Clifford	Brick Kiln
10	Browne	Dulcita	Keys Village
11	Browne	Edna	Jessup's Village
12	Browne	Franklyn	Camps Village
13	Browne	Franklyn	Camps Village
14	Browne	Leonard	Prince William Street

	Last Name	First Name	Address
15	Browne	Roger	Camps Village
16	Budgeon	Joseph	Jessup's Village
17	Budgeon	Luelia	Jessup's Village
18	Carlton	Tom	Brown Hill
19	Chapman	Livinstone	Nevis
20	Charles	Meredith	Low Street
21	Clarke	Edward	Government Road
22	Crandell	Wilson	Hermitage
23	Davis	Everson	Cotton Ground
24	Denning	William	St. Kitts
25	Depusoir	William	Brick Kiln
26	Duzan	Terrence	Brown Hill
27	Edwards	Lionel	Round Hill House
28	Elliott	Ivan	Gingerland
29	Foster	Bertram	Clifton Village
30	France	James	Powell's Village
31	Francis	Rudolph	Rawlins Village
32	Freeman	Samuel	Rawlins Village
33	Hanley	Eustace	Gingerland
34	Harris	Vincent	St. Johnston's Village
35	Hendrickson	Ronald	Gingerland
36	Herbert	Alice*	
37	Hinds	Robert	Round Hill House
38	Huggins	Fitzroy	Cotton Ground
39	Huggins	Phillip	Fothergills
40	James	Jonathan*	
41	James	Leroy	Bath Village
42	Jeffers	Belinda	Bath Village
43	Johnston	Charles	Cayon

Whitman T. Browne, Ph.D.

	Last Name	First Name	Address
44	Johnston	Charles	Jessup's Village
45	Johnston	Llewellyn	Jessup's Village
46	Kelly	Edmund	Gingerland
47	Kelsick	Ian	Cayon
48	Lake	Samuel	Brighton Estate
49	Liburd	Devon	Cole Hill
50	Liburd	Edwin*	
51	Martin	Joseph	Craddock Road
52	Martin	Joseph	St. Kitts
53	Martin	Julie	Bath Village
54	Mason	Samuel	Conaree
55	Matthews	Frank	Cayon
56	Merchant	Edward	Cayon
57	Moore	Charles*	
58	Morton	Franklyn	Gingerland
59	Morlon	Vincent	Cayon
60	Mulraine	Shernelle	The Factory
61	Nisbett	Carlton	Brown Hill
62	Prentice	Gerard	Police Headquarters
63	Procope	Conrad	Dorset Village
64	Rawlins	Clive	St. Kitts
65	Richard	Euste	Gingerland
66	Richardson	Alice	Bath Village
67	Richardson	Wendell	Ponds Pasture
68	Copeland	Roberts	Low Street
69	Robertson	Joseph	Cayon
70	Sage	Leroy	Ponds Pasture
71	Sargeant	Laughton	Cotton Ground
72	Sargeant	Livinstone	Cotton Ground

	Last Name	First Name	Address
73	Scarborough	Clive	Craddock Road
74	Simmons	Malcolm	Low Street
75	Simmons	Victor	Crooks Ground
76	Stapleton	Vincent	Happy Hill Alley
77	Storrod	Earl	Hickman's
78	Swanston	Victor	River Path
79	Tross	Grenville	Nevis
80	Trotman	Livinstone	Rices Village
81	Tyson	Oswald	Cotton Ground
82	Uddenburg	Herman	Cayon Street
83	Walwyn	St. Clair	Craddock Road
84	Ward	Job*	
85	Warner	Cecil	St. Kitts
86	Weekes	James	St. Kitts
87	Wenham	James	
88	Wilkinson	Wendel	Church Ground
89	Williams	Diana	Main Street
90	Williams	Leroy	Cotton Ground
91	Wilson	Aubrey*	
92	Wilson	Lewis Solas	Jessup's Village

N.B. It is possible that there are duplications on this list. Those likely to be are: Arrington Browne, Lambert Inn and Orrington Browne, Liburd Hill; Charles Johnston, Cayon and Charles Johnston, Jessup's Village; also, Joseph Martin, Craddock Road and Joseph Martin, St. Kitts; AUTHOR'S NOTE: The name Franklyn Browne is also a duplicate listing.

APPENDIX VIII

List of Persons Reported Missing
(unconfirmed)

	Last Name	First Name
1	Huggins	Samuel
2	Lawrence	Dawne
3	Liburd	James
4	Morton	Rose
5	Smithen	Calvin
6	Vernon	Joseph
7	Weekes	Marion

APPENDIX IX

Witnesses Who Gave Evidence Before the Commission

Monday, August 17, 1970 (Table One):

	Last Name	Other Names	Address	Occupation
1	Cox	Julian	Bryon La Guerite, Basseterre	Civil Servant
2	Hanley	Herbert	Taylor' Range, Basseterre	Civil Servant
3	Bradley	George	Government House, Nevis	Civil Servant
4	Martin	Joseph	Craddock Road, Nevis	Peddler
5	Swanston	Victor	River Path, Nevis	Butcher
6	Liburd	Helena	Brown Pasture, Nevis	Home Domestic
7	Depusoir	William	Brick Kiln, Nevis	Laborer
8	Mills	Mignol	Chicken Stone, Nevis	Carpenter
9	Dore	Lincoln	Charlestown, Nevis	Taxi Driver

	Last Name	Other Names	Address	Occupation
10	Richens	Hubert	Craddock Road, Nevis	Porter
11	Solas	Wilston	Jessup's, Nevis	Laborer
12	Liburd	Dulcina	Rices Village, Nevis	Housewife
13	Prentice	Gerard	(P. C # 338) Bass. Police Station	Policeman
14	Petty	Rosalie	(W. P. C. # 332) Chs. Police Station,	Female Police
15	Wattley	Landal	I.F. C. # 222) Chs. Town Police Station	Policeman

Tuesday, August 18, 1970 (Table Two):

	Last Name	Other Names	Address	Occupation
16	Miller	Phillip	Cliff Dwellers, Nevis	Captain, *Sea Hunter 1*
17	Liburd	Edwin	Bath Village, Nevis	Fisherman
18	Nicholls	Wentworth	Pinney's Beach Hotel	Hotel Proprietor
19	Matthew	Frank	Cayon, Village, St. Kitts	First Mate, *Christena*
20	Moore	Charles	Cayon, St. Kitts	Engineer, *MV Christena*
21	Skeete	Winston	Nevis	Motor Mechanic, *Sea Hunter 1*
22	Wade	Rupert	Happy Hill, Nevis	Fisherman
23	Hinds	Robert	Round Hill, Nevis	Student, McGill University
24	Nisbett	Evan	Potworks, Nevis	Civil Servant

Last Name	Other Names	Address	Occupation

Wednesday, August 19, 1970:

25 Martineau	John, Martin	Charlestown, Nevis	Asst. Sup. of Police

Monday, August 24, 1970:

26 King	Michael Lynch	Olivees, Basseterre	Company Director
27 Kelsick	Phillip, Ian	Cayon St., Basseterre	Pilot
28 Cox (Recalled)	Julian, Byron	La Guerite, Basseterre	Civil Servant
29 Lewis	Cpl. Leonard	#172, Charlestown Police Station	Cpl. Of Police
30 Uddenberg	Herman, James	Cayon St., St. Kitts	Architect
31 Dash	Rev. Michael	Sandy Pt., St. Kitts	Methodist Minister
32 France	James	Herbert St., Basseterre	Lighter-man
33 Browne	Dulcita	Key's Village, St. Kitts	Home Domestic
34 Starznski	Zygmut	St. Kitts	Master of *MV Barfish*
35 Daniel	Jean	Fiennes Avenue, St. Kitts	Home Domestic
36 Joseph	Lilian	Conaree, St. Kitts	Housewife

Tuesday, August 25, 1970:

37 Nicholls	Catherine	Seaside Hotel, Basseterre	Manager

Whitman T. Browne, Ph.D.

	Last Name	Other Names	Address	Occupation
38	Merchant	Radford	Old Road, St. Kitts	Civil Servant
39	Wade	John, Lynch	Basseterre, St. Kitts	Chief of Police
40	Hanley	Herbert (Recalled)	Basseterre, St. Kitts	Civil Servant

Tuesday, September 1, 1970:

41	Wynter	Stanley	Jamaica	Master, *Hawthorne Enterprise*
42	King	Stephen	St. Vincent	Seaman *Hawthorne Enterprise*

Saturday, September 5, 1970:

43	Miller	Phillip (Recalled)	Cliff Dwellers, Nevis	Captain, *Sea Hunter 1*
44	Anslyn	Arthur	Charlestown, Nevis	Seaman
45	Yearwood	Reginald	Basseterre, St. Kitts	Student, College of the VI

APPENDIX X

The St. Kitts-Nevis Observer

February 1, 1997

Sacrilege or History? Diving the Christena Wreck.

This article first appeared in the Nevis based newspaper, The St. Kitts-Nevis Observer, February 1,1997. It is reproduced here with permission from the editor.

If they're allowed to dive the *Christena,* they should be allowed to go in the cemetery and dig up the dead," maintains Kenneth Samuel, owner of Kenneth's Dive Shop, the first and oldest of the four commercial scuba dive operation in St. Kitts-Nevis. While Samuel isn't the only person with this view, some feel that its history and people should know something about it, In the words of Chief Fisheries Officer, Joe Simmonds, "There is nothing in the law to prevent diving there. However, it is clear that many in the community feel vehemently that it should be prohibited.

Whitman T. Browne, Ph.D.

Some Background

The *Christena* sank on the afternoon of August 1, 1970, in the channel on its way from St. Kitts to Nevis. Of the nearly 320 people on the overloaded ferry at the time, about 90 survived. Family and/or friends of nearly every person in the Federation can be counted among the 57 who were identified; and 170 who were still missing when the search was called off. "After four days of efforts to recover additional bodies, identification of the bodies became virtually impossible and so had to be abandoned," according to the official report on the tragedy. There were 66 unidentified bodies which were recovered, six of which were buried on Nevis and 60 on St. Kitts. A little arithmetic reveals that the remains of just over 100 people remained on the sea floor. "A decision was made to leave the boat and bodies undisturbed," notes Arthur Anslyn, Captain of the *Caribe Queen*, who was hired by the Commission of Inquiry to dive the site in the period after August 1. In the late 1980's a foreign dive operation was observed diving at the site of the *Christena* wreck. Protests from Anslyn and Samuel led to the practice being stopped. However, in recent times both these men and others report seeing an increasing number of dive-boats in the vicinity of the *Christena*.

The Diver's Discretion

Some assert that there is no need for special regulation of the site of the wreck. "I don't have any problem with it," says Sam Lake, a survivor of the wreck who now operates a sailboat. "I wouldn't want to dive it," he says, recalling "when I'm sailing over that area I get a bit of chill." Ian Kelsick, another survivor, feels "it's alright to dive just to look at it but people shouldn't touch anything." Simmonds, who dove it last August for the first time, calls it "the most interesting dive I've ever done."

Simmonds, a very experienced diver, describes the boat as sitting upright in the sand with human remains clearly visible. While he is concerned about reports that some divers "have disturbed the remains," Simmonds doesn't believe special regulations are needed. *Ellis Chatterton's Scuba Safaris* occasionally takes people to dive there. "It's a solemn dive, not an enjoyable dive," he relates. He said, "It's a grave yard basically." Chatterton points out that he had family on the boat. He asserts "We treat it with the uttermost respect and don't advertise it as a regular dive site." It is the only wreck in close proximity to Nevis," notes Chatterton who has been diving it for close to five years now. Austin McLeod of *Pro Divers* insists that he doesn't dive the *Christena,* telling *The Observer,* "I don't even know exactly where it is." However, several divers with whom we spoke reluctantly admitted that they have dived the site with *Pro Divers.*

One of the other operators said that a recent visitor was very eager to dive the *Christena,* but he told her they wouldn't take her there. The following week the tourist returned to say she had gone to the site with Pro Divers. Mc Leod declined to discuss the issue in a follow-up call, reiterating that he doesn't dive there.

The Prohibitionists

"After about 15 minutes at the site, 1 decided that 1 would never go back and would never take anyone else there," says Riley Copple, the dive master at *St. Kitts Scuba.* He says that many visitors ask, "Can we dive the wreck?" His answer is "No." "I think government should restrict people from going there," argues Kenneth Samuel. "Kenneth: ~ *Dive Center* has never been there and will never go there," he said emotionally. A prominent Nevisian used more temperate language, saying, "I don't think it is wise. 1 don't think they should take people down there. The people who they take wouldn't have any real feeling toward it. We really wouldn't want them inspecting our dead," she says. The question of foreigners diving the site and not respecting what it means to the people of St. Kitts and Nevis was a common thread among those who don't want diving at the *Christena*. "I can only compare it to a circus carnival side show," says Copple who is not a native of the Federation. Some people expressed the belief that local people diving the site is fundamentally different from allowing tourists to do so. Although divers are generally advised against touching or picking up pieces of coral, shells or other objects from the ocean floor, most dive operators acknowledge that this happens anyway. Cutting right to the point, Copple declares, "I don't want remains ending up on a desk or entertainment center in Canada, England or the US."

While it is not likely that anyone would condone such an occurrence, one of the disagreements is how well regulations can be enforced. Of course, the same can be said for a prohibition on diving the site itself. Several of those who have dived the wreck recently believe that human remains have been moved. They note that there are exposed skulls and bones which show little sign of weathering. Samuel says that they would normally be covered with moss and other growth. He believes that they were disturbed by divers not by hurricanes or other natural causes.

Prospect For Change

"This is the first time it's been mentioned to me," said Minister of Agriculture, Timothy Harris, whose portfolio includes the Fisheries Department. He feels that "the area may be considered special and requires some policy." He said that he would like to study the issue in greater depth before taking any action, noting the importance of forming "some public consensus," on the question. Joe Simmonds says that his department would have to coordinate with the Department of Environment to prohibit diving there. The National Conservation and Environment Protection Act, 1987, clearly give the department the power to make such regulations. Perhaps the forging of a general public agreement on this issue can help people to take an additional step in overcoming the grief caused by this terrible event 27 years ago.

APPENDIX XI

The Kitts-Nevis Observer

August 1-7, 1998

28 years after the M. *V. Christena* sank
by Paula Warner

The sinking of the *M. V. Christena* 28 years ago, today August I, is still a very vivid memory for many persons in St. Kitts and Nevis. The incident touched almost every family in the Federation. Since that Saturday in August, 1970, some survivors have managed to put the dreadful incident behind, but for many others it still remains a haunting memory they don't care to discuss. On the eve of the anniversary of this fateful event, *The Observer* remembers those who perished and those who survived. We also look at measures that have been put in place since, to guard against the occurrence of similar incident today. Some of the survivors tell how the incident changed their lives, while others say the effects of the tragedy have long been worn out. Romeo Parris of Craddock Road in Nevis is one of those whom the incident continues to touch today. At a tender age of five, he lost his mother in that incident. Speaking to *The Observer* earlier this week Parris said he often wonders what his life would be like if she had remained alive. "There are moments when, especially around that time in August, I always try to think back and even during some lonely times when I am stressed from work I think about my mother. If I think too long about her I begin to cry," he said. It is for that same reason he dislikes celebrations for Mother's Day.

"1 don't have a picture of her in my head but for some strange reason I am always thinking of her. I feel proud of her, and I just sense there was a closeness between us even though I was very young." Romeo said.

Older persons have confirmed the closeness for when she was alive she was always seen carrying him along wherever she went, he was told. After her tragic death he said "My family split up. My mother had eight children and we split up then." Today Romeo has turned out to be a practicing Pharmacist and the proprietor of Parris Pharmacy which operates both in St. Kitts and Nevis. He gives thanks to his foster parents for his upbringing and will always be grateful to them. In return he is living his life as "an example to young people to let them know that even though you have lost a mother figure or you have been brought up in a separate home, you can still make something of yourself," once you are determined he said.

The manner in which he travels between St. Kitts and Nevis has also been affected as a result. Even a few times when he has ventured to commute via ferry, he said, it bothers him every time he passes in the area where the incident occurred. "Just last week I had a frightening experience. I was going up on the Sea Hustler and the rain started falling and the sea began stirring up and it was really rough and I was very frightened. As a matter of fact I have developed a fear of the sea. I am not a swimmer. 1'd prefer to fly than go on the water," he said. His adoptive parents never allowed him to go to the sea, because of the 1970 incident, and so the first time he attempted to swim in his life was in 1986, while visiting a friend in Anguilla. But for one lady of Gingerland who preferred to remain anonymous, the loss of a brother, a sister, two aunts, and a cousin, did hurt for a long time, particularly as their bodies were never recovered for burial. "Burial brings closure and the healing process in the normal scheme of things," she said. "The healing process stays that much longer. Even if you do not want to admit it you are hoping this person will turn up," she said. There was this feeling of disbelief until it eventually sank in that these people had gone for good. For her, that feeling has come and gone, "I cannot mourn for 28 years, that's murder I cannot do that to myself," she noted. "I have accepted what there is and have moved on."

As for Franklyn Browne, a former headmaster who resides in Camps Village, he was one of those who had boarded the *MV Christena* on what was to be her final journey from the St. Kitts port. At the time he was 42 years old. He was accompanying his 14 year old son Roger Browne who had travelled to St. Kitts for a doctor's visit to remove stitches from eye surgery done some weeks before. "It has been so long now, but it has not affected me in any way. I still live a normal life and carry on with my business," he said. "I continued using the ferry after, though I hardly travel these days. Mr. Browne said the incident instilled no fears in him despite being raised in the mountain village of Fountain. In his younger days his stepfather taught him to fish for his relish. So, the family came along and had a lot to do with the sea. Mr. Browne noted that he has had no difficulty relating his experience to anyone over again. The former headmaster said he is also thankful for the survival of his son. And in hind sight it was a lucky decision to accompany Roger on that fateful day. Although he does not take the credit for his son's survival, he acknowledges the fact that during their ordeal, he urged him on.

Twenty-eight years later Roger is a doctor with the United States Army. His father believes that because of his achievements, his son was not adversely affected by the fatal incident. "He went away in 1974 and has studied at Bradford University and then at the New Jersey University of Dentistry and Medicine. I think he is getting on fairly well,' the proud father said. To others whom the 1970 incident has touched, Mr. Browne lends words of comfort. "Cheer up, we can overcome some of our losses and we can bear these things with fortitude and carry on with our lives as we would like it." But what of the medical doctor who was available on Nevis at the time to attend to the victims of the sunken *Christena?* Doctor Kennedy Simmonds told *The Observer* that incident has a lasting impact on his life. "It has stayed with me for a long time and I think it has made me appreciate what life is and how fleeting life can be," he said. The survivor's cries of praise and thankfulness that somehow they were able to survive the incident as they were brought in rubbed off on him and as a result he became a more spiritually minded individual. The doctor regards the incident as being the "most harrowing experience" of his medical career up to that time. He said he dealt with both survivors and persons who had died. Some he had known as friends others as acquaintances, others he had seen very shortly before. "And once you saw them as a medical doctor in that situation, in some cases being unable to do anything for them was a very frustrating and sobering experience," he explained. Dr. Simmonds, who later became the first Prime Minister of St. Kitts-Nevis, said when he graduated from medical school he never envisaged being thrown into that type of situation and "I think if there is one thing it has done for me, is made me more conscious of the medical needs of each person as an individual, who must get the best effort that you can give to see if one could make that person survive. It really brought that home to me."

The doctor said it just so happened on that fateful day in August, 1970, he was on Nevis to replace another doctor who normally visited to hold clinic on the island. Along with the nursing staff at the Alexandra Hospital, he had the task of caring for the living and the dead. An inquiry investigating the circumstances surrounding the sinking of the Motor Vessel *Christena* on her scheduled voyage between the islands of St. Kitts and Nevis, during the afternoon of Saturday 1 August, 1970, was commissioned by the then acting governor. According to the report from the Commissioner J.D.B. Renwick, the incident occurred as a result of overcrowding. There were more than three hundred men, women, and children on board a vessel which had the capacity to carry only 150 persons.

The Commissioner's recommendations included the enactment of new legislation to govern and regulate coastal trade for passenger and cargo with prime consideration given to the safety of passengers. The legislation should also provide for the licensing of all vessels irrespective of ownership and size engaged in coastal trade, after inspection, licenses should be issued and certification of safety for the carriage of passengers, regulations regarding the number of passengers the vessel is allowed to carry, the issuance of certificates of competency for the captains of the ships, that the practice of collecting fares during the voyage cease immediately and should be replaced with a system of ticket sales and collection prior to leaving port. Since that time, the Commissioner's recommendations have been addressed in the Merchant Shipping Act, No 15 of 1985. The comprehensive legislation covers certificates of competency, passenger ships, safety and provision for inspection by authorities among other areas. In the meantime the memory of those who suffered from the events of August 1, 1970, continues to surface at this time of year, while the M.V. *Christena* remains in her watery grave just one mile off the coast of Nags Head in St. Kitts.

APPENDIX XII

St. Kitts-Nevis Observer

July 28-August 03, 2000

And the Sea Shall Tell

By Lisa Eddy

The day started out with a calm sea, moderate to high winds and visibility was good. The only anxiety present was travelers rushing to reach the Basseterre Roadstead to board the only ferry for the 11 mile ran from St. Kitts to Nevis. The trip ended in tragedy so horrifying, people are still reluctant to talk about it. The ferry was the Motor Vessel *Christena*. On Aug 1, 1970, for reasons that still remain a dark mystery, *Christena* plunged to the bottom of the ocean and more than 90 [*] passengers drowned. Everything had begun so ordinary. It all seemed business as usual when *Christena* disembarked at around 3:30 p.m. from Basseterre Roadsted with a full load of passengers who were heading home for a long holiday weekend, some traveling to Nevis to visit their loved ones and friends. The sinking of the ferry and the many lives lost—the worst disaster in the Federation's history—will never be forgotten by those who survived and by the loved ones of those who didn't.

[* 57 bodies recovered; 172 missing; 92 survivors. These numbers were revised].

Michael Brisbane was one of the lucky ones. Now a leading businessman in St. Kitts, Birsbane was just 16 years old when the tragedy struck. He still recalls how overcrowded *Christena* was when he sat down at the back of the ferry with a group of other young men to converse until the boat reached its destiny. "We took off from the pier and when we reached the channel, there was a small fishing boat passing alongside us on the right," he said. "People on the left side of *Christena* came over on the right side to see what was going on outside because all the people in the fishing boat were waving." They thought the crew members were being friendly. Nobody realized that the people on board the fishing boat were trying to alert the captain that his boat was taking on water. Less than six minutes later, the *Christena* was swallowed by the sea.

The *Christena* was equipped with 25 life jackets for adults in the Captain's cabin and 58 in the rack on the upper deck. On the lower deck were 95 adult jackets and 40 life jackets for children. Tragically, there wasn't enough time for the people to grab a life jacket and put them on, witnesses said. Brisbane and several of the young men who survived were excellent swimmers. Many of those who lost their lives were not good swimmers. If they were, some drowned because they panicked. Brisbane told The Observer, "I was young and strong and used to spend a lot of time in the water." But even Brisbane despite his swimming ability, felt there were times he would not make it.

It took the young Basseterre man and the other swimmers nearly two hours to fight the waves and make it to Nags' Head, where they were picked up by one of the rescue boats. In an effort to recreate the tragedy and remember the victims 30 years later, The Observer contacted a number of survivors. Despite the passage of time, many of them were reluctant to talk about what had happened. The question of what caused *Christena* to sink may never be fully answered. Divers who inspected the hull said the steering mechanism was malfunctioning at the time the boat went down. However, investigators said there is insufficient evidence to prove the malfunction caused the ferry to sink.

APPENDIX XIII

A memorial service was held in Charlestown, Nevis, along Samuel Hunkins Drive, on August 1, 2009. It marked 39 years to the day that *Christena* sank. The updated lists of the dead and the survivors from that ceremony follow. The booklet lists 90 survivors and 233 dead from the tragedy. There was a moment of silence in honor of the 233 persons listed as dead. Special remarks were presented by Premier of Nevis, Mr. Joseph Parry. Scripture reading was done by Oswald Tyson, a survivor, and who has since published a personal account of his ordeal on the *Christena*, that afternoon. The sermonette was presented by Pastor Eric Maynard. There was also a laying of wreaths after the ceremony.

LIST OF THE DEAD

#	Last Name	First Name	From Where(Origin)
1	Allen	Ezekiel	St. Kitts
2	Allen	Miriam	Nevis
3	Allen	Shirley	Nevis
4	Archibald	Floretta	Nevis
5	Archibald	Samuel	Nevis
6	Arthurton	Amy	Nevis
7	Arthurton	Bertranne	Nevis
8	Arthurton	Emily	Nevis

#	Last Name	First Name	From Where(Origin)
9	Arthurton	Rodney	Nevis
10	Audain	Valentine	St. Kitts
11	Bartlette	Errol	Nevis
12	Bartlette	Froncille	Nevis
13	Barzey	Ellen	Nevis
14	Barzey	Mavis	Nevis
15	Belle	Austin	St. Kitts
16	Belle	Franklyn	St. Kitts
17	Bertie	Sherwin	St. Kitts
18	Bloyce	Adolphus	St. Kitts
19	Browne	Harold	Nevis
20	Browne	Josephine	Nevis
21	Browne	Monroe	Nevis
22	Browne	Muriel	Nevis
23	Browne	Olga	Nevis
24	Browne	Robert	St. Kitts
25	Budgeon	Gwendolyn	Nevis
26	Bussue	Lilian	Nevis
27	Bussue	Welseen	Nevis
28	Byron	Millicent	St. Kitts
29	Cable	Allan	St. Kitts
30	Carr	Orilda	St. Kitts
31	Chapman	Sharon	Nevis
32	Charles	Clementina	Nevis
33	Clarke	Anita	Nevis
34	Clarke	Brenda	Nevis
35	Clarke	Euphina	Nevis
36	Clarke	Leslie	Nevis
37	Clarke	Sarah	Nevis

#	Last Name	First Name	From Where(Origin)
38	Claxton	Dahlia	Nevis
39	Claxton	James	Nevis
40	Claxton	Vernon	Nevis
41	Comeau	Sister Amelia	St. Kitts
42	Condelle	Anthony	Nevis
43	Condelle	Christene	Nevis
44	Condelle	Irene	Nevis
45	Cornelius	Loretta	Nevis
46	Daniel	Leontine	St. Kitts
47	David	Carl	St. Kitts
48	David	Christina	St. Kitts
49	David	Joseph	St. Kitts
50	David	Leon	St. Kitts
51	David	Mavis	St. Kitts
52	David	Verna	St. Kitts
53	Davis	Lanyel	St. Kitts
54	Dineen	Sister Patricia	St. Kitts
55	Dore	Christine	Nevis
56	Dore	Jessica	St. Kitts
57	Dore	Myra	Nevis
58	Duporte	Amelia	Nevis
59	Duporte	Wendell	Nevis
60	Elliott	James	Nevis
61	Elliott	Kennedy	Nevis
62	Esdaille	Albertha	Nevis
63	Esdaille	Florence	Nevis
64	Farrel	Zenneth	St. Kitts
65	Ferguson	Albertine	Nevis
66	Ferguson	Emile	Nevis

#	Last Name	First Name	From Where(Origin)
67	Francis	Kluiverth H.	St. Kitts
68	Frank	Moses	Nevis
69	Freeman	Augusta	Nevis
70	Freeman	Tamar	Nevis
71	French	Daniel	St. Kitts
72	Forbes	Clarent	St. Kitts
73	Forbes	Emily	Nevis
74	Glasford	James	Nevis
75	Griffin	Lorraine	Nevis
76	Gumbs	Melvina	St. Kitts
77	Halliday	Lillian	Nevis
78	Hanley	Bertram	St. Kitts
79	Hanley	Conrod	Nevis
80	Hanley	Eglantine	Nevis
81	Hanley	Hugh	Nevis
82	Hanley	Melford	Nevis
83	Hanley	Rose	Nevis
84	Hanley	Rosetta, Zena	Nevis
85	Hendrickson	Marilyn	Nevis
86	Henry	Rosalyn	St. Kitts
87	Herbert	Maxwell, King	Nevis
88	Huggins	Alice	Nevis
89	Huggins	Nelson, Leroy	Nevis
90	Huggins	Samuel	
91	Hutton	Frances	Nevis
92	Hill	Bethia	Nevis
93	Hobson	Marilyn, Myrna	Nevis
94	Holland	Emily	USA
95	Irvine	James	St. Kitts

#	Last Name	First Name	From Where(Origin)
96	James	Esther	Nevis
97	James	Vernon	St. Kitts
98	Jeffers	Clifford	Nevis
99	Jeffers	Dwight	Nevis
100	Jeffers	Maurina	Nevis
101	Jeffers	Ralph	Nevis
102	Jeffers	Rosalie Agatha	Nevis
103	Johnson	Clothilda	Nevis
104	Johnson	Michael	Nevis
105	Jones	Edith	Nevis
106	Jones	Emily	Nevis
107	Jones	Iris	Nevis
108	Jones	Olga	Nevis
109	Jones	Oretha	Nevis
110	Jones	Vida	Nevis
111	Joseph	Carmen	Nevis
112	Joseph	Louisa	St. Kitts
113	Joseph	Sheila	St. Kitts
114	Joseph	Vennetta	St. Kitts
115	Joseph	Vernon	
116	Kelly	Avril(Cynthia)	Nevis
117	Kelly	Eugene	Nevis
118	Lanns	Verna	St. Kitts
119	Lawrence	Dawne	
120	LeBlanc	Sister Marie	St. Kitts
121	Lewis	Calvin	Nevis
122	Liburd	Beryl	Nevis
123	Liburd	Castro	Nevis
124	Liburd	EdricPaul	Nevis

#	Last Name	First Name	From Where(Origin)
125	Liburd	Elvira	Nevis
126	Liburd	Emerson	Nevis
127	Liburd	EvelynP	Nevis
128	Liburd	Iris	Nevis
129	Liburd	James	
130	Liburd	Kirsten Olivia	St. Kitts
131	Liburd	Kirtley	Nevis
132	Liburd	Lillian	Nevis
133	Liburd	Louisa	Nevis
134	Liburd	Marianne	Nevis
135	Liburd	Marion	Nevis
136	Liburd	Mildred	
137	Liburd	Thomas	Nevis
138	Liburd	Samuel	Nevis
139	Marson	Eva	Nevis
140	Martineau	MaudeLucilla	St. Kitts
141	Martineau	Sheryl	St. Kitts
142	Masters	Leroy	Nevis
143	Maynard	Charles	St. Kitts
144	Maynard	Sadie	Nevis
145	McQuilkin	Linda	Nevis
146	Michael	Idetha	Nevis
147	Mills	Henetta	Nevis
148	Mills	Maude	Nevis
149	Mills	Vivian	Nevis
150	Morris	Ursula	St. Kitts
151	Morton	Calvin	Nevis
152	Morton	Clarice	Nevis
153	Morton	Inez	Nevis

#	Last Name	First Name	From Where(Origin)
154	Morton	Irma	Nevis
155	Morton	Orville	Nevis
156	Morton	Pearl	Nevis
157	Morton	Rose	
158	Natta	Annie	St. Kitts
159	Nisbett	Govan	Nevis
160	Nisbett	Herbert	Nevis
161	Nisbett	Lilian	Nevis
162	Nisbett	Tony	Nevis
163	Nolan	Doldria	Nevis
164	Nolan	Eulita	Nevis
165	Nolan	Tessa	Nevis
166	Parris	Florence	Nevis
167	Parris	Hannah	Nevis
168	Pemberton	Calvin	Nevis
169	Pemberton	Helen	Nevis
170	Pemberton	Rufus	Nevis
171	Phillips	Berdie	UK
172	Phipps	Conrad	St. Kitts
173	Ponteen	James	St. Kitts
174	Powell	George	Nevis
175	Powell	Marion	Nevis
176	Powell	Miriam	Nevis
177	Powell	Sheryl	Nevis
178	Powell	Yvette	Nevis
179	Prentice	Evanston	Nevis
180	Prince	Anthony	St. Kitts
181	Reid	Austin	Nevis
182	Richards	Assinette	Nevis

#	Last Name	First Name	From Where(Origin)
183	Richardson	Yvonne	Nevis
184	Ritchens	Joseph	Nevis
185	Rouse	Leroy	St. Kitts
186	Saddler	Vernarine	Nevis
187	Scarborough	Alicia	Nevis
188	Scarborough	Duane	Nevis
189	Scarborough	Inez	Nevis
190	Smith	Edward	Nevis
191	Smithen	Calvin	
192	Smithen	Christena	Nevis
193	Smithen	Ivan	St. Kitts
194	Springette	Keith	Nevis
195	Stanley	Vivian	Nevis
196	Stapleton	Yvonne	Nevis
197	Sutton	Stanley	Nevis
198	Swanston	Daryl	Nevis
199	Swanston	David	Nevis
200	Swanston	Hanschell	Nevis
201	Swanston	Theodosia	Nevis
202	Sweeney	Samuel	Nevis
203	Thompson	Marilyn	Nevis
204	Tross	Alston	Nevis
205	Tross	Marilyn	Nevis

Whitman T. Browne, Ph.D.

#	Last Name	First Name	From Where(Origin)
206	Trotman	Alton	Nevis
207	Trotman	Iris	Nevis
208	Trotman	Irvine	Nevis
209	Tyson	Dave	Nevis
210	Tyson	Kirsten	Nevis
211	Tyson	Theodosia	Nevis
212	Wade	Yvette	Nevis
213	Wallace	Candy	St. Kitts
214	Wallace	Lorna	St. Kitts
215	Walters	Judith	Nevis
216	Walters	Virginia	St. Kitts
217	Walwyn	Wentworth(Parks)	Nevis
218	Wattley	Violet	St. Kitts
219	Watts	Velcine	Nevis
220	Webbe	Adina	Nevis
221	Weekes	Avonell	St. Kitts
222	Weekes	Benjamin	Nevis
223	Weekes	Elroy	St. Kitts
224	Weeks	Elroy	Nevis
225	Weeks	Louisa	St. Kitts
226	Weeks	Louisa	Nevis
227	Weeks	Marion	
228	Weeks	Nicholas	Nevis
229	Weeks	Rita	St. Kitts
230	Wheeler	Amelia	Nevis
231	Williams	George(Jinks)	Nevis
232	Williams	Kirtly	Nevis
233	Williams	Vernon	Nevis.

LIST OF SURVIVORS

#	Last Name	First Name	Address
1	Allen	Reuben	Montserrat
2	Arisbeth	Carlton	Nevis
3	Bartlette	Joseph	Nevis
4	Benjamin	Vincent	St. Kitts
5	Blake	Robert	Nevis
6	Brisbane	Michael	St. Kitts
7	Brookes	Ivor	Nevis
8	Browne	Arrington	Nevis
9	Browne	Clifford	Nevis
10	Browne	Dulcita	St. Kitts
11	Browne	Edna	Nevis
12	Browne	Franklyn	Nevis
13	Browne	Leonard	Nevis
14	Browne	Roger	Nevis
15	Budgeon	Joseph	Nevis
16	Budgeon	Luella	Nevis
17	Carlton	Tom	Nevis
18	Chapman	Livinstone	Nevis
19	Charles	Meredith	Nevis
20	Clarke	Edward	Nevis
21	Condelle	Wilson	Nevis
22	Davis	Everson	Nevis
23	Denning	William	Nevis
24	Depusoir	William	Nevis
25	Duzan	Terrence	Nevis
26	Edwards	Lionel	Nevis
27	Elliott	Ivan	Nevis

#	Last Name	First Name	Address
28	Foster	Bertram	
29	France	James	Nevis
30	Francis	Rudolph	St. Kitts
31	Freeman	Samuel	Nevis
32	Hanley	Eustace	Nevis
33	Harris	Vincent	St. Kitts
34	Hendrickson	Ronald	Nevis
35	Herbert	Alice	
36	Hinds	Robert	Nevis
37	Huggins	Fitzroy	Nevis
38	Huggins	Phillip	Nevis
39	James	Jonathan	
40	James	Leroy	Nevis
41	Jeffers	Belinda	Nevis
42	Johnston	Charles	Nevis
43	Johnston	Llewellyn	Nevis
44	Kelly	Edmund	Nevis
45	Kelsick	Ian	St. Kitts
46	Lake	Samuel	St. Kitts
47	Liburd	Devon	Nevis
48	Liburd	Edwin	
49	Martin	Joseph	St. Kitts
50	Martin	Joseph	Nevis
51	Martin	Julie	Nevis
52	Mason	Samuel	St. Kitts
53	Matthews	Frank	St. Kitts
54	Merchant	Edward	
55	Moore	Charles	St. Kitts
56	Morton	Franklyn	Nevis

#	Last Name	First Name	Address
57	Morton	Vincent	St. Kitts
58	Mulraine	Shernelle	St. Kitts
59	Nisbett	Carlton	Nevis
60	Prentice	Getrard	St. Kitts
61	Procope	Conrad	St. Kitts
62	Rawlins	Clive	St. Kitts
63	Richards	Euste	Nevis
64	Richardson	Alice	Nevis
65	Richardson	Wendell	St. Kitts
66	Roberts	Copeland	Nevis
67	Robertson	Joseph	St. Kitts
68	Sage	Leroy	St. Kitts
69	Sargeant	Laughton	Nevis
70	Sargeant	Livinstone	Nevis
71	Scarborough	Clive	Nevis
72	Simmonds	Malcolm	Nevis
73	Simmonds	Victor	Nevis
74	Stapleton	Vincent	Nevis
75	Storrod	Earl	Nevis
76	Swanston	Victor	Nevis
77	Tross	Grenville	Nevis
78	Trotman	Livinstone	Nevis
79	Tyson	Oswald	Nevis
80	Uddenburg	Herman	St. Kitts
81	Walwyn	St. Clair	Nevis
82	Ward	Job	Nevis
83	Warner	Cecil	St. Kitts
84	Weekes	James	St. Kitts
85	Wenham	James	

#	Last Name	First Name	Address
86	Wilkinson	Wendell	Nevis
87	Williams	Diana	Nevis
88	Williams	Leroy	Nevis
89	Wilson	Aubrey	
90	Wilson	Lewis Solas	Nevis

NOTE: There is still uncertainty about the exact number of persons who died, and who survived the tragedy. One certainty is that many more Nevisians than Kittitians died on the *Christena*.

INDEX

A

The Agricultural Department 132
Alexandra Hospital xxxviii,
    16-17, 24, 136, 139, 143,
    229, 318
Anita Liburd 51
Annette Lewis 67, 262
Arrington Browne 10, 47, 49,
    81, 168, 266, 303
Arthur Evelyn xxxvii, 86
Associated Statehood 190
August Monday xxii, 2, 31, 40,
    84, 105, 126, 264
Australian Cricket Team 71, 239
Automation 275

B

Barry Renwick 129
Breadfruit 12, 42, 60, 73, 75,
    111, 118, 224, 252
Brimstone Hill tragedy 89
Bulkheads 70-1, 161, 178, 213,
    222, 232, 239-41

C

Captain Ponteen 4-6, 18, 23,
    39, 41, 44, 46, 76, 179-80,
    214, 218, 237
Captain Wynter 11, 13, 71,
    75-6, 133, 228-9, 235-6,
    242-4, 246-8
Carelessness 45, 70, 76, 90, 194
Caribe Queen 85, 89, 91, 310
Cash Receipts 214, 219
Catherine 97, 307
Central Foundry Limited 215
Certificates of Competency
    233, 318
Charles Chapman 110, 115, 169
Charles Cozier 131, 148
Charles Freeman xxxviii, 72,
    261, 265, 279
Charlestown xvi, xxi, xxxi,
    xxxvii, 4, 15, 37, 43, 47, 52,
    62, 128, 141, 152-3, 307-8
Christena xi-xliii, 3-13, 19-27,
    29-93, 101-35, 137-51,
    153-61, 175-89, 191-203,
    205-25, 235-9, 241-59,
    261-7, 269-83, 309-23

Christena Disaster Fund 67, 69, 74, 80, 125, 156-7, 250-1

Christian Churches 268

Clemontina Nisbett 59, 61

Cliff Dwellers Hotel 80

Clifford Browne 10, 38, 63, 65, 81, 168, 266

Coalition 85, 204, 206

Controls 4-5, 39

Conversation 25, 28, 31-3, 53, 67, 71, 77, 94, 143, 226-7, 242, 244-5

Corsair 75-6

Coury's Hardware Store 50

Cricket 22, 71, 219, 239, 272-3

Culturama 57, 65, 259, 272-4

Curtis Mathes 274

D

Democrat ix, xli, 123, 134-5, 139, 143-4, 194

Demographic Changes xxviii, 275

Devon Liburd 105, 111, 162

Diana Williams 47

Disaster Preparedness 38

Disease xxxv, 230

Divers 4, 9, 26, 89, 133, 222-3, 253, 311-12, 321

Doris Richards 92

Dreams xx, xxxvi, xl-xli, 2, 21, 24, 33, 43, 52, 55, 81, 93, 114-15, 121

Dulcina Wallace 95, 262

Dulcita Browne-David 117

E

Earle Parris 6, 12, 166

Edna Browne 12, 25, 73, 168, 252, 264

Elections xxxv, 148, 198, 200, 203

Emigration xxxix, 176-7, 196, 258-60, 270, 274, 278

Enterprise xxv, 10-11, 13, 26, 47, 55, 71, 75, 78-9, 83, 134, 224-7, 229, 242-8, 308

Extended Families 260

External Assistance 17

F

Fares 5, 39, 41, 53, 124, 142, 221, 234, 318

Federal Queen 147

Female Passenger 242-4, 247

Ferry Service 79, 85, 91, 124, 142, 147, 154, 177-8, 182-4, 194, 277

Fitzroy Bryant xxxiii, 91, 106

Floating Bench 46-7, 106

Foreign Industries 274

Four Seasons Hotel 79-81

Francis Griffin 116, 262

Frank (Matthew) Tyson 5, 12, 39, 70

Frank Morton 40, 111

Frank Tyson xxiv-xxv, 12, 25, 70, 83-4, 161, 182, 240

Fred Parris 140, 156, 197, 205

G

Gingerland   44, 143-4, 151-2,
    174, 269, 291-2, 298,
    301-2, 316
Government's Neglect   267
Grenville Elliott   58
Gwenneth Budgeon   46

H

Hawthorne Enterprise   xxv,
    10-11, 13, 47, 55, 71, 75,
    78-9, 83, 127, 134, 224-7,
    229, 242-8, 308
Helicopters   18, 136
Hospital   xxxvii-xxxviii, 4, 16-17,
    23-4, 40, 43, 47, 50, 55,
    64-5, 82, 87, 106, 136, 143-4
House of Assembly   xxxiii, 131,
    134, 140, 142, 155, 184,
    196-7, 199, 250
Hucksters   3, 41, 74, 177, 179

I

Ian Kelsick   37, 49, 54, 168,
    252, 310
Illegal Rum   98
Independence   xxvii,
    xxxiii-xxxiv, 21, 66, 187,
    190, 196, 202-3, 205, 207,
    271, 273, 278
Inter-Island Travel   xxiii, 91,
    183, 288

Iona and Lennox (Ted) Tross   61
Ivor Stevens   xxxii-xxxiii, xxxvii,
    85-6, 141, 193, 199-200,
    206, 270

J

James (Frayco) Weekes   107
James Ponteen   3, 124, 179, 214
James Weekes   83, 169
Joe Martin   47, 167
Joseph Astaphan   178, 180
Joseph Budgeon   8, 279
Joshua Guishard   75, 242, 244
Julian Byron Cox   217

K

Kennedy Simmonds   16, 21, 84,
    92, 136, 143, 201, 317
King of Delisle Walwyn and Co
    130, 194

L

Labor Party   xxxiii-xxxiv, xli, 11,
    91, 123, 148-9, 184, 191-2,
    196, 198-9, 201, 203-4,
    207-8, 240, 255-6
Labor Union   255
Labour Spokesman   285, 287
Lady Christian   109
Lady Nisbett   xxiii, 26, 177
Lee Moore   130, 134, 184, 243,
    246, 257

Letters 157, 184, 194, 217-18, 227
Life Jackets 222, 320
Life-saving equipment 71
List of Persons Identified 290
List of Persons Reported Missing
    (unconfirmed) 304
List of Survivors 16, 113, 230,
    300, 331
Livinstone Sargeant xxvi,
    xxix-xxx, 8-9, 106, 108, 111,
    167, 252, 272
Luella Budgeon 46, 77, 166

M

M. V. Lavina 154
Malcolm Simmonds 52, 167
Marketing Depot 132
Mechanization 200
Medical Service 125
Memorial xvi, xxi, xxxi-xxxii, 88,
    113, 120, 138, 174-5, 206,
    208, 240, 265, 269, 322

N

Naval Vessels 18
Nevis Reformation Party xxxiii,
    193, 256
New Directions 206, 209
Nicholls 133, 141, 156-7,
    196-7, 306-7
Number of persons xix, 19, 39,
    91, 144, 203, 230, 249,
    252, 334

Nuns xxiv, 3, 27, 40, 53, 136,
    220, 252

O

Obeah 23, 49, 61, 83, 98,
    237-8
Operations 90, 102, 125, 136,
    194, 225
Orlando Browne 68
Orville Morton xvi, 4-5, 9, 22,
    31, 70, 83
Oswald Tyson 51, 80, 167, 322
Overcrowding xv, 84-6, 88, 185,
    194, 218-19, 238-9, 318
Overloading 130, 154, 184, 239
Overthrow Attempt 238

P

PAM xxxiv, xxxvii, xli, 11, 23,
    85-6, 156, 192, 197-202,
    204-9, 243, 246, 251,
    256, 278
Party Politics 11
Peddlers 132
People's Action Movement xxxiv,
    xli, 11, 123, 135, 192, 256
Peter Maynard 14
Philanthropists 259, 263
Phillip Miller 12, 124, 130, 223
Plastic 10, 50, 136, 139-40
Population xviii, xxxix-xl, 189,
    195-6, 198, 249, 270, 272,
    275, 288

Premier Bradshaw 11, 43, 87,
    89, 92, 141, 193, 195
Premonitions 3
Princess Royal xxiii, 154, 177, 183
Prisoners 18, 131, 148
Proper Training 180, 182
Proston's LTD 71

R

Radio Equipment 242
Reasons 2, 43, 50, 63, 113,
    180-2, 196, 206, 223, 227,
    253-4, 287, 319
Recovery of Bodies 131, 136, 148
Regulation 216, 234, 310
Regulations 216, 233, 240,
    277, 311-13, 318
Remittances 278
Resolution of Sympathy 131
River Tar 107, 109
Romeo Parris xxxvi, 97-8, 314
Rupert Wade 6, 12, 116, 162

S

S. L. Horsford & Co. Ltd. 76
San Juan Star 132, 197
The Sane Society 209
Sea Hunter xxx, xxxvii, 11-15,
    17, 25, 43-5, 54-5, 78, 86,
    110-11, 223, 225-7, 229,
    242-7, 306
The Sea Hustler 57, 113, 120,
    315

Secession Politics 57
Selfishness 251
Service xvi, 15, 45, 79, 85, 91,
    113, 120, 124-5, 138, 177-9,
    182-4, 276-7, 282-3, 286
Sherwyn Bertie 49
Silopana 41
The Sinking xiv-xv, xl-xli, xliii,
    10, 12-13, 23, 61-2, 82,
    84-5, 88-90, 127-9, 237,
    239-40, 244-6, 249
Skerritt's Drug Store 102
Social Mobility 278
Social Networks 278
Social Welfare Department 102
Sonny Skeete xxvi, xxx-xxxi,
    xxxvii, 13, 57, 78, 90,
    111, 113, 116, 120, 208,
    243-4, 246
Special Welfare Program 203
Sports Program 100, 272
Sproston's Limited 176
Sprostons Limited 124, 212
St. George-St. James seat 199, 205
St. Kitts xviii-xxvi, xxx-xl,
    13-17, 19-32, 43-51, 57-65,
    83-93, 176-80, 192-6,
    200-13, 235-41, 253-60,
    262-83, 306-12, 322-33
St. Paul and St. John
    constituency 199
Standard Safety of Lives 89
Stanley Wynter 227
Strange Happenings 21
Superstition xl, 53, 92

Whitman T. Browne, Ph.D.

Survey   208, 213, 266
Survivors   xvi, xx, xxv, 10,
    13-16, 86-8, 113-15, 136-7,
    144, 207-8, 225-6, 229-30,
    248-9, 314, 320-2
Sydney Anderson   147
Sympathy Resolution   127, 197

T

Telegram   137, 228-9
Telephone   16, 29, 87, 104,
    144, 155, 260
Telephone Link   155
Terrence Duzan   39
Testimony   xi-xii, xxvi, 10, 184,
    227, 242, 247-8
Tickets   3, 29-30, 89, 147,
    183-5, 214, 234, 277
Treasury Pier   3, 136, 141, 154,
    220-1, 285

U

United National Movement
    196
U.S. Coast Guard   136, 229,
    242

V

Vacuum Chambers   84, 88
Viability   231, 278
Victor Swanston   10, 28, 44-5,
    111, 113, 166, 221
Volunteer Prisoners   18

W

Warner Park   134, 272
Welders   241
Wentworth Nicholls   133
West Indies Industrial
    Development Company
    Limited   124
William Charles Demming   49
Witnesses   129, 227, 236, 305, 320
Wyclide Condell   10, 26, 83,
    166, 240
Wynter   11, 13, 71, 75-6, 127,
    133, 227-9, 235-6, 242-4,
    246-8, 308

Z

Z.I.Z   114, 131, 136, 157

Printed in the United States
By Bookmasters